USS *Bogue*

ALSO BY DAVID LEE RUSSELL
AND FROM MCFARLAND

*David McCampbell: Top Ace of U.S. Naval
Aviation in World War II* (2019)

*Early U.S. Navy Carrier Raids, February–April 1942:
Five Operations That Tested a New Dimension
of American Air Power* (2019)

*Oglethorpe and Colonial Georgia:
A History, 1733–1783* (2013 [2006])

*Eastern Air Lines: A History,
1926–1991* (2013)

*The American Revolution in the
Southern Colonies* (2009 [2000])

USS *Bogue*
The Most Successful Anti-Submarine Warfare Carrier in World War II

DAVID LEE RUSSELL

McFarland & Company, Inc., Publishers
Jefferson, North Carolina

LIBRARY OF CONGRESS CATALOGUING-IN-PUBLICATION DATA

Names: Russell, David Lee, 1947– author.
Title: USS Bogue : the most successful anti-submarine warfare carrier in World War II / David Lee Russell.
Other titles: Most successful anti-submarine warfare carrier in World War II
Description: Jefferson, North Carolina : McFarland & Company, Inc., Publishers, 2023 | Includes bibliographical references and index.
Identifiers: LCCN 2023028496 | ISBN 9781476692036 (paperback : acid free paper) | ISBN 9781476649528 (ebook) ∞
Subjects: LCSH: Bogue (Escort aircraft carrier : CVE-9) | Anti-submarine warfare—History. | World War, 1939-1945—Campaigns—Atlantic Ocean. | World War, 1939-1945—Naval operations, American. | World War, 1939-1945—Naval operations—Submarine.
Classification: LCC D783.5.B594 R87 2023 | DDC 940.54/5973—dc23/eng/20230616
LC record available at https://lccn.loc.gov/2023028496

BRITISH LIBRARY CATALOGUING DATA ARE AVAILABLE

ISBN (print) 978-1-4766-9203-6
ISBN (ebook) 978-1-4766-4952-8

© 2023 David Lee Russell. All rights reserved

No part of this book may be reproduced or transmitted in any form or by any means, electronic or mechanical, including photocopying or recording, or by any information storage and retrieval system, without permission in writing from the publisher.

On the cover: *top*: ACV-9 (later CVE-9) USS *Bogue* underway in Puget Sound, Washington, on November 3, 1942 (photographer: LT. W.O. Moore, Official U.S. Navy Photograph, from the collections of the Naval History and Heritage Command, Catalog #NH 106563). *Bottom*: Air attack on German submarine *U-1229* by Lieutenant (jg) M.J. Sherbring, VC-42 plane from USS *Bogue* (CVE-9), incident #6972. The submarine was sunk, 17 crew members died, and 41 individuals survived (U.S. Navy Photograph, August 20, 1944, #80-G-244761, in the collections of the National Archives). *Background* © Porcupen/Shutterstock

Printed in the United States of America

McFarland & Company, Inc., Publishers
Box 611, Jefferson, North Carolina 28640
www.mcfarlandpub.com

This book is dedicated to the memory of all the naval forces of the United States, Canada, and the United Kingdom who fought and died in the Battle of the Atlantic in World War II. It is also dedicated to the memory of all of the Allied merchant seamen who served, and often died, aboard the Atlantic convoys.

Acknowledgments

I was able to undertake this project to develop a manuscript telling the full story of the USS *Bogue* ASW escort carrier only due to the extensive and comprehensive research material available at the National Archives at College Park, Maryland. They provided complete online digital copies of actual month-by-month war diaries and summary histories of the carrier and the U.S. Navy Composite Squadrons that sailed aboard her in World War II. I have nothing but respect for all the quality work of the staff of our true national treasure, the National Archives.

Table of Contents

Acknowledgments	vi
Introduction	1
1. Birth of the USS *Bogue*	3
2. Operational Training	18
3. First War Cruise	26
4. Second War Cruise	31
5. Third War Cruise	34
6. Fourth War Cruise	46
7. Fifth War Cruise	56
8. Sixth War Cruise	63
9. Seventh War Cruise	66
10. Eighth War Cruise	78
11. Ninth War Cruise	90
12. 10th War Cruise	102
13. 11th Cruise	119
14. The Last ASW Combat Cruise	132
15. Transport Duty	149
16. USS *Bogue* Legacy	152
Appendix A. USS Bogue: *Commanding Officers*	155
Appendix B.. USS Bogue: *Executive Officers and Department Heads*	156

Table of Contents

Appendix C. USS Bogue: *Composite Squadrons (VC) Aboard*   157

Appendix D. USS Bogue: *Presidential Unit Citation*   158

Appendix E. USS Bogue: *Task Organization in the Atlantic 1943–45*   160

Appendix F. USS Bogue: *Submarines Sunk or Contacted by* Bogue *Task Groups*   162

Appendix G. Chart of U-boat Losses 1939–1945   165

Chapter Notes   167

Bibliography   179

Index   185

"You were right about the predominant place which submarine warfare should have in our plans. There is no question in my mind but that the German submarine menace is the most dangerous thing we have to face in our efforts at victory over Hitler."
—Secretary Knox to Admiral Stark
November 27, 1941

"The 'tonnage war' is the main task for the submariners, probably the decisive contribution of submarines to winning the war. This war on merchant shipping must be carried out where the greatest successes can be achieved with the smallest losses."
—Großadmiral Dönitz, in B.d.U. War Diary
December 1, 1942

Introduction

The Battle of the Atlantic began on September 3, 1939, when the German submarine *U-30*, in defiance of treaties that Germany had signed, fired four torpedoes, with one hitting the British passenger steamship SS *Athenia* at 7:40 p.m. in the engine room on the port side. She was carrying 1102 passengers and a crew of 316, for a total of 1418 people on board. Lost with the sinking were 112 persons, including 50 Canadian and British, 30 Americans, 7 Polish, 4 Germans, 2 stateless and 19 from the crew. Three-quarters of the passengers were women and children. The ship sank 200 miles northwest of Ireland. World War II had already started that same day at 11:00 a.m. in response to Hitler's invasion of Poland, when allies Britain and France declared war on Germany.[1]

On that date, Germany had only 57 U-boats, of which only 22 were operational.[2] The Germans had now begun a program of unrestricted submarine warfare against British shipping, a strategy that would come very near to starving England out of World War II. Although the British navy began convoying ships as soon as the war started, the lack of escorts cost these convoys dearly. As more and more German submarines entered the battle, British shipping losses increased at an alarming rate. By the end of 1940, the British had lost 886 merchant ships representing 3,223,000 gross tons of shipping.[3] British Prime Minister Winston Churchill wrote, "The Battle of the Atlantic was the dominating factor all through the war. Never for one moment could we forget that everything happening elsewhere, on land, at sea or in the air depended ultimately on its outcome."[4]

At the beginning, the Royal Navy had an inadequate number of escorts, and the Royal Canadian Navy even a year later in the fall of 1940 was barely able to provide two escorts in the western Atlantic for a convoy to/from Halifax and Sydney, Nova Scotia.[5] Churchill appealed to President Franklin Roosevelt for aid. Although the United States was neutral, on September 2, 1940, President Roosevelt signed a "Destroyers for Bases"

Introduction

agreement in which the United States gave the British 50 obsolete four piper destroyers in exchange for 99-year leases to territory in Newfoundland and the Caribbean, which would be used as U.S. air and naval bases. In December 1940, Churchill indicated that Britain was running out of money. In his December 29 Fireside Chat, Roosevelt envisioned the U.S. as the "arsenal of democracy," using its industrial and agricultural might to aid nations that stood against brutal Nazi aggression. With continued work in Congress to gain support for the Lend-Lease Program, on March 11, 1941, the Lend-Lease Act was signed by the president.[6]

By this time there were more escorts available, but there was another problem: the German use of U-boat wolfpacks made it difficult to provide full convoy protection. The optimum need was air protection over the convoy across the entire route. An air gap, known as the "Black Pit," consisted of a giant hole in the air cover over the main trade routes between Britain and North America that stretched 300 miles across from east to west and 600 miles north to south from Greenland to the Azores Islands. In 1942 and early 1943, Germany focused the majority of its U-boat fleet against Allied convoys in this area. Free from the aircraft threat, U-boats were easily able to move on the surface at night and press home attacks on poorly protected convoys. The results were devastating, as shipping sunk in this 1942–1943 period amounted to over six million tons, a great deal of which was due to U-boats operating in the air gap.

One of the greatest issues of the Battle of the Atlantic for the Allies was the need to provide adequate numbers of aircraft to close the air gap and thereby ensure that the convoys had complete air coverage throughout their voyage. Although the British recognized this problem by late 1941, the air gap was not in fact closed until the spring of 1943.[7]

It is this requirement to provide air protection for convoys and the destruction of the U-boat threat to which this book is devoted. This is the story of the USS *Bogue*, an escort carrier built for anti-submarine warfare (ASW) that was tasked to support the Battle of the Atlantic, the longest battle of World War II. The manuscript covers in comprehensive detail the steps that were followed to devise, fund, build, launch, and commission the carrier, and to the many war cruises with her squadron aircraft and escort destroyers to search for and sink U-boats. The *Bogue* headed out to sea on its first war cruise mission in March 1943. When the war ended in Europe on May 8, 1945, the USS *Bogue* had become the most successful ASW carrier in World War II.

1

Birth of the USS *Bogue*

> *"Suitable merchant ship vessels and their earliest conversion to auxiliary aircraft carriers."*

The history of ships being used to carry operational airplanes aloft for any navy began in 1916 when an Italian passenger ship was converted into the British HMS *Argus*. This ship and all that would follow it were to become known as "carriers." The first U.S. Navy carrier, the USS *Langley*, had been converted from the *Jupiter*, a collier, and was commissioned in 1922. These small-type carriers were to evolve, using converted battle cruiser hulls to become larger U.S. carriers like the *Lexington* and *Saratoga*. When World War II became a reality, the carriers became the major combat vessel for the Japanese, British, and American navies.

Interest grew in American naval leaders in the potential for conducting anti-submarine warfare (ASW) from carriers. The commander-in-chief of the U.S. fleet, Admiral J.M. Reeves, accurately predicted in 1934–36 that convoys could not adequately be protected from enemy aircraft and submarines without using carrier-based aircraft.

The chief of naval operations (CNO), Admiral Stark, paid attention to Rear Admiral William F. Halsey (commander, aircraft battle force) on December 13, 1940, when he conveyed his concern that a new war would quickly consume the six available fleet carriers, the aircraft, and trained naval aviators. Halsey recommended quick procurement of "suitable merchant ship vessels and their earliest conversion to auxiliary aircraft carriers" with specified speed and flight deck requirements to give them an adequate landing deck platform. President Franklin D. Roosevelt moved a week later to recommend that Admiral Stark fit out 15-knot merchant ship hulls with short flight decks to handle autogiros or a few planes with low landing speeds.[1]

This was the time of the birth of what would soon be known as the "escort carrier." The U.S. Navy and the Royal Navy were both driven to acquire (convert or construct) these escort carriers as soon as they could. The Royal Navy was deep in the throes of finding full protection for convoys against German bomber aircraft and U-boats. They had converted a captured German ship and completed their first escort carrier, HMS *Audacity*, in June 1941. Though it was sunk by a German torpedo the next December, its planes and surface escort destroyed five U-boats during a Gibraltar-U.K. convoy.

The U.S. Navy built its first escort carrier by converting the SS *Mormacmail* to the USS *Long Island*. With President Roosevelt's active involvement, the conversion was delivered from January to June 2, 1941. Back in March 1941, the General Board of the Navy approved the conversion of an unspecified number of C3 hulls and other merchant hulls to escort carriers. The Royal Navy asked the U.S. to build escort carriers under Lend-Lease, and on April 29, 1941, the British Admiralty asked to convert six C3 hulls to become what they called "fighter carriers" for convoy defense. Just a week later, on March 6 (date it was acquired by the Royal Navy), the conversion of the SS *Mormacland* to the HMS *Archer* was started, to be completed (and commissioned) on November 17, 1941.[2]

The origin of this story may well have begun on June 29, 1936, when the United States Congress passed the Maritime Commission Act (MARCOM), which replaced the United States Shipping Board (USSB) that had been established as an emergency agency on September 7, 1916, during World War I. The primary role of MARCOM was to establish a merchant ship-building program to design and build 500 merchant ships to replace the vintage World War I vessels. From 1939 through the end of World War II, the commission funded the largest and most successful merchant ship-building program in history. The ships built included the infamous Liberty ships and Type C1, Type C2, Type C3, and Type C4 freighters and the T2 tankers. By the end of the war, U.S. shipyards under Maritime Commission contracts built a staggering 5,777 oceangoing merchant and naval ships.[3]

The freighters began to be constructed under designed Type C1 and C2 specifications, but soon Type C3 hulls were started.[4] The earlier hull types for escort carriers had problems with the reliability of their diesel engines, so it was decided that the *Bogue* class would use two boilers from Foster-Wheeler that fed steam to an Allis-Chambers steam turbine engine driven by a single shaft. The engine provided 8,500 bhp to propel the ship at 18 knots. It could sail 26,300 nautical miles at 15

1. Birth of the USS Bogue

knots. The *Bogue* class displaced 8,390 long tons at standard load and 13,980 long tons at full load. The ships were 465 feet long at the waterline with an overall length of 495 feet 8 inches. The beam was 111 feet 6 inches overall. At full load the draft was 24 feet 8 inches. For weapons, the USS *Bogue* carried two five-inch guns and 10 40mm and 27 20mm antiaircraft guns.[5]

As the need for escort carriers was identified as a priority by the U.S. Navy, the *Bogue* class was designated to be built on C3 cargo ship hulls. Some 45 *Bogue* escort carriers were built in the United States, each of them being named for sounds (defined as a narrow stretch of water forming an inlet or connecting two wider areas of water such as two seas or a sea and a lake, e.g., Bogue Sound, North Carolina).[6] Thirty-four of the 45 ships of the *Bogue* class were transferred to the Royal Navy under the provisions of the Lend-Lease program and were given new names. Out of the first group of 22 ships, all built on completed converted keels based on C3-S-A1 or C3-S-A2 plans, 11 were retained by the U.S. Navy and the remaining 11 were transferred to the Royal Navy and reclassified as the *Attacker* class.[7] The second group of 23 ships was built from the keel up based on C3 designs and transferred to the Royal Navy and reclassified as *Ruler* class, or *Ameer* class.[8]

The USS *Bogue* was the fourth of the class. The hull was ordered by the War Shipping Administration (under MARCOM) to be a type C1-S-A1 with MC hull number 170 as the name *Steel Advocate* originally intended to be operated by the Isthmain Steamship Company. The contract was awarded on September 30, 1940, to the Seattle-Tacoma Shipbuilding Corporation of Tacoma, Washington. The cost was $3,733,124. The keel was laid on October 1, 1941, in Yard number 9, Way number 1. It was launched on January 15, 1942, by sponsor Mrs. W. Miller, Jr., wife of Lieutenant Commander Miller. It had spent 106 days on the ways. The U.S. Navy was allocated the ship on May 1, 1942. It would spend 254 more days in the water completing the build-out.[9]

After Pearl Harbor, the demand for C3 hulls was coming from most of the branches of the U.S. Navy. They were in great need of all types of vessels, including transports, tenders, repair ships, and escort carriers. The Maritime Commission held the overall power over the merchant hulls, while the Auxiliary Vessels Board of the Navy sought to press the commission to give up completed hulls for its ship conversion requirements. In December 1941, the Maritime Commission released 20 C3 steam-powered freighter hulls under construction at the Seattle-Tacoma Shipbuilding Corporation. Ten went to the *Bogue* class escort carriers. The other 10 were converted for the Royal Navy. On April 2, 1942, Admiral Reeves's commission of the Joint Munitions Assignment Board voted for 15 additional C3 conversions, and on May 1, 20 more were contracted for West Coast shipyards.[10]

The USS *Bogue* was originally designated as AVG-9 (auxiliary aircraft ferry-escort carrier) during conversion but was redesignated on August 20, 1942, as ACV-9 (auxiliary aircraft carrier). A year later, on July 15, 1943, she received a further redesignation as a CVE-9 (escort carrier).

On September 26, 1942, at the Puget Sound Navy Yard at Bremerton, Washington, the USS *Bogue* was tied up to Pier 5D. The crew was in formation in their dress blues assembled on the flight deck. At 1212, Rear Admiral S.A. Taffinder stepped up to the microphone and read the authority document placing the ship in commission. Next to the microphone was Captain Giles Elza Short, who read his orders as the first commanding officer of the USS *Bogue*. The *Bogue* was under the operational control of CINCPACFLT with type commander assigned to Commander Air Forces, Pacific Fleet.[11]

Captain Short of the *Bogue* commanded a crew of 97 officers and 921 men. The USS *Bogue* captain was a man with significant career experience. Giles E. Short was born in the small rural town of Lohrville, Iowa, on March 25, 1895. He was appointed to the Naval Academy in 1915 and graduated as an ensign on June 7, 1918. In June 1919, Short was ordered to the USS *Conyngham* (DD-58), which was based in Queenstown, Ireland. The next December, Short was transferred to the U.S. Naval Headquarters at Brest, France. In February 1920, he served on the ex-German ship *Graf Waldersee*, a transatlantic liner that was launched in Germany in 1898 and surrendered as part of Germany's World War I reparations to the Allies. Then Short assisted in fitting out the USS *Thornton* as a senior engineer officer until December 1920.

That same month, Short began flight training at NAS Pensacola, gaining his wings in November 1921. He was ordered in June 1922 to NAS Anacostia, where he received advanced training in radio. He served with Scouting Squadron One aboard the USS *Wright* (AZ-1), a unique type of auxiliary "lighter-than-air" aircraft tender, until August 1924. He was then ordered to NAS Coco Solo in the Panama Canal Zone and supported various squadrons attached with the USS *Wright* in June 1927. From January 1930 until April 1932, he was stationed at NAS Norfolk, Virginia. He served with Bombing Squadron Five aboard the USS *Langley* and then transferred to take command of the squadron stationed at NAS Coco Solo. He spent six months preparing prior

1. Birth of the USS Bogue

USS *Bogue* (ACV-9) commissioning ceremony at the Puget Sound Navy Yard, Bremerton, Washington, September 26, 1942. (U.S. Navy Photograph, now in the collections of the National Archives and Records Administration [NARA], #80-G-266407.)

to commissioning and assumed command of Bombing Squadron Seven deployed aboard the USS *Yorktown* from January 1937 to June 1938.

Next, Short took command of Carrier Air Group aboard the USS *Enterprise* the next year. He fitted out the USS *Patoka* for recommissioning and commanded the ship until June 1940. After completing the senior course at the Naval War College in June 1941, he served with the staff until June 1942, when he worked on preparation for the commissioning and command of the USS *Bogue* at Puget Sound Navy Yard, Bremerton, Washington.[12]

The *Bogue* had some work left to be handled and remained at Pier 5D until September 30, 1942, when at 0725 the ship sailed to the drydock 5 and moored at 0805. On October 4 at 1216, the ship sailed back to Pier 5D, arriving an hour later.

At 0745 on October 26, the *Bogue* got underway from the Puget Sound Navy Yard and headed for deperming (naval term: deperming, or degaussing, is a procedure for erasing the permanent magnetism from ships and submarines to camouflage them against magnetic-detection vessels and enemy marine mines) at Orchard Bay at Illahee, Washington, mooring at buoy at 0945. The next day, the ship rebirthed to complete deperming from both sides (east and west side buoys). The process of loading ammunition aboard was begun and was completed at 1533 on October 28. At 1615, the *Bogue* departed Illahee for Puget Sound Navy Yard, where it moored at 1705 to Pier 5D.

The USS *Bogue* was off on another rotation to another site, the Fuel Oil Dock at Manchester, Washington, at 0734 on October 29 for ship fueling. After fueling was completed at 1549, the ship sailed back to the Navy Yard at Bremerton and moored to Pier 5C an hour and 15 minutes later.[13]

On October 30, the first aircraft landed aboard the USS *Bogue*. It was an SOC-3A flown by the carrier air officer, Commander Jack Pendleton Monroe.

During the period from November 1 through November 16, the men of the USS *Bogue* conducted a myriad of important shakedown exercises, tests, calibrations, and repairs to prepare the ship for operational sea duty. Examples of these activities included trial speed runs, steering gear and engine order telegraph testing, course changing and zigzag testing, gyro/compass adjustments, gun loading drills, fire drills, abandon ship (station) drills, general quarters drills, gun test firing, casualty drills, broiler testing, catapult testing, engine room annunciator and telemotor testing, runs over a measured mile to gather tactical data, ship inspections (various decks), fueling, ammunition loading, pumping gas over the side, and air alert drills.

USS *Bogue* (ACV-9) off Puget Sound Navy Yard on October 27, 1942. (Naval History and Heritage Command, Catalog #NH 56501.)

1. Birth of the USS Bogue

ACV-9 (later CVE-9) USS *Bogue* underway in Puget Sound, Washington, on November 3, 1942. (Photographer: LT. W. O. Moore, Official U.S. Navy Photograph, from the collections of the Naval History and Heritage Command, Catalog #NH 106563.)

One special event occurred at 1340 on November 4 when Navy pilot Lieutenant Moore took off the first plane from the *Bogue* using the catapult. After completing all the necessary shakedown events, on November 16 at 0751, the *Bogue* headed to refuel at the fueling dock at Manchester, then returned to dock at Pier 5C. Having been prepared for getting underway, at 1106 on November 17, 1942, the USS *Bogue* sailed from Puget Sound Navy Yard en route to San Diego, California, in company with the USS *Gillespie* (DD-609). Heading toward the sea zigzagging according to plan #19, the *Bogue* at 1445 called General Quarters and launched and recovered one aircraft. At 1602, the ship's utility plane, piloted by LTJG Norton, landed aboard. She secured from General Quarters at 1604 and set condition III. After varied course changes, at 1809 the darkened ship passed 7.2 miles to port of Port Angeles lighthouse heading 280°T.

In early morning on November 18, the USS *Gillespie* was steaming some 2,000 to 2,500 yards ahead of *Bogue* on anti-submarine patrol making 17 knots zigzagging as before. At 0200 in open ocean, the *Bogue* changed course to 180°T heading south. The *Gillespie* had a main engine problem, which was repaired and in commission by 0730. At 0956 a radar contact was reported by the escort destroyer, which was identified as Army bomber Number 123450. The next day at 1116, the *Gillespie* reported seeing an Army observation bomber. The force changed the base course to 168°T following the same #19 plan zigzagging.[14]

After numerous course changes eastward on the 20th, the *Bogue* reported for duty with the Commander Fleet Air West Coast (COM-FAIRWESTCOAST) and was assigned a training period with the squadron. The *Bogue* air officer, Commander Jack P. Monroe, noted, "we found that the quality of our pilots was not anywhere near that of the old carrier groups. In spite of the long training period, they were pretty ragged, and, in fact, we found a few pilots who had to be detached because they were not suitable for this work."[15]

On Saturday, November 21, the *Bogue* sighted Los Coronados Island bearing 134°T some 30 miles ahead. Harbor Pilot Johnson boarded the *Bogue* to guide the ship to its berth. They passed Point Loma Lighthouse to port at 1026. The *Bogue* was secured to the starboard bow of Navy Tug YT199 as it moored to berth J at the Naval Air Station Dock at 1123. The *Bogue's* engines were secured, and the usual port routine condition was set. At 1440 the ship began taking on 65,677 gallons of fuel oil. At 1449 Ensign R.D. Lapham USNR came aboard with $50,000 from the Bank of America, San Diego.[16]

USS *Gillespie* (DD-609) off Mare Island Navy Yard, California, on March 17, 1943. (National Archives Catalog #19-N-42265.)

1. Birth of the USS Bogue

On November 22, 1942, Escort Scouting Squadron Nine (VGS-9) reported aboard the USS *Bogue*. The squadron was commanded by Lieutenant Commander William McClure Drane, USN. The squadron had been originally formed for training and commissioning in June 1942 at Sands Point Naval Air Station at Seattle, Washington. The NAS site had been selected back on June 19, 1920, on a peninsula in north Seattle that juts into Lake Washington. The squadron had been formally commissioned on August 6, 1942 (redesignated on March 1, 1943, as Composite Squadron Nine [VC-9]).[17]

The VGS-9 commanding officer, William McClure Drane, graduated from Annapolis and was issued his wings from NAS Pensacola in 1933. He took part in the search operations for Amelia Earhart while serving with Patrol Squadron Six (VP-6) at Pearl Harbor. He reported on June 6, 1942, for duty as the commanding officer of Escort Scouting Squadron Nine.[18]

The squadron was later designated as a "composite squadron" (VC-9) because, contrary to other Navy squadrons, it flew two different type aircraft: the F4F-4 Grumman Wildcat fighter and the TBF Grumman Avenger torpedo bomber. The squadron was supplied with eight Avengers and 12 F4F fighters. The *Bogue* usually carried between 18 and 24 aircraft loaded aboard. The squadron had 32 pilots, but all except five or six were straight out of pilot training with no carrier experience. It was obvious that the squadron needed additional training. The training had begun at the NAS Sands Point at Seattle, then at Long Island when they moved south to get better weather and then on to San Diego.[19]

F4F-4 Wildcat was a single pilot fighter powered by a 1,200-horsepower Pratt and Whitney R-1830 engine with a top speed of 330 miles per hour, a range of 770 miles, and a cruising speed of 155 mph. It had wings that rotated 90 degrees and folded back along the fuselage, self-sealing fuel tanks, and pilot protection armor, and it carried six deadly .50-caliber machine guns. The U-boat deck crews came to fear this roughed fighter aircraft.

Also aboard the *Bogue* was the Grumman TBF Avenger, which was the heaviest single-engine plane in World War II, weighing eight tons. It was a mid-wing monoplane powered by an 1,850-horsepower Wright Cyclone engine with a maximum speed of 276 mph and a range of 1,000 miles. Its hydraulic system folded its wings back along the fuselage and retraced its wheels in flight. The rugged Avenger carried a crew of three: a pilot, radioman, and gunner. The armament included two .50-caliber wing guns and another a .50 caliber mounted next

Grumman F4F-4 "Wildcat" fitted with drop tanks of VF-4 takes off from USS *Ranger* (CV-4) on a photo-recon mission over French North Africa, during operation "Torch," November 1942. (National Archives Catalog #80-G-30311.)

to the gunner in a glazed rear-facing electrically powered turret. The plane had seal-sealing wing fuel tanks, armor for the pilot and the turret gunner. The bomb bay carried up to 2,000 pounds of bombs or one 2,000-pound torpedo.[20]

On November 24, the *Bogue* got underway at 0816 from its berth J at the Naval Air Station Dock and headed out the channel and into international waters off San Diego to begin flight training operations. Changing courses as required to position to gain wind over the bow, at 1047 the first AGS-9 plane from North Island Naval Air Station landed aboard. Later the *Bogue* returned to berth J at the dock. The next day the ship returned again to international waters to the assigned operating area and commenced flight operations steaming northwesterly and southeasterly at 1300. Operations consisted of qualifications and refresher takeoffs and landings in SOC1 and F4F aircraft. The flight operations were suspended at 1606. The *Bogue* changed course to 191°T at 17 knots and darkened ship for the evening. The next day (November 26) saw the USS *Gillespie* sailing 2,000–2,500 yards ahead of the *Bogue* on anti-submarine patrol. At 0740 she went to flight quarters with qualifications with takeoffs and landings with F4F fighters staying as before on northwesterly and southeasterly courses. At 1550 the carrier ceased flight operations.

1. Birth of the USS Bogue

On November 27, still cruising offshore with the *Gillespie*, the *Bogue* continued with seven more hours of flight training operations. The following day the ships headed back to San Diego. The *Bogue* was off Point Loma at 0815 and soon moored at the North Island NAS Dock at berth I at 1118. The ship remained moored until November 30.[21]

On December 2 at 1143, the *Bogue* departed San Diego Harbor for the assigned operating area in open sea escorted by USS *Gillespie* for flight training operations and gunnery practice specified in dispatch 29716 from COMFAIRWESTCOAST. Flight training was held in the afternoon. The next day, flight operations were again held in the afternoon. On December 4, flight training operations were continued. At 1129 the Avenger plane #9 (BuAer 00545) was attempting to land on the flight deck but veered too far to the port side, fell over the side, and sank immediately. Thankfully, the crew consisting of pilot Ensign H.C. Carby, ARM3c F.E. Ellingsworth, and AMM3c D.L. Clark were rescued by a boat from the *Gillespie*. The crew was uninjured and returned aboard the stopped *Bogue* at 1148. The ship resumed sailing at 17 knots.

Formation of TBF Avenger Aircraft of Air Group Four, USS *Essex* (CV-9) Task Group 38.3, approaching the coast of French Indochina on the way to bomb and torpedo airfields and shipping in the Saigon area on January 12, 1945. (National Archives Catalog #80-G-300673.)

The *Gillespie* conducted 30 minutes of test firings from the 40mm battery at 1700.

Saturday, December 5, was going to be the toughest day of flight training operations for its attached squadron since its launching. At 1140 plane #17, piloted by Ensign P. Perabo, crashed on the flight deck during landing. He was uninjured but the plane sustained damage to the propeller and landing gear.

Incredibility, just three minutes later, AGS-9 Commanding Officer Drane radioed the *Bogue* that two of his Avenger TBF-1 torpedo bombers (BuAer numbers 00597 and 00547), while flying in formation with five other Avengers, had collided some eight miles bearing 270°T from the ship. The two pilots were seen deploying their parachutes. The *Bogue* and escort destroyer *Gillespie* changed courses to retrieve the pilots and crews. The remaining planes in the formation were ordered to circle the location where the planes had hit the water.

The *Gillespie* picked up two men: AMM3c Harold Eugene Bucholtz, with no injury noted, and ARM3c Sylvester Peter Schmaltz, who suffered from shock and a broken arm. One man was spotted from the *Bogue* at 1225 off the port bow as the whale boat was lowered to pick up pilot Ensign William Valentine, Jr., at 1235. He had not been injured. At 1240 a boat from the escort picked up Ensign James Oren Pfeffer, who had suffered severe injuries.

The search continued to locate the two remaining crash victims: ARM3c Clarence Manly Marlette and S1c Gerald Laughlin. As the TBF planes were low on fuel and survivors reported that the missing crew members were obviously killed in the collision and went down with the planes, the search was abandoned. Unfortunately, at 1520 Ensign Pfeffer was pronounced dead aboard the *Gillespie*. It was a dark day for the members of AGS-9.

Flight training operations continued the next day until 1115 as the *Bogue* entered the channel entering San Diego Harbor. At noon the ship moored at berth H at the Naval Air Station. Through December 10, 1942, the *Bogue* remained moored at the same berth. On the 8th, CINCPAC dispatch 260915 was received releasing the USS *Gillespie* from escort duty for the *Bogue*. It was replaced by the USS *Kendrick* (DD-612). At 0930 on the 9th, the *Bogue* began fueling. She completed taking on 142,506 barrels of fuel oil at 1255.[22]

As the flight training continued, the squadron, as well as the *Bogue* crew, was anxious to get in the action in the Pacific against the Japanese. VGS-9 skipper Drane recalled, "I had been told by Commander Fleet

1. Birth of the USS Bogue

Air Alameda that the *Bogue* would be heading West. I was much surprised when I discovered that the *Bogue* was headed South instead of West."[23]

Following CINCPAC's dispatch 26915 and COMFAIRWESTCOAST dispatch 82215, the USS *Bogue* sailed on December 11, 1942, out of the San Diego Harbor en route to Balboa, Canal Zone, at 0957 escorted by the USS *Kendrick* (DD-612). Engaged in calibrating radio transmitters aboard the *Bogue* between 1055 to 1330 some eight miles off Point Loma, the group commenced steaming at 17 knots at 1500 on a course southward.

En route to the Canal Zone, beginning December 12 the *Bogue* held various daily drills and flight training operations. At 1600 on the 13th, the *Kendrick* reported a submarine sonar contact and dropped a single depth charge. The next day at 1100, a periscope was sighted, but the group was unable to prosecute the contact. On the 15th, a radar contact was obtained at 0730 that was later identified as the SS *Sague*. The *Kendrick* came close in to start fueling from the carrier *Bogue* at 0953. The escort took on 33,000 barrels of fuel oil by 1145. Flight training was canceled due to poor weather, a low ceiling and rain squalls.

Still steaming as before, the *Bogue* on December 17 continued its routine activities. At 1147 a radar contact was reported bearing 112°T distance, 17 miles off, which was determined to be an Army B-17. Another contact of a flight of planes was detected at 1240 and

USS *Kendrick* (DD-612) underway off the Mare Island Navy Yard, California, on December 6, 1942. (Official U.S. Navy Photograph, from the collections of the Naval History and Heritage Command, Photo #NH 107215.)

USS *Bogue*

USS *Corry* (DD-463) with nets over her side, rescuing *U-801's* survivors after the submarine had been sunk by aircraft and surface ships of the USS *Block Island* (CVE-21) group in position 16 41 N, 29 58 W, 17 March 1944. (Official U.S. Navy Photograph, now in the collections of the National Archives, #80-G-222851.)

confirmed as friendly by IFF (*Identification, friend or foe* is an identification system to avoid firing on friendly forces. It uses a *transponder* that listens for an *interrogation* signal and then sends a *response* that identifies the friendly target to the broadcaster). The Commander Western Sea Frontier informed the *Bogue* that the SS *Ulua* reported a submarine contact at 1815. On the 19th, flight training was canceled with more poor weather, a low ceiling and rain squalls.

During the Sunday morning of the 20th, the carrier held drills and flight training. Approaching the Canal Zone, the *Bogue* squadron VGS-9 launched aircraft under Army escort to land bases while the ships transited the Panama Canal. The F4Fs were dispersed to Chance Field while the Avengers flew to Fort Cobbe. Inland waters of the Canal Zone were reached at 1325 and at 1425 the *Bogue* was moored at berth 16 at Balboa.

The next day the squadron duty officer reported that F4F-4 number 9, flown by Ensign Stewart E. Doty, was engaged in a forced landing at Chance Field. Doty suffered minor scalp wounds, but the fighter was

1. Birth of the USS Bogue

totally destroyed. Skipper Drane noted that at the "Army Air Base on the Atlantic end of the Canal … we practiced Carrier Landings on one of the runways. Many of the Army pilots wondered why in the hell we didn't spin out making those steep banked turns into the final approach to the landings."[24]

On Wednesday, December 23, at 0705 the *Bogue* got underway from its berth 16 at Balboa to transit the Panama Canal en route to Hampton Roads at Norfolk, Virginia. The ship completed the transit at 1650 and moored on the port side to Pier 16C at Colon, Panama, at 1752. Two days later, the *Bogue* left Colon Pier and moved to temporarily anchor at berth 212. At 1416 the ship got underway to Hampton Roads in accordance with CINCLANT dispatch 141620 in company with the USS *Corry* (DD-463) as the escort. Underway during the afternoon, VGS-9 squadron planes recovered aboard the *Bogue*.[25]

At 0650 on December 26, the *Bogue* launched an anti-submarine patrol plane, which landed back on the carrier at 0909. The carrier continued morning and evening flight training operations, as well as other drills. The next day two anti-submarine patrol aircraft took off at 0702. They recovered at 0831. Flight training was held daily through December 30. On the 31st, the *Bogue* passed the Norfolk buoy at 1019, entered inland waters, sailed past Cape Henry, and anchored at berth 21 at Hampton Roads, Norfolk, Virginia, at 1528.[26]

2

Operational Training

"We had to have a big catapult to get our torpedo planes off with a decent load."

Anchored at Hampton Roads on January 1, 1943, the *Bogue* got underway and moved to moor to the port side of Pier 5 at berth 56 at the Naval Operating Base (NOB) at Norfolk. On the 3rd, Rear Admiral A.D. Bernhard, the commander Air Force, U.S. Atlantic Fleet, and his staff conducted a reporting-aboard inspection of the USS *Bogue*. Four days later at 1117, the carrier got underway and proceeded to the Norfolk Navy Yard at Portsmouth to comply with COMAIRLANT dispatch 061841 of January 1943. The *Bogue* then moored at 1300 to Pier 4.

At the Norfolk Navy Yard, a number of repairs and changes were made to the USS *Bogue* as recommended by the commander Air Force, U.S. Atlantic Fleet. Concrete ballast was added to improve the stability. The four 4.1s were doubled to eight 40mm and the 10 20mm guns were doubled to 20 20mms. The five-inch 51-caliber guns were converted to five-inch 38-caliber guns. The 1.1-inch antiaircraft guns were changed to 50mm Bofors guns. Anti-fire systems were also upgraded. The old Mark 2 catapult was replaced with the Mark 2 Mod 1 catapult for good reason.

Commander Jack Monroe, the *Bogue* air officer, explained the need for the new catapult: "These ships were merchant ship designed and had a top speed of barely 18 knots and in light winds, you simply could not get a heavily loaded plane off. This deck is 438 feet long and there just is not enough room. Therefore, we had to have a big catapult to get our torpedo planes off with a decent load."[1]

On January 22, the *Bogue* was underway without using power at 1155 assisted by tugs to the Navy Yard Drydock #3 at Portsmouth. The *Bogue* on January 24 was underway with tugs using no power to Pier 4, mooring at 1704. On Friday, January 29, the Commander Carrier Division One (COMCARDIVONE) assigned the USS *Belknap* (DD-251) and

2. Operational Training

USS *George E. Badger* (AVP-16) to the USS *Bogue* for duty for training exercises and as surface escorts. The last day of January 1943, just after noon, the carrier was underway to berth 56 at Pier 5 at the NOB at Norfolk.²

From the first use of World War II merchant convoys escorted by British, Canadian, and then American destroyers to defend against German U-boats, the issue of a potential centralized organization was on the minds of the senior leadership. If the decentralized anti-submarine warfare organizations split up among different sea frontiers, naval districts, and fleet commanders of Britain, Canada, and the United States was to continue, there was little hope in seeing the elimination of the U-boat threat anytime soon.

In December 1942, Air Chief Marshal Sir Philip Joubert of the R.A.F. Coastal Command "proposed a single supreme control for the whole anti–U-boat war, with a central planning staff to coordinate the separate and often conflicting policies of the British, Canadian and

The U.S. Navy destroyer seaplane tender USS *George E. Badger* (AVP-16) underway, circa September 5, 1940, by which time she had been redesignated AVD-3. She wears her APD number (16) and the aviation star insignia on her bow and is armed with two 102 mm/50 guns (one forward, one aft) and four 12.7 mm anti-aircraft machine guns (mounted two on each side atop the midship's deckhouse). (Naval History and Heritage Command photo #80-G-466188.)

American naval and air authorities."[3] U.S. Navy Captain L.H. Thebaud, working in Londonderry, suggested a combined general staff directed by a single admiral be established to control all British and American escorts, convoys, and anti-submarine warfare. With either Prime Minister Churchill or President Roosevelt giving anti-submarine control to the other government being an impossibility, there would be no supreme commander for this anti-submarine warfare role.[4]

On January 19, 1943, at the Casablanca Conference of the Combined Chiefs of Staff with Roosevelt and Churchill, it was agreed that the "defeat of the U-boat must remain a first charge on the resources of the United Nations."[5] On the British side, some changes were made in their anti-submarine warfare (ASW) organization, but they were still left with a rather loose organization. The British commands involved were the commander in chief Western Approaches (CINCWA), the Coastal Command (a branch of the Royal Air Force), and the Admiralty. The idea of a British central command under a single anti-submarine warfare commander, as recommended by the leader of the House of Commons on November 30, 1942, was rejected by Churchill with a response that "it is always tempting in times of stress to set up a local dictatorship, but it is very easy thereby to rupture the constitution."[6]

On March 1, 1943, Admiral Ernest King, the commander in chief, United States Fleet (COMINCH), delivered the opening address at the Atlantic Convoy Conference in Washington attended by British Admiral Percy Noble, and Vice-Admiral Henry Moore, and Rear Admiral Victor Brodeur of the Royal Canadian Navy, as well as the Royal Air Force and United States Army Air Forces Anti-Submarine Command. King told of his support for convoys by protecting merchant ships even as they were "attractive bait for U-boats." He felt the best answer was the hunter-killer groups to be associated with the convoys. A number of recommendations came out of the conference, and they were presented to the Combined Chiefs of Staff for approval. The first recommendation was that the British and Canadian navies would take complete control of all transatlantic convoys, not including those from Halifax to Boston and New York. Other significant recommendations were setting up increasing convoy cycles (timetables), adding more long-range aircraft from Newfoundland, extending the high-frequency direction finder (HF/DF) network, and significantly employing escort carrier ASW groups as soon as possible. The USS *Bogue* group would be the first organized.

Admiral King was ready to execute on the American side. On April

2. Operational Training

6, 1943, he appointed Rear Admiral Francis S. Low as his assistant chief of staff for ASW. Low immediately began to study the disorganized ASW material from the British and U.S. By April 20, he submitted his report, entitled "Appreciation of the Antisubmarine Situation," to King, in which he declared that the answer to the problem was having enough escorts, aircraft, and trained forces. King submitted the recommendations to the Combined Chiefs of Staff on April 30 and asked that each Allied nation adopt a centralized control of ASW and to coordinate closely among them.

The next day King formally submitted to the U.S. Joint Chiefs of Staff the following:

> "It is arranged that to set up immediately in the Navy Department an antisubmarine command to be known as the Tenth Fleet. The headquarters of the new Fleet would consist of all existing antisubmarine activities of the U.S Fleet headquarters, which will be transferred intact to the Commander Tenth Fleet. Such additional officers will be assigned to the Commander Tenth Fleet as are necessary for its function, in the same manner as any other command. In addition, a research-statistical analysis group will be set up composed of civilian scientists, headed by Dr. Vannevar Bush. The Commander Tenth Fleet is to exercise direct control over all Atlantic Sea Frontiers, using sea frontier commanders as task force commanders. He is to control allocation of antisubmarine forces to all commands in the Atlantic, including the Atlantic Fleet, and is to reallocate forces from time to time, as the situation requires. In order to ensure quick and effective action to meet the needs of the changing antisubmarine situation, the Commander Tenth Fleet is to be given control of all LR and VLR aircraft, certain groups of units of auxiliary carriers, escort ships and submarines which he will allocate to reenforce task forces which need help, or to employment as 'killer groups' under his operational direction in appropriate circumstances."[7]

Admiral King appointed himself to be the commander of the 10th Fleet. Rear Admiral Low was the chief of staff with the authority to issue direct orders to the operational commands. In fact, Low did not issue orders but sent instructions to the commanders that all knew had the full weight as if they had been issued by Admiral King. The staff of the 10th Fleet, consisting of 50 people, were in the Navy Department Building in Washington, D.C. They were organized into five divisions:

1. Operational Division: This division directed sea frontier forces, escort groups, and all units of the Naval Air Arm assigned to ASW work. It also used the Atlantic section of Admiral King's (COMINCH) Combat Intelligence Division (CID), including the situation room where a large map was maintained on which was

plotted convoy positions, the forces at sea, and the U-boat positions 24 hours a day. It served as the clearinghouse for the Navy's HF/DF network.

2. Anti-Submarine Measures Division: This division coordinated all ASW research, material development, and training, as well as the ASW Operational Research Group (ASWORG) that analyzed the statistics of ASW activities.

3. Convoy and Routing Division: This division managed the effective interlocking convoy system.

4. Civilian Scientific Council: This group was headed by Dr. John T. Tate.

5. Air Anti-Submarine Development Unit Atlantic Fleet (AIRASDEVLANT): This Division tested ASW equipment, developed the best operational use for the equipment, and developed anti-submarine tactics and communications procedures between aircraft and surface vessels.[8]

One of the problems with the 10th Fleet was it did not provide a place in the organization for the Army Antisubmarine Air Command, which had been providing the role since June 1942. In March 1943, the War Department began to deal with the important issue. A disagreement between the Army and Navy had existed since the beginning of the war. The essence of the problem was that the Navy under Admiral King believed the primary function of use of aircraft in anti-submarine war was supporting convoys, and further that being involved in this support increased the chances of sinking enemy submarines. The Army Antisubmarine Air Force felt the Navy's approach was too "defensive oriented," while their motto was "Search, Strike, Sink!"

At the TRIDENT Conference in May 1943, King asked General Hap Arnold to send a group of B-24s to Newfoundland to strengthen air support of the northern transatlantic convoys. The general sent the aircraft to Gander Airport in early June 1943 but required the squadron commander to engage only in offensive search and attack and forbade him to protect convoys. King was outraged. The conflict revealed itself in a meeting held on June 10, 1943, among General Arnold, Lieutenant General Joseph T. McNarney, Rear Admiral John S. McCain, and Captain M.B. Gardner. The two air generals said they never wanted to take over anti-submarine warfare in the first place and declared they would be glad to withdraw as soon as the Navy planes were ready to take over the duties of the Army anti-submarine bombers.

2. Operational Training

Captain Gardner suggested that the Army turn over its anti-submarine-equipped B-24 Liberators to the Navy in return for an equal number of unmodified B-24s from the Navy. General Arnold agreed, which prompted Admiral King to write to General George C. Marshall that the Navy would be prepared to take over anti-submarine operations by September 1, 1943. The agreement was formally accepted by the Navy and War Departments on July 9.[9]

On Monday, February 1, 1943, the USS *Bogue* was still moored to berth 56 at Pier 5 at the Naval Operating Base at Norfolk. Then at 0828 the carrier was sailing out to Chesapeake Bay to conduct training exercises in flight operations, gunnery, general drills, and fueling at sea as specified in CINCLANT dispatch 181438 of January 1943. The surface escorts USS *Belknap* and USS *George E. Badger* tracked along with the *Bogue*. In the afternoon, in addition to drills, the carrier calibrated the radio direction finder and checked out the magnetic compass. At 1628 the *Bogue* anchored in 75 fathoms off Wolf's Head.

For the next five days, the *Bogue* and the escorts continued daily underway training, practiced refueling the escorts, and held torpedo defense drills, gunnery practice, fire drills, general quarters, and the like. After 1600–1700 each day, they anchored at various locations in the Bay, including Rappahannock Spit, Cherry Point Lighthouse, Windmill Point, and Wolf Trap Lighthouse.

On February 7, 1943, the *Bogue* left its anchorage and got underway at 0800 cruising at various speeds and directions to conduct flight training operations. At 1018 F4F Wildcat fighter (plane #03440), piloted by Lieutenant (jg) Robert Lamar Steward, crashed upon landing and fatally injured the landing signal officer (LSO), Lieutenant George S. Friend. The fighter came in to land into the wind at the aft end of the carrier and drifted diagonally across the flight deck, hit Lieutenant Friend with the nosewheel, and went over the port side. As it went over the side, it crashed into the gun platform, which damaged four 20mm guns, two 20mm gun sights, and three-gun mounts. A life raft was torn loose. The fighter fell into the sea and sank immediately in eight fathoms of water.

The *Bogue* immediately stopped its engines and search efforts were begun. The exact spot (Lat. 37° 39' 43" N, Long. 76° 00' 50" W) where the aircraft sank showed an oil slick where a marker buoy was set. The USS *Belknap* lowered a boat and attempted to recover the pilot and plane. The search was unsuccessful. The raft from the carrier and the fighter's rubber boat were recovered. At 1055 an escort was ordered to stand by and continue the search. The *Bogue* headed to the Naval Operating Base at Norfolk and anchored (bearings to Fort Wool 087°T and Point Comfort 138°T) at berth 21 at Hampton Roads in 11 fathoms.[10] This was a tragic loss of two fine officers of AGS-9.

The next day, the *Bogue* moved to Pier 5 berth 56 at the NOB and loaded aircraft and ammunition aboard. Just after noon on the 9th, the carrier got underway for flight training escorted by Coast Guard Cutter *482*. At 1653 they anchored off Rappahannock Spit in the Bay. The following day, the carrier held flight training in the morning and anchored off the Degaussing Barge before moving to a new anchorage. She continued using the Degaussing Range at various speeds and directions on the 11th. The next day the carrier conducted drills and gunnery practice.

February 13 saw the *Bogue* underway landing the squadron of TBF-1 Avengers and F4F-4 Wildcat fighters aboard, followed the next two days with flight training. The carrier fueled the Coast Guard cutter with 1,200 gallons of aviation gas. On the 16th at 1115, Avenger Number 8 crashed into the sea 50 yards ahead of the ship due to a failure of the catapult to launch the plane. The plane sank immediately, but thankfully the crew, pilot Ensign W.S. Fowler, AOM3c H.E. Bucholtz, and AEM3c C.J. Wojcik (suffered a scalp laceration), was able to escape. The *Bogue* then continued flight training operations for a few more hours before anchoring off Wolf Trap Lighthouse.

There were more flight training operations the next day, as well as fueling the Coast Guard cutter with 750 gallons of aviation gas. On February 18, the carrier was fueled with 1,214 barrels of fuel oil. The next day, the *Bogue* received ammunition from the Naval Ammunition Depot at Saint Juliens Creek in Portsmouth. The carrier remained moored at Pier 5 berth 55 at the Naval Operating Base through February 23, with the USS *Belknap* and USS *George E. Badger* reporting for duty to the USS *Bogue* as specified in the COMAIRLANT dispatch 221436 of February 1943.

At 1148 on the 24th, the *Bogue* with its two surface escorts got underway en route to Argentia, Newfoundland, for North Atlantic convoy duty. At 1835 the group commenced zigzagging according to Plan #30. On Thursday morning, February 25, the group was steaming at 16 knots on a 106°T course. A radar contact was reported at 0045 out 3,850 yards on a bearing of 188°. The *Belknap* was ordered to investigate. The contact was reported as negative. At 1000 flight operations were commenced and 43 minutes later Avengers numbered 7, 4, and 9 were launched on morning anti-submarine patrol. Avenger #9 reported at

2. Operational Training

1230 an oil slick bearing 060°T off four miles. This prompted Avengers 6, 1, and 3 to be launched at 1331 to relieve the morning patrol. At 1346 the morning patrol planes landed aboard. Flight training exercises were commenced with launching and recovering of F4F fighters. At 1647 the afternoon patrol was recovered, and the flight training operations were secured. The carrier darked ship at 1822 and soon Readiness Condition Two was set.

The next day the carrier practiced gunnery exercises. No flight operations were conducted. The 27th saw the *Bogue* group continuing northerly courses and speeds as several merchant ships and a small sailing vessel were noted. At 1055 a freighter with two funnels was challenged by the *Belknap*. The ship was identified as a Norwegian merchant vessel bound from Halifax to Avonmouth.

Steaming as before at 16 knots changing courses as required, the *Bogue* entered Placentia Bay at 0953. At 1333 they passed through the submarine net and moored portside at 1433 to berth AB at the Naval Operating Base at Argentia, Newfoundland. The USS *Bogue* reported to COMTASKFOR 24 for duty. Later the carrier moved to moor to Buoy Prep I, Little Placentia Harbor, Newfoundland, in 15 fathoms of water. The *Bogue* and its escorts were ready for action.[11]

3

First War Cruise

"...the bombs failed to release."

Remembering back on the USS *Bogue* Commissioning Ceremony of September 26, 1942, at Pier 5D at the Puget Sound Navy Yard at Bremerton, it was finally time for the escort carrier to begin its first war cruise and build a legacy of achievement that history was about to give her.

On March 1, 1943, the Escort Scouting Squadron Nine (VGS-9) aboard the *Bogue* was redesignated as Composite Squadron Nine (VC-9). The carrier and the two escorts remained moored through March 4 at Little Placentia Harbor, Newfoundland. On the 4th, the *Bogue* (and escorts *Belknap* and *George E. Badger*) received Operation Order 1–43 (Serial 0034) from COMTASKFOR 24 to join the convoy HX-228 as COMTASKUNIT 24.4.1 of the Mid–Ocean Carrier Escort Group. The HX-228 convoy had sailed from New York on February 28, 1943, with 60 ships bound for Liverpool carrying war materials.

The Mid–Ocean Escort Force group B3 with eight escorts (destroyers HMS *Harvester*, HMS *Escapade*, ORP *Burza*, and ORP *Garland*; corvette HMS *Narcissus*; and FNFL ships *Aconit*, *Renoncule*, and *Roselys*) joined the convoy from Saint John's, Newfoundland. The escort group was led by the well-respected Royal Navy Commander Arthur Andre "Harry" Tait of the HMS *Harvester*. Even though he was just a commander, the commodore of the convoy also reported to Tait.[1]

Before the *Bogue* joined the convoy, a conference was held with Commander Tait. Air Officer Commander Monroe was impressed with Tait and his experience. The escort commander made it clear that the *Bogue* under Captain Short reported to him as the convoy commodore. Tait provided a comprehensive account of the available U-boat intelligence information as well as "what we were to do and how much cover to give the convoy." Otherwise, he gave no orders for the planes and did not interfere with the *Bogue's* operations. He listened in on the aircraft frequencies to keep up with activities.[2]

3. First War Cruise

On March 5, Commander J.E. Broome, DSC, of the Royal Navy, came aboard the *Bogue* as an observer. The carrier and escorts got underway at 1044. The next day at 1110, the *Bogue* sighted convoy HX-228 and maneuvered to take up its position in the center of columns 8 and 9. The convoy was in columns of five ships each with about 700 yards between them. A double spacing was made for the *Bogue*, with the escort ships placed in a half-circle around the convoy.

On the early morning of the 7th, the carrier was sailing in position in the convoy some 2,000 yards bearing 030°T from the commodore's ship. The *Bogue* launched anti-submarine patrol aircraft at 0705 as they maneuvered as required into the wind. The carrier patrol sighted the Allied convoy ON-168 at 1055 ahead of their convoy HX-228 bearing 210° at speed 10 knots. At 1115 maneuvering from behind the convoy, the carrier recovered the patrol planes before moving back into their assigned column position.

No anti-submarine patrols were possible on the 8th or 9th due to weather conditions of low overcast, rain, and visibility of three-quarters to two miles, with SSW surface winds 34 to 50 knots in a rough sea. On the afternoon of the 9th and morning of March 10, attempts were made to fuel the escorts *Belknap* and *Badger* with the escort tanker equipped to use a stirrup-and-trough method with no success.[3]

On the 10th, the *Bogue* was sailing at nine knots when anti-submarine planes were launched at 0651. At 0913 Ensign Alexander C. McAuslan was flying an Avenger on the last leg of his search when he came out of a cloud bank and saw a surfaced submarine revealing a conning tower bearing 000°T at a distance of 10 miles from the carrier. He was flying at 180 knots at only 50 feet altitude when he pressed to release two MK 17 depth bombs. Nothing happened, as the bombs failed to release. McAuslan tried to yank his stick and shake loose the release, but again nothing.

The enemy submarine was obviously surprised and immediately began to dive. McAuslan made another run and tried firing his .30-caliber cowl gun while again attempting to release the bombs. Again, no joy. Now totally frustrated, the pilot flew to the nearest destroyer and alerted it of the contact, urging it to head to the submarine position. By this time, the submarine was gone. The *Bogue* was not happy about landing an Avenger with two armed World War I depth bombs aboard. McAuslan was ordered to gain altitude and go into a steep dive and pull the emergency bomb release. No response. He climbed again and pushed over, generating negative Gs as he pulled the bomb release. No luck again. Finally, Captain Short gave McAuslan permission to land.[4]

The last patrol aircraft landed at 0957. At 1137 Avenger #9 was launched to investigate the previous submarine contact. It recovered aboard at 1256.

In view of the escort fuel situation and the rough weather limiting air patrols, it was decided that it was prudent to detach from the convoy and head back to Argentia. This was in agreement with the Escort Task Unit commander and in compliance of COMTASKFORCE 24 orders. At 1308 the *Bogue* and the two escorts detached from the convoy on a course 185°T and soon was maintaining 16 knots zigzagging according to Plan #12. There was another anti-submarine patrol launched at 1634. They were all recovered by 1744 having encountered no contacts.[5]

Tragically, during the evening of March 10/11, there were a number of attacks made against convoy HX-228 by *U-221*, *U-444*, *U-757*, *U-86*, and *U-406*. In the morning of March 11, the HMS *Harvester* sighted *U-444* on the surface and moved into attack. The destroyer opened fire on and then rammed *U-444*, but her propellers were damaged. While it lay helpless in the area unable to move, it picked up 50 survivors from the *William C. Gorgas* and one from the *U-444*. She called for help from the French corvette *Aconit* but was seen by *U-432* and torpedoed, with the loss of 149 aboard, including Commander Tait. The *Aconit* came in and depth charged to bring the *U-432* up and finished her off with gunfire. The battle was called off by Karl Dönitz on March 12. The convoy HX-228 arrived in Liverpool on March 15 with the loss of the four merchant ships.[6]

Early morning of March 11, 1943, the *Bogue* was steaming at 16 knots on course 257°T zigzagging using plan #12 with the *Badger* and *Belknap* positioned to port and starboard as anti-submarine screen. At 0907 the *Belknap* sighted a suspicious object off 6,000 yards bearing 315°T, location 47° 43' N Lat, 35° 31' W Long. The escort was ordered to investigate. It turned out to be a lifeboat with 21 survivors aboard. The Liberty cargo ship SS *Jonathan Sturges* (7,176 tons of American registry) had been torpedoed by *U-707* some 120 miles from their current location at 2010 on February 23, 1943, while en route from Liverpool to New York in convoy ON-166.

During a squall the *Sturges* was a straggler behind the convoy and had been hit by two torpedoes in the first and second holds. The ship was flooding. The engines were stopped and eight officers, 36 crewmen, and 31 armed guards abandoned ship in three lifeboats and four rafts.

3. First War Cruise

Unfortunately, one of the boats swamped in rough seas but the occupants were picked up by the other lifeboats. Four crew members and 11 armed guards went down with the ship.

Of the 21 survivors picked up by *Belknap*, three were from the Dutch SS *Madoera* (9,382-ton motor merchant), which had also been torpedoed in convoy ON-166 in station #13 at the bow by *U-653* on February 23. The master of the Dutch ship curiously reboarded his ship with 15 other crewmen and managed to save the ship. Making four knots, it reached Saint John's, Newfoundland, on March 1. Of the remaining 18 survivors of the 21, seven were members of a U.S. Navy gun crew.

The *Belknap* conducted rescue operations. At 1006 Avenger #9 launched from the *Bogue* to search for more survivors. The *Bogue* resumed the base course with zigzagging.

At 1203 the *Badger* reported a probable submarine contact on the port quarter. The *Bogue* launched Avenger #4 at 1229 to investigate the submarine contact. As the executive officer, Lieutenant H.S. Roberts, was preparing to land aboard the *Bogue* when he noticed a swirl in the water 3,000 yards behind the carrier. Roberts felt it was a submarine and attempted an attack. He pressed the bomb release button, but the bomb rack failed. He tried a second pass to bomb the swirl and a depth charge fell out when the bomb bay door opened. Analysis of the event determined the contact was not a submarine. At 1230 Avenger #9 landed and at 1445 the Avenger #4 was recovered.

At 1907 Avenger #9 launched to conduct a dusk patrol, which was later recovered. At 2000 the *Bogue* group changed base course to 262°T and continued zigzagging from Plan #12.[7]

On March 12 the *Bogue* was steaming as usual at 16 knots to Argentia when at 0528 radar reported an object bearing 098°T out 4,200 yards. The *Badger* investigated and it turned out to be the wake. An anti-submarine patrol plane saw a periscope about 2,000 yards on the port bow at 0913 and two minutes later dropped two MK 17 depth charges at bearing 160°T some three miles from the carrier. Two Avengers were launched at 0940, and soon the previous patrol plane landed. The last plane was landed at 1159. Captain Short reported the bomb rack failures to Admiral King. It was a serious problem.

The next day the *Bogue* steamed as before with the *Badger* and *Belknap* positioned at 30° to port and starboard as the anti-submarine screen. The Avenger #5 took off at 0722 and returned to land at 0834.

The *Bogue* and escorts sailed into Little Placentia Bay, Argentia,

Newfoundland, at 1050 on March 14, 1943. Twenty-five minutes earlier, 12 F4F fighters and three Avengers launched with Commander J.E. Broome DSC of the Royal Navy occupying Avenger #9. The carrier was moored to Buoy P1 at 1235. The *Bogue* remained moored from the 15th through the 19th. The cruise had logged only 15 hours of flight time.[8]

4

Second War Cruise

"We pitched and plowed through the ragging waves."

In accordance with CTF-24 Secret Dispatch Number 200033, on March 20, 1943, at 1305 the *Bogue* and escorts *Badger* and *Belknap* got underway. They set a course to rendezvous with convoy SC-123 (under CTF 24 Operational Order 2–43 of March 19). The USS *Bogue* was the flagship of the Mid–Ocean Carrier Escort Group, Task Unit 24.4.1. The convoy SC-123 had left New York on March 14 and was en route to Liverpool.

The task group sighted the convoy at 0635 on Sunday, March 21, and assumed its center position between columns 6 and 7 on a base course of 090°T steaming at seven knots (this was a slow convoy). The other escorts guarding the convoy were TU 24.1.16 HMS *Whimbrel*, HMS *Whitehall*, HMS *Vanessa*, HMS *Gentian*, HMS *Heather*, HMS *Sweetbriar*, HMS *Clematis*, and TU 24.12.1 HMS *Salisbury* and HMS *Chelsea*. At 1602 and 1630, the *Bogue* launched planes, which were recovered by 1730.

At 0040 on the 22nd, a radar contact at bearing 135°T off 21,000 yards from the carrier was identified as friendly. Another friendly group of ships passed through the convoy at 0240. The carrier entered ice floes during the day. The next day saw the *Bogue* Task Group and convoy steaming at seven knots through various icebergs. As *Bogue* increased speeds to launch aircraft into the wind, Avenger #8 was launched at 0927 and, after a short patrol, recovered aboard at 1020. Later, at 1655, another plane took off on patrol, recovering 54 minutes later.[1]

The weather was deemed by the flight squadron to be worse that the first war cruise had been. Ensign McAuslan recalled: "Some of the waves were as high as the bridge. We were rolling, pitching, and yawing almost all at the same time. We kept our headway, with difficulty, as we pitched and plowed through the ragging waves."[2] Lieutenant Commander Drane noted: "On one particular flight that I was not on, the ship was really lying on its heels. The plane taking off got just about even with the island about halfway up the deck and it looked like to me that he stopped completely-just ran into a hill he couldn't climb. Then the old bow went down and he got off all right. Coming up the landing groove, quite frequently I have seen the screws out of the water."[3]

On March 23, Ensign Harry Fryatt, making a landing in an Avenger, bounced over the barrier in a heavy pitching flight deck, went off the deck at the bow, and somehow was able to bring the plane up from almost hitting the water and regain altitude. He was able to make a normal landing, having cheated death.

Another major problem with maintaining flight operations was the situation with the new catapult failing. Because the catapult was unreliable, the torpedo bombers had to reduce the number of depth charges to only two and the aviation gasoline to only three hours' supply. The winds over the deck would get to 41 knots, which limited flights to only the most skilled and experienced pilots.[4]

Anti-submarine patrols flew two flights on the 24th, but by 1651 the winds were too high for flights. The winds continued to be too severe the following day for flight operations.

Escorts with the *Bogue*, USS *Badger*, and USS *Belknap* could not be fueled by the escort tanker. The anti-submarine patrols were active during March 26, 1943, with no contacts reported. It was decided appropriate as authorized by CTF 24 that the *Bogue* Task Group would detach from convoy SC-123. The movement was executed at 1710 to return to Argentia.

Meanwhile on the 26th, the German wolfpack named *Sea Devil* had been shadowing convoy SC-123. *U-663* sighted a carrier and reported back to Admiral Dönitz at headquarters. Dönitz replied to the *U-663* with "the sinking of the aircraft carrier is particularly important for the progress of the convoy operation. Do not on that account, however, let any other chances slip."[5]

Thirty minutes after the *Bogue* Task Group had departed, the wolfpack U-boats attacked the convoy. The escorts were able to fight off the attackers. The *Bogue* group suffered communications problems and played no part in the event.

The next day radar picked up icebergs as the *Bogue* Task Group moved at 16 knots toward Argentia. The anti-submarine escort screens were maintained at 30° from the port and starboard bow ahead of the *Bogue*. No flights were made until 1045 on the 29th. On the 30th, the

4. Second War Cruise

Bogue fueled the USS *Badger* with 800 barrels of fuel oil at 1423. At 1539 the task group entered the channel at Little Placentia Harbor at Argentia. The *Bogue* was moored at 1707 to Buoy P-1 in 15 fathoms of water. The squadron had been able to log only 24.5 hours of flight time on this second war cruise.[6]

5

Third War Cruise

"I got the son-of-a-bitch. He's straight up and down."

The *Bogue* remained moored at Little Placentia Harbor, Argentia, Newfoundland, until Monday, April 5, 1943, at 1425 when the carrier launched Avenger #7, F4F #10, and F4F #13 from the catapult. Later the three planes were recovered. The carrier returned to the mooring.

On April 6 the air officer of the USS *Bogue*, Commander Jack Monroe, reported his thoughts regarding the *Bogue* war operations through the period of the second cruise.

> It was not considered that combination of types of planes we had on board was correct for this type of work. We had twelve fighters and nine TBFs on board. We didn't fly the fighters at all because we had no use for them. I understand now that the plane complement of these escort carriers has been changed to twelve TBFs and six fighters. I, personally, feel that four fighters would be enough. I also feel that the SOC type aircraft could be used to more advantage than the TBF. Although the TBF is an excellent airplane, the upkeep due to the great amount of hydraulic gear and the large size of the airplane is considerable. The SOC is a much slower plane but rugged and reliable, can stay out three hours, carry two depth bombs and do the work. We had very heavy anti-aircraft armament on the ship which required a great number of men to man and we had absolutely no use for it on this type of work. It takes a lot of men to sea uselessly to stand cold, miserable watches, and if the ship was sunk, would take a lot of trained men down with it. The complement of these ships is getting up around 750 to 800 men. A great many of them do no constructive work except training, but please remember that I am referring only to an ACV devoted exclusively to the North Atlantic convoy.[1]

At 0820 on April 7, the *Bogue*, *Badger*, and *Belknap* stood out and got underway. The carrier began launching at 1010 the F4F fighters #11, #15, #18, and #12. They were recovered by 1255. Underway the *Bogue* began fueling the *Badger* using the two-blocked fueling operation. The fueling was completed by 1204.

5. Third War Cruise

At 1518 the *Bogue* passed the submarine net and then anchored to Buoy P6 off Low Room Point at 1543. The tug Y.S.D. 23 (*Mary Ann*) came out and delivered F4Fs #2 and #7 onboard the *Bogue*. At 1838 the carrier was underway again, departing from Point X-Ray at 1909. The *Bogue* was on course 186°T speed 14 knots en route to the Navy Yard at Philadelphia in compliance of CTF 24 dispatch 071731 for urgent repairs to the catapult.

On the 8th, the *Bogue* was steaming at 16 knots on a course 186°T with its two escorts positioned as an anti-submarine screen as usual ahead of the carrier at 30° to the port and starboard. CTF 24 modified its previous dispatch ordering the *Bogue* to Boston for repairs. Radar and sound contacts were confirmed as friendly all day. The zigzagging Plan #12 was observed as usual. The following day, the carrier launched six F4Fs on CAP. They were recovered by 1223. At 1419 two Avengers took off for anti-submarine patrol. They landed at 1611.

On April 10, at 0954 the USS *Bogue* launched seven Avengers and six F4F fighters en route to land at Naval Air Station Quonset Point, Rhode Island. Passing Graves Lighthouse at 1305, the *Bogue* came into inner waters. At 1558 the carrier was moored to the south jetty at the Navy Yard, South Boston Annex. The ship was connected to dock services telephone, steam, fresh and salt water, and electricity.

The carrier remained moored as before through April 15. On the 13th, four SOC aircraft were received from the USS *Tuscaloosa*. The next day the carrier was delighted to receive 50 gallons of fresh milk from Shawmut Dairy for the general mess at 0630. At 1655 F4F #12 was received aboard.

On April 16, the *Bogue* cast off her lines and steamed out of the outer Boston Harbor. At 1453 she exited the submarine net and moved out of the port with *Belknap* as plane guard. At 1545 the carrier launched the first F4F, #10, using the repaired catapult, followed by F4Fs #18, #11, #13, and #12. At 1632 she commenced landing F4F planes #10, #12, #11, #18, #14, and #13 and Avengers #10, #4, #5, #3, #7, #1, #2, #11, and #8. All the aircraft were aboard the *Bogue* by 1735. At 17 knots the carrier returned to the harbor and moored as before at the South jetty at the Navy Yard, South Boston Annex.

The following day, the *Bogue* cleared Boston Harbor by 1730, passed through the submarine net, passed off Point Z at 1921, and steamed on course 090°T at 15 knots en route to Argentia, Newfoundland. The carrier was escorted by the USS *Belknap* and the USS *Lea* (DD-118) in accordance with CTF 24 dispatch 151307 of April 1943.

USS *Bogue*

During the trip back to Argentia, the surface escort screens were maintained, and anti-submarine air patrols were launched and recovered as appropriate. On April 20, 1943, the *Bogue* and escorts arrived at Little Placentia Harbor, Argentia. The carrier was moored at Buoy P6 off Low Room Point at 1022. On the 21st, the *Bogue* launched the four SOC aircraft from the *Tuscaloosa* to land at Naval Air Station, Argentia.[2]

When the *Bogue* arrived back at Little Placentia Bay, the crew and VC-9 were delighted to sight the fleet carrier USS *Ranger* moored there. The carrier was conducting training exercises. Apparently, a few of the *Ranger's* officers had been barred from the base officers' club. In an act of revenge, they and others decided to damage the club. The club manager took swift action to alert the shore patrol when someone used a fire ax on the club piano. The VC-9 personnel exited the scene, as did the *Ranger's* officers, who headed back to their carrier. The admiral commanding the *Ranger* barred their squadron officers from leaving the ship.[3]

The *Bogue* remained moored until April 23, 1943, at 1601 when it got underway to proceed to rendezvous with convoy HX-235 in accordance with CTF 24 Operation Order No. 2–43. Task Group 92.3 consisted of the *Bogue*, USS *Belknap*, USS *Greene* (DD-266*)*, USS *Osmond Ingram*, and USS *Lea*. Task Unit 24.1.14 consisted of the convoy escorts

USS *Lea* (DD-118) underway in San Diego Harbor, California, on April 17, 1933. (Original negative given by Mr. Franklin Moran in 1967, Naval History and Heritage Command #NH 64522.)

5. Third War Cruise

HMS *Churchill*, HMCS *Restigouche*, HMCS *Brandon*, HMCS *Collingwood*, HMS *Trent*, and HMCS *Baddeck*.

The following day, the *Bogue* and her escorts steamed on courses around base course 095°T at speed 15 knots to intercept the convoy. Escort screen and anti-submarine air patrols were conducted all day.

On Sunday, April 25, at 0516 an aircraft of the anti-submarine patrol sighted the convoy 40 miles from the carrier bearing 095°T. The *Bogue* had launched and recovered six Avengers by 1240 when the *Bogue* Task Group joined with convoy HX-235 and took up its position between lanes 6 and 7 ahead of the second ship in the convoy. At 1434 the *Bogue* commenced fueling the USS *Lea* with 16,400 gallons of fuel oil, finishing at 1521. Avengers #6 and #12 were launched at 1539 for patrol duties. Later, at 1629, the USS *Belknap* fueled from the carrier and received 21,279 gallons by 1735. The carrier recovered the last two Avengers by 1756.

The 26th was without anti-submarine air patrols and all was uneventful except at 1150 when a straggler merchant ship escorted by the HMS *Trent* rejoined the convoy. The next day saw the carrier task group with convoy HX-235 and escorts on a base course of 095°T. A number of anti-submarine air patrols were launched and recovered during the day traveling at 16 knots while the convoy plodded along at 10 knots. The USS *Ingram* was refueled commencing at 1446, delivering 33,600 gallons by 1558. Two more Avengers were launched at 1621. At 1713 a senior officer of an escort reported an HF/DF submarine contact bearing 223°T at 50 miles. It was investigated, but the Avengers #4 and #5 were landed by 1837.[4]

The convoy, escorts, and *Bogue* continued along as usual on April 28 until 1650, when Lieutenant Santee from the anti-submarine patrol attacked a totally surfaced submarine bearing 028°T speed some 50 miles from the carrier. Santee dropped four depth charges immediately, but they ricocheted before they exploded, and the U-boat escaped. There was a problem with the depth charge nose configurations, which was soon corrected. The next morning the commodore over the convoy sent a message to the *Bogue*: "Please thank pilot whose attack certainly prevented interception of the convoy by a U-boat."[5]

At 1821 on the 28th, Avenger #2 crashed into the barrier on landing. The 29th saw continued patrols with Avengers and even some F4F fighters. At 1655 radar reported an unidentified aircraft flying at bearing 055°T at 55 miles from the carrier. It was soon discovered to be a friendly B-24 Liberator bomber.

USS *Bogue*

On April 29, 1943, the *Bogue* Task Group 92.3 (in compliance with the Commander-in-Chief, Western Approaches [CINCWA] dispatch 261020 of April) detached from the convoy at 1952 with its four escorts en route to Belfast, Northern Ireland.

The *Bogue* Task Group was steaming on a course of 030°T at 17 knots on April 30 with its four escorts. At 0443 the first Avenger anti-submarine patrol plane was catapulted. The patrols continued all day. At 0703 an RAF Sunderland Flying Boat flew over the carrier. When landing at 0829, Avenger #10 crashed into both barriers on the deck and damaged the plane. The crew was uninjured.[6]

On May 1, 1943, TG 92.3 was steaming with the escorts positioned at their anti-submarine screen ahead of the carrier by 4,000 yards, with the USS *Lea* at 60° on the port bow, the USS *Greene* at 15° on the port bow, the USS *Belknap* at 15° on the starboard bow, and the USS *Ingram* at 60° on the starboard bow. Another RAF Sunderland Flying Boat flew 15 miles away from the task group.

In the early morning of May 2, the TG and escorts were approaching Belfast steaming on the base course 054°T at 14.5 knots when at 0102 the group sighted the Isle of Aran Light bearing 098°T off 27 miles. Land was sighted at 0403 and the group soon passed Fanad Head Lighthouse and then Inishtrahull Lighthouse. The *Belknap* and *Greene* were detached while the *Lea* and *Ingram* maintained their anti-submarine

USS *Greene* (DD-266), circa 1919–1920. (U.S. Naval Historical Center, Photograph NH 70868.)

5. Third War Cruise

screen positions ahead of the *Bogue*. At 0950 the *Lea* and *Greene* detached to proceed to Londonderry. After numerous course changes, at 1355 the *Bogue* was anchored at Belfast Harbor in Bangor Bay, Northern Ireland. Fifty minutes later, Captain Short was visited by the liaison officer, Commander T.J. Keane, USNR, and a party: LT (jg) A.J. Hoffman, USNR; LT (jg) E.E. Eager, USNR; Ensign H.B. Beauregard, USNR; Ensign R.H. Lidey, USNR; Third Officer S. Morrison of W.R.E.N.; and Miss D. Kirkpatrick. Later, at 1620, Commander Fillmore of the Royal Navy called on the captain.

On May 3 the *Bogue* got underway and moved to moor at 1149 at the Sydenham Aerodrome Jetty, Belfast. The captain was visited by Rear Admiral R.H.L. Bevan and his 10 aides. The carrier and her escorts stayed for two weeks for training at the British Anti-submarine School at Bally Kelly in Northern Ireland. During this time in port, the *Bogue* was outfitted with HF/DF equipment. This was a critical enhancement to the U-boat search capability. When the *Bogue* left Belfast, Royal Navy officer Commander Jack Broome was aboard to supervise the operation of the new HF/DF set.

Captain Short spoke of the convoy tactics used during the early cruises and remarked that the "ship's aircraft must be flown and safely

USS *Osmond Ingram* (DD-255) underway, probably circa 1922. (Courtesy of Donald M. McPherson, 1975. Naval History and Heritage Command Photo, Catalog #NH 78138.)

recovered to justify even an ACV gamboling about in the playgrounds of the U-boats."[7] The old procedure, as used in the previous convoys in March and April, was to protect the carrier by positioning it in the middle of the convoy, giving it at least a two-column spacing behind the leading ship (usually the convoy commodore's ship). The problem with this positioning was that the tactical diameter of the carrier operations was 690 to 750 yards, which was not available in the center. Of like significance was that the carrier needed wind over the deck of 31 knots to properly take off a fully loaded Avenger and 27 knots wind for a loaded F4F Wildcat. The usual convoy was steaming around seven knots, so when flight operations were underway the *Bogue* had to exit the center location and move away from the convoy, choose the best wind speed direction, and begin takeoffs and recovery operations. Later the carrier had to regain its convoy center position. It was a great strain on the crew to carry out these actions. The decision was made that the *Bogue* and her escorts on the next mission would take up station at the rear of the convoy to allow for freedom of action.[8]

Captain Short noted in his interview on June 22, 1943, that he recommended "the reduction of fighter complement from the previous number of twelve planes to six in order to carry more TBFs because it did not seem that we would use fighters in this work. However, as the submarines started shooting, the problem comes up again as to what is now the best complement for the carrier." It was at this time at Belfast that VC-9 had the number of Avengers increased to 12, with the number of F4F Wildcats reduced to six.[9]

The *Bogue* remained moored at Sydenham Airdrome Jetty until May 13 when tugs *Audacious*, *Empire Medal*, and *Empire Cherub* directed the carrier into the channel to anchor at 1912 at bearing 16° 45' to Black Head Light. The next morning at 0110, the carrier got underway from Bangor Bay, Belfast, Northern Ireland, to anchorage in the Firth of Clyde, Scotland, for calibration of the new HF/DF equipment. By 0715 she was anchored in the Firth of Clyde in 21 fathoms of water at Skelmore Bank Bell Buoy. The HF/DF calibration officer and his party came aboard at 0755, and after completing their work, they departed the ship at 1932.

The *Bogue* got underway at 2002 heading to anchor at Bangor Bay at 0105 May 15, bearing to Mew Island 090°. At 1637 the carrier got underway followed by escorts *Greene*, *Belknap*, *Badger*, and *Ingram* joining it by 2010. On a course 330°T at 16 knots, CTG 92.3 steamed without the USS *Lea* en route to Iceland in compliance with Commander-in-Chief,

5. Third War Cruise

Western Approaches (CINCWA) dispatch 121933 to refuel, join, and support convoy ON-184.

On May 17 at 2040, the carrier anchored at Hvalfjordur, Iceland, and cut its engines. The Royal British Navy tug *Golden Emblem* came along to receive 46 bags of mail. At 0035 the next morning, the *Bogue* exited the channel with its four escorts to rendezvous with the ocean liner SS *Toltec* off Grotta Light, Iceland, and headed to join with the convoy ON-184. This action was directed in dispatch 172258 from the Flag Officer Commanding Iceland to CTG 92.3. The USS *Lea* joined up with the *Bogue* task force at 0854 and positioned as before in the anti-submarine screen.

Convoy ON-184 had left Liverpool on May 15 en route to New York with 36 merchant ships and 17 escorts (not including the *Bogue* Task Group).

On May 19, 1943, the *Bogue* Task Group (also known as the 6th Escort Group) steamed on course 195°T at 16 knots with the five escorts ahead in the anti-submarine screen, with the SS *Toltec* behind the carrier 600 yards in column. Three Avengers were launched to find the convoy, which was located at 0545 off 20 miles. Convoy ON-184 was sighted at bearing 108°T, and the *Bogue* and escorts joined at 0745 on convoy course 264°T, with the carrier positioned astern of the escort tanker in the commodore's column. This action was specified in CINCWA dispatch 151029. The HMCS *Itchen* came alongside to allow an officer to speak with Captain Short. Avengers #9, #11, and #7 took off on patrol at 1844. They were recovered aboard by 2103.

The convoy continued westward the next day on base course 238°T averaging 10 knots as the *Bogue* Task Group steamed at 16 knots. At 0955 the USS *Lea* reported that ship 93 was dead in the water to transfer an injured man to the rescue ship.[10]

As the convoy was steaming along, Admiral Dönitz had directed the wolfpack code-named *Donau-Mosel* made up of 42 U-boats to attack and overwhelm the convoy. The U-boats formed a barrier between the Grand Bank and Greenland. With Enigma intercepts and HF/DF plots, the 10th Fleet for the first time alerted the *Bogue* of the German force in front of them.

On May 21 at 2110, dusk, convoy ON-184 was steaming south by west some 520 miles southeast of Cape Farewell (the southern tip of Greenland) as the VC-9 skipper, Lieutenant Commander Drane, was patrolling on his second leg of his search in an Avenger. Suddenly he sighted the wake of *U-231* some eight miles to his starboard, 60 miles from the carrier. He alerted the *Bogue* and hurried toward the submarine, circled around to approach dead ahead, dropping from 3,000 to 50 feet, lowered his wheels, and dropped four Mk 44 flat-nosed bombs on the submarine. Drane continued on his course for 10 seconds to allow his crew to take pictures, but the submarine was obscured by smoke and sea spray from the bombs. He came around to see if he could find the submarine. It was gone. He then climbed to 7,000 feet and tried to contact the *Bogue*. As it happened, *U-231* was severely damaged in the bridge, but it was able to dive and escape any further attacks. The submarine reached its base at La Pallice, France, for repairs. Low on fuel, with only 30 gallons left, Drane had to head back to the *Bogue* as the escorts USS *Ingram* and HMCS *Saint Laurent* raced ahead of the convoy to search for the submarine.[11]

Starting at 0430 on May 22, Avengers #9, #2, #5, and #1 launched on the morning anti-submarine patrol ahead of the convoy. At 0535 Lieutenant (jg) Roger C. Kuhn in Avenger #2 was dogging rain squalls flying in and out of clouds when he spotted *U-468* surfacing three miles away and about 55 miles southeast of the carrier. He climbed up to 3,000 feet and when he broke through the cloud cover, the U-boat gunners immediately fired at him with their 20mm guns. Kuhn accidently switched on his VHF radio instead of his intercom and said, "Well. I'll be damned! They're shooting at us!"[12] His voice was heard on the *Bogue*. As the *U-468* gun crew continued to fire, he pushed over and executed a 50-degree dive, started firing his .30-caliber cowl guns, and released four depth bombs at 150 feet that exploded aft and under the stern of the submarine.

The submarine, unable to submerge, stopped and began circling by the stern, leaving a trail of oil on the water. Compressed air and steam was sent skyward up to 50 feet high on two occasions as the U-boat crew tried to blow her tanks. Kuhn radioed the *Bogue:* "She's down by the stern, but fighting back." The *U-468* remained on the surface for an hour and two minutes after the attack, moving slowly and making a small circle until, with only the conning tower showing, she slid under the water by the stern with her bow pointing up at 30 degrees.

When Kuhn had reported his position to the carrier, it was in error. Since the carrier could not get a radar fix on his aircraft, the plot was wrong. As time passed, Kuhn wondered where the relief planes were and called the carrier. Finally, the *Bogue* plotted a correct position and relief planes and escorts were sent to search the area. Despite the damage inflicted, *U-468* was able to make repairs and return to port.

5. Third War Cruise

In a debrief aboard the *Bogue*, Kuhn described the action: "By the time I got my bombs armed, the tracers were coming pretty close. Then I got within range and opened up with my forward machine gun. My tracers seemed to disappear right into the conning tower. I don't know whether I hit the gun crew but at any rate they stopped firing a couple of seconds before I released my load. When I looked back the submarine was completely enveloped in spray. When she came out, her stern was down and she was slowly in a circle at about two knots."[13]

After more than an hour after the attack on *U-468*, while Lieutenant (jg) O.J. Donahoe was looking for Kuhn flying in his F4F Wildcat fighter, he saw *U-305* off 30 miles ahead of the convoy. Before he could close on the submarine, it immediately dived and disappeared. An Avenger piloted by Ensign Stewart E. Doty sighted a long wake of the same submarine out nine miles away. When he dropped out of the clouds, Doty saw the submarine 1.5 miles ahead of him. The captain of the U-boat, Kapitanlieutenant Rudolf Bahr, did not see Doty for the first 15 seconds and sent out an aircraft contact report, which the *Bogue's* HF/DF picked up. The U-boat opened fire on Doty as he executed a 20-degree dive and dropped four depth bombs from 60 feet at the stern.

The crew of Doty's Avenger reported that the entire submarine was enveloped by the explosions and the stern appeared to be thrown off course about 15 degrees and falling aft. They thought *U-305* was out of control, but after a minute and a half it settled below the surface in an oil slick. Two minutes later the conning tower and 20–30 feet of the bow reappeared on a 45-degree angle. Excited, Ensign Doty reported to the *Bogue*, "I got the son-of-a-bitch. He's straight up and down." He asked his crew to get a picture of the submarine. Then *U-305* slowly settled stern first until only eight to 10 feet was visible. Twenty seconds later the bow slipped under the water at 45 degrees. More oil came up. The USS *Ingram* arrived to see no indication of *U-305*. Incredibly the submarine resurfaced a little after noon and was met by another Avenger piloted by Lieutenant (jg) Robert L. Stearns.

Stearns attacked from 1,200 feet when he was 750 yards away using his .30-caliber cowl gun as the submarine fired its 20mm anti-aircraft gun on the conning tower. At 125 feet in a 30-degree dive, Stearns dropped his depth bombs some 25 feet off the port side of *U-305*. It cracked the pressure hull of the submarine as it turned hard starboard and disappeared. Incredibly, *U-305* was able to make repairs and arrived at Brest, France, on June 1.[14]

USS *Bogue*

At 1636 the carrier detected the HF/DF contact on a bearing 067° off 30 miles. This was *U-569*, which had been dodging planes and destroyers for a while. Lieutenant (jg) William F. Chamberlain in Avenger #6 was launched at 1656. He found *U-569* cruising along on the surface some eight minutes later and dropped four depth bombs. *U-569* immediately dived as Chamberlain circled the area hoping to see him resurface.

Lieutenant H.S. Roberts, having taken off at 1717 in Avenger #7, arrived at the scene to assist Chamberlain. At 1740, *U-569* surfaced just below Roberts's Avenger. Roberts reacted quickly and dived from 600 feet, releasing four depth bombs (2 Mk 44 flat-nosed torpex and 2 Mk 17–2 flat-nosed TNT depth charges), which exploded near the stern. The submarine submerged and descended to 350 feet deep before gaining control. The tanks were blown and *U-569* resurfaced out of the water at a 30-degree angle. It slid back under and came back up two more times. Roberts was confident that *U-569* was in trouble. With the submarine now remaining surfaced, Roberts's gunner started shooting at the conning tower. The submarine crew began coming out of the conning tower, with some waving white cloths and jumping into the water.

At this time Chamberlain charged in, having heard Roberts's report of the battle. His gunner added his bullets to the onslaught. Both Avengers circled shooting and waiting for the escort HMCS *Saint Laurent* to reach the scene. At 1900 the destroyer reported that *U-569* had opened up the flood valves, nosed up, and—in rough seas—sank in view of the escort. Of the crew of 46, there were only 24 survivors (21 enlisted and three officers), including the captain (Oberleutnant zur See der Reserve Hans Johannsen), to be rescued. (After taken prisoner, Johannsen was eventually taken to the POW camp at Papago Park, Arizona. On February 12, 1944, he was one of five U-boat commanders to escape from the camp but was soon recaptured some 30 miles across the Mexican border.)

The debrief of the survivors indicated that the second drop of depth bombs caused the most damage, as the high-pressure lines broke, which caused a leak in the aft compartment. By the time the water finally reached the electric power, the boat was too heavy by the stern. With no way to trim the boat, there was no choice but to surface and receive the gunfire from the Avenger. Johannsen ordered the crew to go up to the deck and display white napkins. The chief engineer was sent down to flood valves, but he never returned.

The *U-569* was scuttled and sank east of Newfoundland, in position 50.40 N, 35.21 W. At 2040 all aircraft were recovered for this long

5. Third War Cruise

day of May 22, 1943, aboard the *Bogue*. The sinking of *U-569* was the first successful sinking by the USS *Bogue*, which would become a bellwether of events to follow.[15]

The U.S. Atlantic Fleet was impressed with the performance during the attack on *U-569*. Since the USS *Bogue* was assigned to operate from April 22 to May 30, 1943, under the command of the Royal Navy, the British awarded the Distinguished Service Cross to Lieutenant Commander Drane, Lieutenant Roberts, and Lieutenant (jg) Chamberlain for their part in the submarine attacks during the cruise. The Avenger gunners ARM1c James O. Stine and AOM2c Rex Boyd received the Distinguished Service Medal.[16]

The next morning on May 23, the convoy was steaming on a base course of 260°T at 10 knots while the *Bogue* launched four anti-submarine Avengers into the wind by catapult from 0425 to 0429. They were landed by 0751. An HF/DF contact was reported at 1030 bearing 080° at 40 miles from the carrier. The HMS *Woodstock* dropped depth charges off the starboard bow at 8,000 yards. No contact was acquired.

Anti-submarine and ice patrols were maintained with the *Bogue's* five escorts screening ahead of the carrier as usual from May 24 through the 25th. At 0859 CTG 92.3 detached from convoy ON-184 and headed to Argentia. At 1212 on May 26, as the weather had cleared, the *Bogue* and escorts passed Cape Saint Mary's Lighthouse. By 1515 the *Bogue* was moored in Little Placentia Harbor to Buoy Prep 6 with Fox Island bearing 327°T.[17]

While in port, a test was tried to launch an F4F from the catapult while at anchor. Lieutenant (jg) Frank Fodge's plane captain, AMM2C Bud Snyder, said that "my fighter was on the catapult ready to be launched at full power, when the hold-back ring broke prematurely, and the plane taxied off the deck into the cold waters of Argentia Bay. Fodge was OK but cold and wet."[18]

On the 27th, the Y.S.D. 23 (*Mary Ann*) stood off the starboard side for salvage of the F4F aircraft catapult test plane. At 1220 Lieutenant (jg) Chamberlain crashed his F4F Wildcat on landing aboard the *Bogue* after gunnery drill at Argentia Field, Newfoundland. At 1815 the USS *Clemson* reported for duty with the task group.

The *Bogue* remained moored through May 30, 1943, receiving supplies. During this cruise, the flight hours of VC-9 were increased to 182 hours.[19]

6

Fourth War Cruise

"We have been chasing you for fourteen days."

The Sixth Escort Group consisting of the USS *Bogue*, as flagship, and CORTDIV 1 (USS *Belknap*, USS *Clemson*, USS *Greene*, USS *Osmond Ingram*, and USS *George E. Badger*) was designated as CTG 21.12 (CINCLANT 301616) under the operational control of the Commander-in-Chief, U.S. Atlantic Fleet (Admiralty 301210B). On May 31, 1943, the *Bogue* was moored at Buoy P-6 in Little Placentia Harbor, Argentia, and got underway at 1052 (without the USS *Belknap*) out of the harbor. The carrier recovered at 1112 Avengers #1, #6, and #10, followed at 1215 by landing aboard six F4F fighters.[1]

The CTG was en route to 40° N, 50° W, in support of North African convoys. But there was a change in the orders. Admiral Royal E. Ingersoll, commander in chief of the Atlantic Fleet, had stated "that close air support of central transatlantic convoys was a waste of effort." He deemed it better to give the commanders of escort carriers complete discretion to hunt these U-boats by HF/DF fixes or transfer their support to another convoy that needed close protection. Now Captain Short would have more freedom to operate as he saw fit.

The results of the third war cruise for the *Bogue* along with other Allied positive developments seemed to prove that events were turning in the favor of the Allied forces in the North Atlantic against the U-boat campaign. Back in January 1943, the total tonnage losses were 180,000 tons of shipping, rising to 576,000 tons for March. But the losses in May dropped to 211,929 tons, while U-boat sinkings were increased to 41 U-boats.[2]

> As evidence on this new situation, on May 24 Admiral Dönitz sent a message to all his U-boat captains: "The situation in the North Atlantic now forces a temporary shift of operations to areas less endangered by aircraft."[3]
> On the same day, he broadcast an appeal to all officers of submarines: "You alone can, at the moment, make an offensive attack against the enemy

6. Fourth War Cruise

and beat him. The U-boat must, by continuous sinking of ships with war material and the necessary supplies for the British Isles, force the enemy to continual losses which must slowly but steadily sap the strength of the strongest force. The German people have long felt that our boats constitute the keenest and most decisive weapon and that the outcome of the war depends on the success or failure of the Battle of the Atlantic.... The time will soon come in which you will be superior to the enemy with new and stronger weapons and will be able to triumph over your worst enemy-the aircraft and the destroyer."[4]

Two days later Dönitz ordered what he felt was the best opportunity to regain higher Allied merchant tonnage with a new Group "Trutz" of 17 U-boats to form a patrol line along the meridian between the latitudes 32° and 39° N.[5]

It was ironic that in May 1943, the number of U-boats reached their peak level at 240 operational boats and 118 at sea. But on May 23, Admiral Karl Dönitz withdrew almost all of his U-boats from the North Atlantic as a result of losing 43 of them in convoy battles with Allied forces. This loss of a fifth of his U-boat fleet became known as "Black Friday." Another sad fact for Dönitz was that during this period his 21-year-old son, Peter Dönitz, was killed on May 19 when *U-954* was sunk along with all hands by hedgehog attacks from sloop HMS *Sennen* and frigate HMS *Jed* of the Royal Navy, both escorting convoy SC-130.[6]

This Allied success in protecting North Atlantic convoys was caused by the effectiveness of the HF/DF network, improved radar and sonar, improved tactics and weapons, and most of all the use of Ultra intercepts to reroute convoys away from U-boat wolfpacks. The latest code to be broken on December 12, 1942, was the *Triton* key network (a separate key network for Atlantic U-boats), so the German submarine radio messages could be read. The decoded messages were relayed to the 10th Fleet and Submarine Tracking Room of the British Operational Intelligence Center for quick message distribution to Allied ships and escort carriers like the USS *Bogue*.[7]

On June 1, 1943, CFG 21.12 was ordered by CINCLANT (011406) to operate offensively in appropriate areas against submarines in support of African convoys normally outside a 500-mile circle from Bermuda unless necessary to continue offensive operations in the area. Captain Short was directed to protect convoys steaming from the U.S. to Gibraltar, while simultaneously attacking U-boats. Back on May 24, Short had been advised of the existence of Group Trutz by COMINCH in Washington.

USS *Bogue*

When *Bogue's* CTG 21.12 reached the patrol area at 35° N, 45° W on June 1, Short was faced with two options: (1) head directly for the concentration of U-boats or (2) support the westbound convoy GUS-7A among the other convoys UGS-9 (eastbound NYC to Port Said, Egypt with 79 merchant ships/14 escorts) and Flight 10 (eastbound with 19 British LCI[L] landing craft ships convoy Norfolk-Bermuda-Gibraltar). He decided to support convoy GCS-7A, which was diverted south of the line and steaming around the southern end of the Trutz line, while CTG 21.12 maintained near constant anti-submarine patrols while refueling his four escorts.[8]

On June 3 convoy GCS-7A appeared to be clear of the U-boat area, and with the good weather, the *Bogue* planes covered an eastward search area 120 miles wide and ahead of UGS-9 hoping to locate the U-boat line. During the evening, the *Bogue* Task Group changed course northeastward with no contacts until the afternoon of June 4. At 1615 the *Bogue* changed course to 205°T to launch aircraft on an HF/DF contact.

At 1640 while Oberleutnant Edwin Christophersen was on the bridge of *U-228*, Lieutenant (jg) Fryatt and Lieutenant E.W. Biros, flying in their Avengers at 2,500 feet, spotted his submarine 1.5 miles to their starboard. They both peeled off with Fryatt in the lead and came in to attack from the rear. Fryatt salvoed his depth bombs from 50 feet that exploded near the conning tower, sending up high towers of spray. The U-boat shuttered and turned violently to the right. Biros turned sharply to maneuver to line up with the submarine to drop his depth bombs from 50 feet as the explosion sent debris around while the submarine's bow came out of the water and then settled. Christophersen immediately took his submarine down by the stern and was able to escape, though he was damaged.[9]

At 1715, flying at 2,500 feet heading back to the *Bogue*, Edward R. Hodgson saw *U-603* commanded by Oberleutnant Rudolf Baltz cruising on the surface three miles ahead. The submarine was some 50 miles north of the carrier and just 10 miles south of the vulnerable Flight 10 convoy. As Hodgson came in to attack, the submarine fired antiaircraft shells at him. Coming in at 200 knots, Hodgson came up on the track and dropped four depth bombs 30 feet ahead of the U-boat. One of the bombs bounced off the submarine's jumping line before exploding. The Avenger came around to strafe and was met with heavy antiaircraft fire. By the time Hodgson made another pass, *U-603* had submerged to escape.

Meanwhile, radioman ARM2c C.J. Wojcik, flying with Lieutenant

6. Fourth War Cruise

(jg) Wilma S. Fowler's Avenger, spotted the battleship-gray-colored *U-641* on the surface five miles away. Fowler came out of the sun racing at 200 knots. With the submarine in his crosshairs, he reached his release point but decided he was coming in too fast. He came around again, which gave *U-641* time to man the guns. The Avenger arrived at 165 knots on this second pass as he was met with heavy antiaircraft fire. He released only two depth bombs, which dropped on the starboard side midway between the bow and conning tower. These caused only minor damage. *U-641's* Kapitanleutnant Horst Rendtel had his submarine turning constantly to the starboard to keep his attacker from getting a straight-in run as his gun crew fired shells at the Avenger.

At 1728 VC-9 skipper Lieutenant Commander Drane arrived to join the attack against *U-641*. He came into the fight from the starboard quarter and dropped four Mk. 17 depth bombs from 65 feet as he endured heavy flak. His engine was hit but he could still fly. Drane's bombs exploded 20 yards off the *U-641's* port quarter. The bombs caused the stern of the submarine to come out of the water. As a third plane came in, *U-641* dived at a steep angle near 40° and submerged. The American Avenger pilots thought the submarine was sunk, but Rendtel's submarine had escaped.

Since Captain Short believed the three U-boats were indeed part of the Trutz line, and he did not want to pass in the risky area at night, he turned his task group to the southwest until dawn. The next day, June 5, Short turned back to the east to reengage the U-boat line.

With the experiences from the previous day, all the Avengers launched on anti-submarine patrols were paired with an F4F fighter. At 0650 and 63 miles from the carrier, Lieutenant Richard S. Rogers (in #13 F4F) and Lieutenant (jg) Alexander C. McAuslan (in #11 Avenger) saw *U-217* off seven miles ahead cruising on the surface. Rogers raced forward and fired his six .50-caliber machine guns at the deck of the submarine. The deck gunners fired back until six of them were knocked off the deck by Rogers's bullets. By the third pass, Rogers had caused a fire in the conning tower, having expended 1,200 rounds into *U-217*.

Rogers asked McAuslan where he was, and he responded, "I'm in a dive behind you." Coming out of the sun, McAuslan released four depth bombs from 100 feet in a perfect straddle, with two dropped on the starboard side and two on the port side. The explosions were deadly, and the submarine sank with all hands (50) aboard in a steep dive just 33 seconds after the bombs hit. The *U-217* was the southernmost U-boat of the Trutz line at Lat. 30° 18' N, Long. 42° 50' W.[10]

Likewise on June 5, after it became obvious that convoy GUS-7A had slipped past his U-boats, Dönitz, in anger, ordered the Trutz U-boats to break off and fuel to the northeast from *U-488*. *U-488* was a supply and replenishment submarine tanker (a *milchkuh* or *milchcow*). *Bogue's* Task Group 21.12 at 1923 saw the convoy UGS-9, reduced speed to 11 knots, and changed course to parallel the convoy UGS-9.

There were no submarine contacts until June 8 at 0729, when *Bogue* received an HF/DF fix bearing 005°T at distance 50 miles away. As Lieutenant (jg) Letson S. Balliett was returning in his Avenger from a search as a result of the HF/DF contact, his radioman, ARM1c James H. Finch, saw *U-758* cruising along rather fast on the surface two miles away en route to the Caribbean. The U-boat commanded by Kapitanleutnant Helmut Manseck was not part of the Trutz group. He had sent the sighting contact report of convoy UGS-9, which had been intercepted by the *Bogue*.

Balliett took the wrong direction to circle around some 300° to come in from the sun to attack. He was coming in at 200 knots as bullets came past him from the submarine. *U-758* had been the first U-boat outfitted with quadruple-mounted 20mm guns and heavier armored plating fitted on the bridge. The Avenger dropped four depth bombs from 200 feet after a 45-degree angle dive that landed in the aft end of the boat, which raised the stern 15 feet out of the water. Four or five German sailors were seen swimming in the water as the submarine slowed to five knots and turned slowly to starboard to pick up the sailors.

Balliett circled around to strafe as he again was targeted with fierce antiaircraft fire, but his turret gunner silenced the enemy gunners. Kapitanleutnant Manseck sent off two messages, one to alert U-boat Command that he was being attacked by ship-based aircraft. The U-boat straightened out and sped up to 18 knots. Balliett radioed the *Bogue* and they picked him up, but he couldn't hear the carrier until his radioman disconnected the relay and held the antenna in his hand.

At 1547 Lieutenant (jg) "Monk" Fowler arrived on scene and attacked while the submarine's 20 mm shells ripped into the Avenger's engine, right wing, and bomb bay and tore off part of the horizontal stabilizer. The radioman, Wojcik, was hit as Fowler continued forward to release three depth bombs (one got hung up) close aboard the U-boat's stern. The submarine seemed to shake all over and nearly stopped. Fowler left the scene immediately with his wounded man aboard and an engine smoking. He called the *Bogue* and reported his situation. His gunner, Bucholtz, crawled back to help Wojcik. He used his belt to

6. Fourth War Cruise

make a tourniquet for Wojcik's foot, which had been hit by shrapnel. Then Fowler asked Bucholtz if all the bombs had dropped on release and learned that one had hung up. Fowler tried the emergency release and tried to shake the bomb loose, but it would not drop.

Fowler called the *Bogue*, alerting the ship of the bomb left over, and said he might have to ditch. The carrier called back and asked if they could bail out. Fowler called back, "Ship from Monk. Negative, will try to make it aboard."[11] On landing, Fowler learned that one of his tires had been blown out from flak, but thankfully the arresting cable caught the good wheel and it held. Many of the squadron mates had come on deck to witness the landing. The chaplain heard that Fowler had landed and came on deck. He had gone below to pray for Fowler and his crew. Fowler knew he was lucky to be alive when he learned that a shell from *U-758* had hit just six inches from the unexploded bomb onboard.[12]

In the debrief with VC-9 Squadron Intelligence Officer McCreath, Fowler said: "The sub opened up on me as I went in. His first blast took off part of my wing. We were running into their flak." Asked about what it was like, Fowler said it "sounded like rain hitting on a tin roof." He continued to head in, when "the cockpit filled with smoke, an acrid mixture of burnt oil and gunpowder. I pulled open the hatch and just as I released my bombs, I heard my gunner Buchholz [sic] report 'Mr. Fowler—Wojcik (my radioman) is hit!' Then the earphones buzzed with static."[13]

After the Fowler attack, *U-758* radioed U-boat Command to report that he had been attacked from a second plane and noted he was damaged and sinking. U-boat Command responded by sending *U-460* and *U-118* at top speed to Mansek at 29° 09′ N and 33° 26′ W.

Meanwhile the *Bogue* launched Lieutenant (jg) Frank D. Fogde in his Avenger and Lieutenant (jg) Phil Perabo in his F4F Wildcat fighter to join the *U-758* attack. Fogde arrived in the area first and saw the submarine slowly circling. Rather than engage into the flak known to be coming up from the enemy sub, Fogde decided to circle until his fighter partner arrived. When Perabo came in, Fogde signaled for him to strafe the U-boat and silence the gunners. Perabo raced in and engaged with his .50-caliber wing guns. His fire jammed the 20 mm Oerikons and killed and wounded most of the gunners. He did not receive any antiaircraft fire during the two runs on the sub.

Having his deck guns silenced, Mansek decided to dive. As *U-758* submerged, Fogde hurried in to attack from 70 feet with depth bombs. The submarine survived the attack, but Mansek had broken valves and a flooded compartment. He surfaced ten minutes later. Perabo strafed in two more runs at *U-758* and caused explosions near the conning tower but was met each time by heavy antiaircraft fire. Perabo called the *Bogue* for more help, but Captain Short refused to send any of his four remaining serviceable Avengers that he held in reserve for future convoy sweeps.

Captain Short had already sent three of his screening escort destroyers to engage but withdrew two of them after the on-scene pilots had messaged him not to send surface assistance. The third escort, the USS *Clemson*, arrived at 1715 and tried to make a "scare" attack on the submarine, which kept Mansek down until midnight. *U-758* was able to escape in the early morning hours of June 9. Mansek made another radio call to the U-boat Command reporting, "Eight carrier planes warded off; one shot down, four damaged. Am repairing at 27° 45' north, 35° 26' west, request physician." U-boat Command responded in a general message about *U-758* being the first submarine fitted with quadruple antiaircraft guns and repeated Mansek's report of enemy losses. The message ended with a note to Mansek declaring "Well done. Long live your quadruple."[14]

Although *U-758* had not been sunk, its message reporting the damage to U-boat Command did get intercepted by Ultra, revealing a refueling rendezvous location. The *U-460* and *U-118* were a new type of German refueling submarine. The order to aid Mansek was intercepted by the 10th Fleet, but not until June 11. Other messages were delayed when the two tanker subs contacted U-boat Command when they could not find *U-758*. HF/DF plots had defined the area of operations and Captain Short was alerted.

In the afternoon of June 9, *U-118* and *U-758* finally joined up and the next day *U-460* rendezvoused. *U-460* transferred extra fuel to *U-118* and took some of the wounded from *U-758*. *U-460* sailed with Mansek's *U-758* back to port. *U-118* moved to the previous rendezvoused position at 30° 45' N and 33° 40' W, planning to refuel outbound U-boats.[15]

June 9 and 10 found CTF 21.12 searching down the German radio bearings ahead and on the flanks of convoy UGS-9 with no contacts. At dusk on the 10th, when the first Morocco-based B-24 Liberator arrived to take on support for the convoy, the *Bogue* Task Group departed and headed west along the 30th latitude north to look for U-boats. It was not until June 12 at 1147 when a patrol picked up *U-118* cruising on the surface 20 miles astern of the carrier. Avenger pilot Lieutenant (jg) Robert Stearns was patrolling with F4F Wildcat partner Lieutenant (jg) Robert

6. Fourth War Cruise

J. Johnson and saw the submarine just a mile away. Johnson dived at *U-118* from 3,000 feet down to 15 feet on a strafing run that was raking the sub from stern to bow, with Stearns following behind to release his four depth bombs as they straddled amidships. The *U-118* was submerging and only the conning tower showing as oil was streaming behind her. Suddenly the sub surfaced immediately. It circled slowly and then sank to 25 feet below the water.

Johnson made a second strafing run, as Lieutenant (jg) Fowler and Lieutenant (jg) Raymond J. Tennant arrived a few minutes later as *U-118* was resurfacing for a second time. Fowler quickly dropped four depth bombs, with one hitting the deck forward of the conning tower and exploding close alongside it, a second hitting just ahead of the bow, and the other two exploding some 50 feet ahead. All the American planes continued to strafe *U-118* from both sides to prevent the deck crew from manning the guns.

Johnson ran out of ammunition and headed back to the *Bogue*. He was replaced by Lieutenant (jg) Fryatt, who dropped two depth bombs that straddled the conning tower. By this time, *U-118* was listing to the starboard and began to slowly sink by the stern. Fryatt tried to make another attack but there were so many planes around the submarine that he could not get near the enemy sub. The three remaining fighters made more strafing runs. Lieutenant (jg) Chamberlain arrived and

German U-boat *U-118* attacked and sunk June 12, 1943, by aircraft from USS *Bogue* (ACV-9). (Naval History and Heritage Command, Photo #80-G-68694.)

dropped two more depth bombs directly under the conning tower. He came around again and dropped two more bombs under the sub, which blew it up, sending a tower of water, oil, and debris high in the air. One of the pilots flying at 500 feet said the spray was higher than his aircraft.[16] *U-118* was the second U-boat sunk by the USS *Bogue* and VC-9. It was also the first U-boat sunk by Ultra intercepts along with HF/DF contacts.

Ensign Doty had arrived at the *U-118* location with no submarine to drop his depth bombs on. *U-118* had been hit with 16 325-pound depth charges and some 4,410 rounds of .50-caliber and 800 rounds of .30-caliber ammunition. Unknown to the attackers, *U-172* was only a few miles away submerged and waiting to rendezvous with *U-118*. As they waited, the crew could hear the explosions from *U-118* as it was destroyed.

From the survivors of *U-118*, details were soon revealed. As Stearns and Johnson had attacked with strafing, the watch standers in the conning tower were totally unaware. One of the lookouts called out the planes alert, which prompted the bridge watch to man the deck guns while the skipper, Korvettenkapitan (Commander) Werner Czygan, rushed to the bridge and gave the order to dive. Three of the bridge watch had been wounded by the first bullets from Johnson's guns, while the fourth man aided the others to safety and closed the hatch.

When the submarine reached 100 feet, the first depth bombs exploded near the stern, which caused significant damage. The diesel compartment was flooding through the exhaust valves, which caused the submarine to go down a few degrees by the stern. To regain trim, the engineering officer ordered all the men forward. In a few minutes, *U-118* was down to 165 feet when more depth bomb explosions exploded aft. Their two motors went dead, the electrical system failed, and the hydrophones and rudder were wrenched loose. Czygan ordered to blow the tanks.

When the submarine broke the surface, Czygan ordered the gun crews up to the deck to fight. As they gunners opened the hatch, they were shocked to see not two attackers but at least eight planes circling and diving on their boat. The fire from the attackers came in from both sides and most of the gunners who tried to fire were killed or wounded. Only a few magazines were fired from the deck guns. Czygan was hit several times by gunfire but bravely stayed on the bridge. Below deck only one engine was providing propulsion, while the others were blowing the tanks. The engineering officer cried out to Czygan that he could not keep the boat afloat. The skipper gave the order to abandon the boat. At least one-third of the crew was not able to leave the boat. One

6. Fourth War Cruise

survivor saw Czygan covered with blood and kneeling on the bridge as the boat was consumed with spray and debris.

When the spray cleared, the dead and the living were seen floating in the water. Fryatt flew over and dropped a raft to help the survivors. The attack on *U-118* had been terrifying for the crew. The submarine carried a crew of 58 men: six officers, three midshipmen, and 49 petty officers and men. All the officers had been killed in the conning tower. Seventeen sailors were rescued (one died later) by the destroyers USS *Clemson* and USS *Osmond Ingram*, and then were transferred the next day to the *Bogue*. Some of the survivors were wounded from Mansek's *U-758*. *U-118* had been sunk about 1400Z on May 12, 1943, some 600 miles southwest of the Azores at 30^0 14' N., 34^0 00' W.[17]

The VC-9 squadron intelligence officer, Lieutenant McCreath, debriefed the survivors. *U-118* had departed from Bordeaux, France, after May 21. One prisoner stated, "We have been chasing you for fourteen days." The *Bogue* had left Argentia 13 days before. McCreath noted: "They seemed to know when we left Argentia and to be well posted on our movements to date; but did not know our destination. All prisoners expressed a great fear of fighters."[18] *U-118* was a unique submarine, a 1,600-ton combination of a minelayer and refueling tanker, and the first of three in the German fleet at the time. The submarine had sunk four Allied ships (14,989 tons) and she had completed a mission to mine the Straits of Gibraltar.

On June 20, CTG 21.12 steamed into Hampton Roads with USS *Bogue* launching eight Avengers and five F4F Wildcats fighters to NAS Norfolk, Virginia, between 0702 and 0725. The carrier docked at 1330 at Northside Pier 7, Naval Operating Base, Norfolk. The carrier was greeted by a message from Admiral Ingersoll, CINCLANT: "Well done. Results indicate hard work and thorough training." CINCINCH Admiral King added, "Regret that your magnificent performance cannot be given public recognition, but it is still necessary to keep the Germans guessing to what happened to their U/Bs." On June 27, the *Bogue* and VC-9 received the following message from the Royal Navy admiral commanding the Western Approaches, "The Battle of the Atlantic has taken a definite turning in our favor during the past two months, and returns show an ever increasing toll of U-boats and decreasing losses of merchant ships in convoy.... Particularly gratifying is the invaluable success of the aircraft of the Escort Carrier *Bogue* which have given invaluable service in the Battle."[19]

7

Fifth War Cruise

"Loud howling noise which increased in intensity for a few seconds."

Still moored at Pier 7 at NOB, Norfolk on June 21, 1943, the USS *Bogue* got underway at 1513 en route to the Norfolk Navy Yard at Portsmouth. She was moored at 1827 on the port side at berth 29, Pier 4. The *Bogue* remained moored at Portsmouth until July 6 making necessary repairs and checking out systems. At 0706 the carrier got underway and steamed back to the Naval Operating Base at Norfolk, mooring at 1004 on the starboard side to Pier 5, berth 55. That day the *Bogue* commenced loading ammunition and 687,960 gallons of fuel oil. On July 8, the *Bogue* received 161,230 gallons of aviation gasoline.[1]

In a change of command ceremony on July 9, 1943, Captain Joseph Brantley Dunn, the former executive officer of the carrier, took over command of the USS *Bogue* from Captain Giles Short, who headed for duty in the Pacific. Dunn was born in Europe, Mississippi, in 1899, and graduated in the class of 1922 at the U.S. Naval Academy at Annapolis. His early career was spent in various submarines, and he commanded the USS *R-6*. He then shifted his focus to aviation and became a naval aviator, which was a designation held by only a few submarine officers.[2]

The carrier got underway on July 10 and anchored in Chesapeake Bay on a bearing 275° from Wolf Trap. The HF/DF system was calibrated. On July 12, the *Bogue* got underway to the degaussing range, which was completed at 0742.

On July 12, in compliance with CINCLANT 012356, Task Group 21.13—consisting of the flagship USS *Bogue* and escorts USS *Clemson, George E. Badger, Osmond Ingram,* and *Belknap*—departed Chesapeake Bay to join convoy UGS-12 en route to North African waters. The USS *Greene* was ordered to join CTG 21.13 upon completion of repairs at the Norfolk Navy Yard. USS *Belknap* was detached from the TG in response to dispatch 122350 to return to Hampton Roads for urgent repairs.

7. Fifth War Cruise

CTG 21.13 was given full authority by CINCLANT dispatch 102109 to leave the vicinity of a convoy to operate effectively against submarine concentration wherever submarine information indicated that it would be possible to operate against U-boats and yet be in a position to cover a convoy to prevent a wolfpack attack on it.

At 0515 on July 13, the *Bogue*, in company with escorts *Clemson* and *Ingram*, sighted convoy UGS-12 (departed Hampton Roads July 12 en route to Gibraltar with 78 merchant ships and 14 escorts) bearing 250°T at 12 miles away. By 0632 the carrier took its position on the flank of the convoy steaming at nine knots. The anti-submarine air patrols were being maintained all day. The convoy base course was 113°T.

On the 14th, the USS *Badger* joined TG 21.13, and the TG departed the convoy at 1535. The base course was established at 090°T, with the *Bogue* screened by the three escorts ahead in their standard anti-submarine protection positions. The next day, July 15, at 0036, the *Bogue* received an HF/DF contact bearing 097°T at a distance of 45 miles. The carrier shifted the course to 075°T and launched the anti-submarine air patrol of four F4F fighters at 0522. At 1137 it resumed base course to 090°T running at 16 knots. It received another HF/DF contact at 2126, bearing 085°T off at 35 miles, and modified the course to 180°T.

On the 17th, the *Bogue* refueled it escorts: at 0720 it delivered 39,555 gallons to the USS *Ingram*, at 1005 delivered 38,869 gallons to the USS *Clemson*, and at 1203 delivered 37,846 gallons to the USS *Badger*. At 1602 planes reported an object in the water on the port bow. The *Ingram* found the object was a raft bearing the name "Triton." TG 21.13 resumed base course 180°T at 16 knots. The next day at 1434, an Avenger spotted an object 10,000 yards ahead of the carrier, which was investigated by the *Ingram* and found to be another empty raft. The escort dropped a depth charge to sink the raft, but it was unsuccessful. At 2300 the *Bogue* received an HF/DF contact (Class "C" Naval Enigma), bearing 210° at 50 miles away.

A milestone was reached on July 19, 1943, at location 32° 3' N, 40° 33' W. by Lieutenant (jg) H.E. Fryatt piloting Avenger Bureau number 24114 when the 1,000th landing was made aboard the USS *Bogue*. Later, at 2311, a Class B HF/DF submarine contact was received by the *Bogue* at a bearing 291°T. On July 21 at 1045, in company with convoy UGS-12, an HF/DF contact was received by the commander of the convoy escorts bearing 066°T. Anti-submarine air patrol investigated with no contact made.[3]

Sunrise over a convoy photographed from the deck of the USS *Bogue* (CVE-9) in mid–Atlantic, July 14, 1943. (National Archives Catalog #80-G-86005.)

Also on the 21st, the 10th Fleet reported in its daily submarine estimate that there was a concentration of U-boats ahead of convoy UGS-12. It was also the day that the U-boat Command warned U-boats that Allied aircraft from carriers were operating 600 miles south of the Azores and told them to operate far to the west of the Azores. The next day, CTG 21.13 moved away from the convoy and set its base course to 323°T to patrol the U-boat concentration area. Several HF/DF contacts were received that evening.[4]

Flying in intermittent rain squalls with low clouds on July 23 at around 0600, an Avenger/Wildcat team, Ensign Stewart Doty and Lieutenant (jg) O.J. Donahoe, saw a surfaced U-boat 11 miles ahead of the *Bogue* at a bearing of 290°T. Donahoe strafed, and Doty released his depth bombs on the U-boat (possibly *U-613*). The submarine escaped but left a trailing oil slick.

At 0906 the USS *Badger* got a sonar contact 1,100 yards away and 4,000 yards off the port bow of the *Bogue*. Lieutenant Thomas H. Byrd, the *Badger's* skipper, ordered a left full rudder but the submarine was inside the destroyer's turning radius, so it could not attack. Contact was lost for a few moments, then regained by the sonar operator. The *Badger* made two eight-charge patterns set for 600 feet but nothing but water came up to the surface. The U-boat was trying to evade the destroyer by making turns back and forth. A third attack was attempted when the submarine was slowly turning to the right. Contact was lost at 400 yards and another eight-charge attack failed. The depth charges were

7. Fifth War Cruise

reset, and sonar regained contact with the submarine turning inside the radius again. Byrd skillfully countered with a hard left rudder and engaged again for another depth charging. This time the explosions sounded different. It was the sound of the U-boat being ripped open to discharge debris, diesel oil, splintered wood, clothing, and bodies that floated to the surface.

The *Badger's* sonar operator described the sound as a "loud howling noise which increased in intensity for a few seconds, followed by intermittent bubbling and hissing sounds."[5] Postwar evidence revealed that the submarine sunk was the 769-ton *U-613*, which had been en route to Jacksonville on a minelaying mission. *U-613* was sunk at 35° 32' N, 28° 36' W, with 48 dead (all hands lost).[6]

Just after noon, the CFG 21.13 was 42 miles from UGS-12 when Lieutenant (jg) Stearns ran into a pair of U-boats. He was at 300 feet just under the clouds when he saw oil patches. Minutes later his gunner saw two wakes some 50 yards apart. They were being made by the 1,144-ton *U-527* and the 769-ton *U-648* in the process of fueling. The quick-moving crew of *U-648* were able to submerge before Stearns was able to make an attack.

The captain of *U-527* was Kapitanleutnant (Lieutenant Commander) Herbert Uhlig on his second patrol returning from the Gulf of Mexico. Uhlig had been ordered to meet *U-67* and *U-648*. Of course, *U-67* had already been sunk by the USS *Core's* aircraft.

As Stearns's Avenger approached, Uhlig moved to a fogbank at 15 knots while using his newly installed 20mm guns mounted aft of the bridge to fire at Stearns. Stearns came in too fast to get effective gunfire on the sub, but he was able to drop four Mk. 47 depth bombs (fused for 25 feet) dead astern. The stern was covered with spray as the pressure hull of *U-527* was torn open aft of the conning tower by the explosions. One man was sent airward and several others jumped overboard because of the explosions. The entire crew was stunned as the submarine turned slowly to the right. Smoke was rising aft from the conning tower. The bow of *U-527* rose higher and higher in the water until it was nearly vertical. Then she sank stern first.

Stearns circled around, dropped his flaps and wheels, and decreased his speed to 80 knots to fly over the German survivors floating in the water as his gunner, Frank Dittmer, and radioman, Meyers, tried to drop the 12-man raft to the men below. The plane's slip stream caused the raft to become jammed, but Dittmer, held by the belt by Meyers, somehow was able to drop the raft. The USS *Clemson* was dispatched to the scene to recover the 13 survivors, who included Uhlig. After landing back aboard the *Bogue*, Stearns and his crew were called before Captain Dunn and read the riot act for endangering the plane and their lives. *U-527* was sunk at 35° 25' N, 27° 56' W with 13 survivors and 40 dead.[7]

On July 24, the CTG 21.13 was steaming in position 84 in convoy UGS-12 on the base course 120°T at nine knots. The anti-submarine patrol launched three Avengers and the three F4F fighter partners between 0516 and 0522. At 0912 Avenger #12, flown by Lieutenant (jg) Hodgson, dropped a message on the flight deck of the *Bogue* stating "sighted freighter course 250°T, 8 kts, red-yellow-red (equal horizontal stripes) flag, Name Castillo-Bellver, bearing 035°T., 40 miles at 0800 from convoy posit. Cargo not recognizable. No recognition signal attempted. Cad-2 on stern."[8] At 1215 a whaleboat from the USS *Clemson* transferred five German prisoners, including Kapitanleutnant Herbert Uhlig, to the *Bogue*.

At 1700 escort USS *Ingram* reported a submarine radar contact on bearing 307°T at 14,000 yards. An hour and 15 minutes later, an Avenger marked the location of the contact and waited for the destroyer to arrive. At 1850 a plane reported a submarine bearing 290°T turned to the starboard after the dive. No contact was made later. An HF/DF was received by the *Bogue* at 2220 bearing 181°T class C.

On July 26, CFG 21.13 detached from convoy UGS-12 for Casablanca since the *Ingram* was having boiler problems and required repairs. At 1155 on July 26, the *Bogue* received a dispatch warning of the possibility of being attacked by long-range German Focke-Wolf 200 aircraft from FOC Gibraltar. As a response to the possible threat, Captain Dunn maintained continual daytime fighter patrols over the carrier until the TG arrived at Casablanca on August 1, 1943. This was one of the few times an Atlantic escort carrier had to operate in such a manner.[9]

The *Bogue* arrived and moored on August 1 to starboard at Vettee Transversale, berths 21 and 22, at Casablanca, French Morocco, in North Africa. At 1320 eight more German prisoners from the USS *Clemson* were transferred aboard the *Bogue*. Prisoners Metrosengefreiters Kennemund, with a fracture of the right ankle, and Steinmetz, with hemorrhages on the right calf, were admitted to sick bay. At 1900 six prisoners were turned over to Lieutenant White from Naval Operating Base, Casablanca. The next day, five more prisoners were turned over to the NOB, Casablanca and two transferred to Naval Intelligence. While

7. Fifth War Cruise

moored at Casablanca, the #2 40mm and #11 20mm guns were always manned in case of enemy air attack.

Between 1435 and 1504 on Thursday, August 5, 1943, CTG 21.13 with the USS *Bogue*, escorted by the *Clemson*, *Ingram*, and *Badger*, departed Casablanca in compliance with CINCLANT 042020 en route to the U-boat concentrations in the vicinity of the Azores with a mission to conduct offensive operations against submarines in the area until time to support Task Group 63 escorting GUS-11. The escorts maintained their standard anti-submarine screening pattern ahead of the *Bogue* with one at 50° on the port side, one dead ahead, and one at 50° on the starboard side.

The *Bogue* received a message in CINCLANT 060056 on August 6 at best speed to support Task Group 64 escorting convoy UGS-13. The *Bogue* reached UGS-13 on the 8th and took position in the convoy.[10]

Back on August 4, Admiral Dönitz revealed his growing concern when he noted "the supply situation has already had its effect on operation" and "there are no more reserve tankers." Morale was another problem in the German U-boat fleet. On August 6, Dönitz relayed to his U-boat commanders, "Do not report matters which ratings do not need to know by officer's cipher." The admiral also knew his skippers were not taking seriously his message that "the sinking of an aircraft carrier is of greatest importance. If a boat sights a carrier she should attack at all costs; the carrier is always the most important target."[11]

For the following days until returning homeward toward the west, CTG 21.13 continued to occasionally receive moderate to weak HF/DF contacts and some radar and sound contacts, but they yielded only negative results. On August 9, CTG 21.13 received CINCLANT 091837 to detached convoy UGS-13 (departed Hampton Roads on 27 July 1943, en route to Port Said, 97 merchants and 29 escorts) with TG 64 shifting to convoy UGS-11 (departed Hampton Roads on 27 June 1943, en route Port Said, 92 merchants and 30 escorts) with TG 63. The next day at 1852, the *Bogue* sighted convoy GUS-11 (departed Alexandria on 28 July 1943 en route Hampton Roads, 92 merchants and 11 escorts) off 13 miles. The convoy moved at 8.8 knots on base courses between 250°T to 280°T. On August 13, a convoy escort had a sound contact and dropped depth charges at 2358, with negative results.

On August 17, CTG 21.13 received orders from CINCLANT dispatch 171841 to detach from convoy GUS-11 to arrive at Hampton Roads on the 23rd. On August 20 at 1725, the *Bogue* sighted a PBM patrol plane. Later that day Avenger #4 crashed into the flight deck barrier

USS *Bogue*

when the tail hook was detached from the aircraft. On August 23 at 0640, CTG 21.13 passed Hampton Roads. The escorts detached at 0657. At 1249 the USS *Bogue* was moored on starboard side to Pier 7, berth 73 at the Naval Operating Base, Norfolk. The *Bogue* had completed its successful fifth war cruise.[12]

8

Sixth War Cruise

> *"No contacts with the enemy were made on the squadron's first operational cruise."*

On August 23, 1943, VC-9 was detached for a well-deserved rest and replaced by Composite Squadron 19 (VC-19) of 36 officers and 50 men flying 12 Avengers and nine F4F Wildcat fighters. The new squadron commanding officer was Lieutenant Commander Claude Weaver Stewart, USN, of Seattle, Washington.

Still moored on August 24, 1943, to Pier 7, berth 73 at NOB, Norfolk, the *Bogue* got underway at 1158 and steamed up the Elizabeth River Channel. At 1327 the *Bogue* was moored to the N&PBL Railway Pier at the Norfolk Navy Yard at Portsmouth. The carrier got underway on the 29th and moved to a new mooring at Pier 1-A, still at Portsmouth. The next day, the *Bogue* moved to NOB Norfolk to Pier 7, berth 75.[1]

On September 3, VC-19 embarked aboard the *Bogue*, with escorts *Badger*, *Ingram*, and *Clemson* designated by CINCLANT as CTG 21.12. The mission was to escort convoy UGS-17 and act offensively against U-boats. UGS-17 was scheduled to depart Hampton Roads on September 6, 1943, en route to Port Said with 106 merchants and 22 escorts.

On September 5, the *Bogue* steamed from Norfolk again searching Atlantic waters for U-boats. The carrier and Task Group 21.12 joined with convoy UGS-17 on the 7th.

The Atlantic U-boat contacts were slow to come by in September for the escort carriers due to a number of factors: the U-boat sinkings of June and July, most especially the refuelers; the increase in U-boats fitted out with antiaircraft armament; the shift of U-boat concentrations to other locations by Dönitz; the increased long range of land-based ASW aircraft; and, of course, the increase in the number of Allied escort carriers now deployed in the Atlantic.

A new factor that was thought of at the time was due to a decision by Admiral Dönitz to deploy U-boats with the newest version of

USS *Bogue*

an electric acoustic homing torpedo fitted against the North Atlantic convoys. The German navy had been working on developing an effective homing torpedo for some time and had actually used the Falke T4 torpedo in March 1943 in *U-603*, *U-758*, and *U-221* against convoys HX-229 and SC-122. The latest version, called the *Zaunköning* (Wren), known by the British as the "Gnat," came into service during the autumn of 1943. It was originally intended to kill escort carriers, but it was soon countered by the Allied Foxer noise-making decoy. The weapon was designed to lock onto the loudest noise after a run of 400 meters from its launch. The Germans had sunk six merchant ships and three escorts (probably between September 20 and 24) using the new T5 *Zaunköning* version.[2]

Captain Dunn and Lieutenant Commander Stewart had an idea to get the U-boats to reveal themselves. Their plan was to send out the Avenger/Wildcat team searching at 5,000 feet following a known HF/DF bearing in the hope that a U-boat would transmit a sighting report. After 30 minutes a second attack team would launch and fly on the search bearing at an altitude of only 50 feet. Unfortunately, the plan did not work. On the 10th, the task group detached from the convoy and proceeded to the Azores area to operate independently. On September 26, the *Bogue* steamed into the Casablanca port with nothing to talk about.

The task group departed Casablanca on the 29th on its way back to Norfolk in support of convoy GUS-16 (departed Alexandria on 19 September 1943, en route Hampton Roads, 101 merchants and 16 escorts). While leaving the port, the escort USS *Clemson* damaged its propeller

USS *Dupont* (DD-152) at Miami, Florida, during the 1920s or 1930s. (Naval History and Heritage Command, Catalog #NH 82345.)

8. Sixth War Cruise

and had to be detached for repairs to Norfolk. The USS *Du Pont* (DD-152) replaced the *Clemson* and joined the task group on October 6.

On October 1, 1943, the *Bogue* was steaming with the convoy GUS-16 on a base course of 273°T escorted by the *Badger* and the *Ingram* stationed ahead in the standard anti-submarine screen. The next day, the *Bogue* received COMINCH 021655 and CINCLANT 021948 to detach from the convoy and proceed to 43° 00' N, 29° 00' W to sweep for U-boat refueling areas east and northeast of the Azores. On the 6th, Seaman 2c Armand Savelli was killed when he was caught underneath the after elevator. He was buried at sea with full military honors. The task group then continued west and south of Flores. On the 8th, a U-boat was seen but submerged before an attack could be made.

On October 15, the *Bogue* refueled the escorts: *Badger* completed at 1041 with 20,724 gallons, *Ingram* completed at 1100 with 24,427 gallons, and *Du Pont* completed at 1300 with 22,682 gallons.

On Wednesday, October 20, the *Bogue* and escorts steamed into the channel to Hampton Roads at 0808. At 0930 the *Bogue's* aircraft were launched to NAS Norfolk (then moved to the Naval Auxiliary Air Station at Pungo, Virginia), followed at 1127 when the escorts were detached. The USS *Bogue* was moored at 1531 to the starboard side of Pier 7, berth 76 at Naval Operating Base, Norfolk. The USS *Bogue* had completed its sixth war cruise. "No contacts with the enemy were made on the squadron's first operational cruise aboard the USS *Bogue*."[3]

9

Seventh War Cruise

"The most dramatic of any attack we made."

On October 21, 1943, the USS *Bogue* remained moored to the starboard side of Pier 7, berth 76 at the Naval Operating Base, Norfolk until 1110, when the carrier got underway en route to the Norfolk Navy Yard at Portsmouth. She was moored at 1227 on the port side to Pier 4, berth 27.

The *Bogue* remained moored until the 25th, when the carrier got underway using tugs to enter dry dock 4, resting on blocks and receiving services from shore including steam, fresh and salt water, electricity, compressed air, and telephone. On the 29th, the carrier got underway back to moor at 1301 to Pier 5, berth 33 at the Navy Yard at Portsmouth. On November 7, 1943, the *Bogue* moved to Chesapeake Bay to calibrate the HF/DF and prepare other systems for the next mission. She returned on the 10th to NOB, Norfolk.[1]

Back when the year 1943 arrived, Grumman was ready to introduce a new naval fighter, the F6F Hellcat, but the Navy still needed the F4F. These F4F Wildcats were small in size and had modest weight, which made them suitable to operate aboard convoy escort carriers. To make room for Hellcat production at the Grumman plant, the company transferred the Wildcat manufacturing tools and equipment to the Eastern Aircraft Division of General Motors. GM built two versions of the F4F that the Navy designated the FM-1 and FM-2. These versions were being used on the USS *Bogue* now. GM produced the FM-1, identical to the F4F-4, but reduced the number of guns to four and added wing racks for two 250-pound (110 kg) bombs or six rockets. The FM-1 was built at the Linden, New Jersey, Eastern Aircraft Division plant.[2]

On November 14, 1943, authorized by CINCLANT as Task Group 21.13, the *Bogue* departed from Norfolk escorted with *Badger*, *Ingram*, *Du Pont*, and *Clemson* to support the convoy UGS-24 (that had also departed Hampton Roads that same day en route to Port Said with 103

9. Seventh War Cruise

merchants and 24 escorts) and conduct independent search actions against U-boats when appropriate. On the 16th, the USS *Du Pont* left the task group to head to Bermuda for emergency repairs.

On the 17th, the task group left the convoy to move to the southeast toward U-boats reported to be near the Azores. The USS *Clemson* on November 22 get a few contacts and attacked with depth charges at 2040Z at location 41° 23' N, 32° 34' W. No results were confirmed. The USS *Du Pont* rejoined the *Bogue* on the 26th. The next day, while the *Bogue* was topping off the USS *Ingram* with fuel, the USS *Badger* got a sound contact and raced to 39° 24' N, 22° 06' W to drop depth charges. Some oil rose to the surface, but the submarine escaped.

One pilot on air patrol picked up curious radio transmissions over the aircraft frequencies, speaking for 10 minutes with an English accent, "VC-1 from (numerals), how do you receive me?" The *Bogue* picked up a German accent saying, "Blow water ballast 1, 2, 3, 4." Then on the 28th, another German voice was picked up saying, "Watch your step. Aircraft still overhead."[3]

At 1326Z on the 29th, the *Du Pont* and the *Badger* were in the process of investigating a sound contact when Lieutenant (jg) Bernard H. Volm saw *U-86* cruising on the surface 50 miles west of the task group. Volm contacted the *Bogue* and remained astern of the U-boat waiting on reinforcements. Six planes were launched to the site at 39° 33' N, 19° 01' W. Depth charge attacks from the VC-19 Avengers doomed the U-boat. *U-86's* captain, Kapitanleutnant Walter Schug, submerged and sank 385 miles east of Terceira.

The next day, November 30, Lieutenants (jg) James E. Ogle III and Carter E. Fetsch saw *U-238* under the command of Oberleutnant Horst Hepp on the surface cruising at 41° 07' N, 18° 30' W. *U-238* was on its second patrol some two weeks out of Brest on the French Atlantic coast. The experienced commander ordered his crew to fire a heavy barrage from his antiaircraft guns at the attacking planes, but Ogle and Fetsch were able to engage. The Avenger and F4F were able to fire rockets at the submarine, killing two crew members and wounding five more, as well as causing serious damage that forced Hepp to head back to his home base at Brest.[4]

At 0800 on December 1, 1943, the *Bogue* Task Group 21.13, with its escorts *Badger*, *Du Pont*, *Clemson*, and *Ingram*, was operating independently against U-boats as before at 42° 42' N, 19° 00' W. The anti-submarine patrol had been launched earlier at 0648 with four Avengers and two FM fighters. At 0810 Lieutenant (jg) Gallagher reported a one-mile-long oil slick bearing 143°T off five miles. Both the *Du Pont* and *Badger* were dispatched to investigate, and another Avenger was launched at 0842 to the scene. Both escorts reported sound contacts on a submarine at 0855 and began to attack with depth charges. The *Bogue* received an important dispatch from Commander Morrocan Sea Frontier (COMMORSEAFRON) marked 010925.

Another Avenger at 0952 took off to search, as well as a replacement ASW patrol eight minutes later with four Avengers and one FM. The first patrol recovered aboard the *Bogue* at 1038. At 1045 the *Clemson* was dispatched to relieve the *Badger* so it could return to screen the task group. The *Du Pont* was recalled from the attack area to join the screen at 1605. The planes were all recovered by 1720.

The next morning, the 2nd, Task Group 21.13, less the USS *Clemson* (already in the area), returned to the area of the submarine attacks of the previous day. Four Avengers were launched at 0655 for the morning search. Five minutes later, two FMs took off to orbit the carrier. At 0735 another Avenger headed down the catapult. The USS *Clemson* joined the task group at 0900. Another routine patrol was launched with 4 Avengers and at 1034 five Avengers and 2 FMs were recovered aboard. Another dispatch from COMMORSEAFRON 020929 was received.

Forty minutes after noon, Lieutenant (jg) Gallagher in his Avenger #17 dropped a message on the deck of the *Bogue* revealing "CVE 11 and 3 escorts bearing 130°T distant 25 miles at 1220; course 350°T, speed 15." The evening search with five Avengers took off at 1329, with four Avengers recovered at 1355. At 1705 all five Avengers had landed.

On December 3, the task group was en route to Casablanca as it maintained routine ASW patrols and received several radar contacts from friendly ships and a convoy. The *Ingram* was refueled by the *Bogue* by 1255. The evening patrol was sent off at 1424 and was recovered at 1815.

December 4 was uneventful, and on the 5th at 0840, the Task Group 21.13 entered the swept channel at Casablanca. By 1121 the *Bogue* was moored to North Jetty, berth H at Casablanca, French Morocco. Air cover was provided by the Commander Moroccan Sea Frontier. The *Bogue* remained moored until December 8 to replenish necessary supplies, as were the four escorts. The *Bogue* received dispatches from CINCLANT 062155 and COMMORSEAFRON 071531.[5]

The 10th Fleet became convinced that Dönitz had moved his U-boats attack focus to the North Atlantic, but some boats were still concentrating near the area where the *Bogue* Task Group

9. Seventh War Cruise

patrolled. Thus, Task Group 21.13 was ordered to search the area 770 miles south-southwest of Madeira, Portugal.[6] "It was evident that [Admiral Ingersoll] was combing his area of responsibility with a fine-toothed-comb, for the object of his interest was a brief fueling rendezvous of a 1,763-ton supply boat, *U-219*, with a submarine outbound for operations in the Indian Ocean."[7]

At 1218 on December 8, 1943, the Task Group 21.13 departed Casablanca on a northwesterly course toward the convoy GUS-23 (departed Port Said, Egypt, on November 27, 1943, en route to Hampton Roads with 108 merchants and five escorts). The next day around location 34° 51' N, 12° 13' W at 0714, the morning A/S patrol launched with three Avengers and three FMs. Some 36 minutes later, the Avenger #15 with Lieutenant (jg) H. Morrison dropped a message on the deck of the *Bogue*: "Convoy sighted bearing 155°T distant 25 miles, at 0731 course 255°T."[8] The TG joined convoy GUS-23 at 0900. Two FMs landed at 1023 and later, at 1044, four more Avengers took off on routine patrol. Ten minutes later, three Avengers and one FM recovered.

At 1404 the convoy escort USS *Huse* (DD-145) reported a sound contact that developed with negative results, as did the sound contact at 1420 from the USS *Roe* (DD-418). The USS *Bogue* received from COMINCH dispatch 091509, which led at 1600 to the departure of the carrier and Task Group 21.13 from the convoy to a reported concentration of U-boats at 27° 00' N, 30° 00' W. At 1752 all the search aircraft were recovered aboard.[9]

On December 10, the Task Group 21.13 continued to proceed to the U-boat concentration area and maintained search patrols all day, ending with recovery of all planes by 1837. The next day at 0700, the morning ASW patrol was launched with four Avengers. The escorts *Du Pont*, *Ingram*, *Badger*, and *Clemson* were fueled from the *Bogue* during the day ending at 1417. All planes were landed by 1804.[10]

December 12 began with the launch of the morning ASW search at 0645 with four Avengers, followed at 0757 when the support group of two FMs took off to orbit the carrier. At 0823 the Avenger #13, piloted by Lieutenant (jg) E.C. Gaylord, spotted a surfaced submarine, *U-172*, bearing 195°T distance 38 miles from the carrier at 26° 27' N, 29° 44' W. This was the submarine that was supposed to rendezvous with *U-219*. Gaylord immediately sent a contact report and turned in the direction of the U-boat. Unfortunately for Gaylord, a hydraulic line prevented him from opening his bomb bay doors automatically. The U-boat's skipper, Oberleutnant Herman Hoffman, was slow to react to the intruder and did not begin to dive until Gaylord was only two miles away and coming in quickly.

Gaylord worked to open his door manually and decided to drop a Fido instead of a 500-pound depth bomb. The MK-24 Fido was the first American ASW acoustic homing torpedo, released to the Navy in March 1943. The hydraulic problem prevented Gaylord from using his flaps to slow down so he did some erratic maneuvers to lose speed. Gaylord dropped the Fido 35 seconds after the U-boat had submerged. He dropped a sonobuoy, but it seemed to take forever to work. One minute after Gaylord dropped the Fido, the U-boat came up barely out of the water to show it had been damaged. Oberleutnant Hoffman was able to get his boat under control.

Meanwhile, the *Bogue* launched three more planes and at 0830 directed the *Du Pont* and *Badger* to investigate the attack position. The *Badger* arrived at the scene of contact at 1052 GCT and began conducting sound search at 15 knots northward of the original contact area. The *Du Pont* arrived simultaneously and began sound-searching southward. The *Du Pont* first established sound contact with *U-172* at 1214 GCT and attacked with hedgehogs. The *Badger* established sound contact at 1342 GCT bearing 005°T, at 1,200 yards, but she did not attack since the *Du Pont* was still engaged with the U-boat attack.

When the *Du Pont* lost sound contact with *U-172* temporarily, the *Badger* detected the submarine at 1445, bearing 230°T at a distance of 1,000 yards, and attacked with five depth charges. From this attack until 1914, one or the other of the two escorts maintained contact with the submarine nearly continuously. While the escorts were engaged, the aircraft from the *Bogue* kept a constant check on the *U-172* oil slicks and sonobuoy tracking data.

During the afternoon, the *Badger* made 10 depth charge attacks with 68 MK VI charges with settings varying from 150 to 600 feet. Throughout the entire duration of the attacks, oil was seen floating to the surface. At 1734, between the sixth and seventh attacks, *Bogue* aircraft reported hearing three pronounced explosions. In the seventh attack, at 1750 and 1754, two loud explosions were reported by the plane after depth charges had detonated. No other evidence of damage was seen at that time.[11]

After the depth charge attack from the *Badger* at 1914, no contact was regained by either escort. CTG 21.13 ordered the *Badger* and *Du Pont* to remain on scene until the next morning. To the *Badger* and *Du Pont*, the CTG 21.13 visual dispatch at 1836 read, "Use last contact

9. Seventh War Cruise

as center point and each escort steam in 10 mile square AAA Do not overlap, will rejoin you here at daylight."[12] The Commander of Escort Division One (flag in the *Badger*) designated the *Du Pont* to search eastward of the area of last contact, while the *Badger* was to search westward.

At 1948 a box search plan was executed that had been prepared in collaboration with Commander of Escort Division One (COMCORTDIVONE). This plan was thought to be the best option because the U-boat had been submerged almost all day and had to have expended most of its battery power while conducting evasive tactics. The best course of action was to depend on getting a radar contact rather than using sound gear. The U-boat would assume that the escorts had departed and abandoned the search area.

At 2323 while steaming at 15 knots in moderate seas on a course of 000°T, the *Badger* detected a contact on its SF-1 radar at a range of 9,000 yards, bearing 354°T. The CIC maintained an accurate plot, which revealed that the U-boat was on a course of 348°T cruising at seven to eight knots. They discontinued the echo ranging and used a speed of 12 knots on a course 340°T, which moved the submarine into the path of the moon. But at 2351, the plot revealed that the U-boat had stopped at a range of 6,400 yards. Though it was not ideal, the *Badger* fired its 3"/50-caliber gun with a mean fuse range of 7,000 yards hoping to hit the submarine. Four star shells were fired, but one did not work, and none revealed the target.

The U-boat did not submerge but continued ahead, while the escort closed to a range with a speed of 17 knots on course 010°T. At 3,500 yards, the U-boat's wake and silhouette of the conning tower were visible from the *Badger's* bridge, but not from the gun crews forward. The estimated angle to the target submarine was 200°T. The escort sent off two illuminating shells from the 3"/50-caliber gun #1 fused range 4,000 yards and fired three more regular shells ammunition, but no hits were observed. *U-172* fired an acoustic torpedo back at the *Badger* but it missed.

At 2418 on December 13, 1943, the last shell landed close to the starboard bow of the U-boat as it was submerging. A sound contact at 1,800 yards at 15 knots zigzagging was reported. At 0024 an attack was made by the *Badger* with five depth charges set for 125 feet. Another sound contact at 0112 was followed three minutes with four more depth charges set for 175 feet, which left the escort with only three depth charges onboard. There was a strong smell of diesel fuel in the air and visible oil slicks were seen in the moonlight. The *Du Pont* was called by voice radio with the last contact report, and she arrived on scene at 0101. The previous search plan was again executed at 0115. No more contacts or attacks were made, and at 0759 the *Bogue* ordered the *Du Pont* and *Badger* to rejoin the task group.

At 0910 an aircraft from the *Bogue* regained contact with the U-boat by seeing the oil slick and five minutes later the *Clemson* and *Ingram* were dispatched to the scene. The *Badger* was also dispatched later, at 1053, to support maintaining the targets' sound contact. The *Badger* detected a sound contact at 1107 but no depth charge attacks were conducted since the ship had expended all its charges. COMCORTDIVONE coordinated via the TBS with bearings and ranges to the *Clemson* and *Ingram* conducting the attacks. The submarine was submerged as the *Badger* steamed slowly to maintain 1,500 to 2,500 yards, occasionally obtaining range and bearings at will.

At 1213 the *Clemson* dropped depth charges and the U-boat surfaced three minutes later and immediately received overwhelming gunfire from the three escorts. The *Ingram* used accurate and heavy fire on the submarine as two of *Bogue's* Avengers bombed and strafed the boat. The U-boat deck crew fired back at the *Ingram*, killing one and injuring six others. The *Badger's* range to the target with its 3"/50-caliber guns was fouled by the *Clemson*, but the after battery opened fire at 1217 GCT, range 1,400 yards.

Six rounds of 3"/50-caliber common ammunition was expended before the *Ingram* came into the line of fire. The *Badger* hit the U-boat at the waterline below the conning tower, while the other two escorts sent machine-gun fire forward and aft on the boat. During this engagement, the *Ingram*, commanded by Lieutenant Commander Roger F. Miller, was closing at 500 yards to ram the boat, but Commander TG 21.13 ordered the *Ingram* to sink by gunfire.

At 1221, *U-172* sank while 46 survivors were rescued between 1240 and 1315 by the escorts USS *Badger* (23 survivors), USS *Ingram* (eight survivors), and USS *Clemson* (15 survivors).

The German survivors revealed that attacks made by the *Du Pont* and *Badger* on the afternoon of December 12 caused leaks in the fuel and ballast tanks. Partial flooding of the forward torpedo room came with the first attack of the day, assumed to be from the *Du Pont*. They indicated that the night depth charge attack by *Badger* at 0024 and 0115 broke all the gauges, severely damaged the radio and electrical circuits, and put one diesel engine permanently out of commission. The

9. Seventh War Cruise

survivors also confirmed what was readily apparent at the time that the submarine was sunk by shell fire.

In every attack on *U-172*, it either turned sharply at a range of 100 yards or it reversed its engines, threw out a knuckle (a group of turbulent bubbles that a submarine propeller makes when evading another submarine—the bubbles reflect sonar back at the pursuing submarine, causing the torpedo to lock onto the bubbles), and back down into its wake. The survivors indicated that this was standard procedure. The submarine also changed its depth between each run with the range at lost contacts at 150 to 800 yards.[13]

Dr. Philip K. Lundeberg, the American naval historian and author of *American Anti-submarine Operations in the Atlantic, May 1943–May 1945*, wrote of the sinking of *U-172*.

> This action, which lasted a full twenty-seven hours from the time of contact, demonstrated that by the end of 1943 the United States Atlantic Fleet had succeeded in combining the salient features of British surface support group tactics with the rapidly developing technique of carrier warfare, in which American success was pre-eminent. The prolonged 'hunt to exhaustion' illustrated better than any other operation a proper coordination between planes and ships, between two or more ships engaged in sound search and depth charge attacks, a correct choice of weapons and a high degree of individual proficiency.[14]

On December 14, the *Bogue* Task Group 21.13 launched the morning ASW patrol at 0708 with four Avengers, located at 0800 at 30° 07' N, 27° 28' W. The midday search with four Avengers was launched at 1103 and nine minutes later the *Bogue* began recovering the earlier patrol. At 1320 Avenger #13 with Ensign R.L. Revenaugh reported several oil slicks bearing 240°T, distance eight miles. The escorts *Badger* and *Clemson* were dispatched 20 minutes later to investigate. Lieutenant (jg) H.G. Bradshaw reported a submarine contact with Avenger #10 at 1410. More Avengers were launched to the scene as well, and the *Du Pont* at 1445 was dispatched. The *Badger* and *Du Pont* reported sound contacts at 1525 and 1532, respectfully. These two escorts worked to keep the contact between six and eight miles' distance. At 1818 the *Ingram* was dispatched to join the *Du Pont* to remain at the contact area. The rest of TG 21.13 sailed southerly to remain in the area of the contact the next morning. Aircraft were recovered by 1755.

The next day, the 15th, the TG 21.13 steamed northerly to gather in the contact area from the 14th. The morning search took off at 0703 with five Avengers. At 0734 Lieutenant (jg) H. Morrison reported contact with Task Group 21.15 bearing 347°T out 55 miles traveling at 14 knots, which was seen by the *Bogue* at 0930 out eight miles. TG 27.8 was at bearing 071°T, distance 21,000 yards at 0910.

At 0945 Lieutenant (jg) W.J. Gallagher, in Avenger #10, reported a USS light cruiser in company with three destroyers bearing 190°T, distant 15 miles cruising at 12 knots at 31 55' N, 28 00' W. The *Badger* and *Ingram* were recalled from the December 14 sighting area to rejoin the task group screen at 1005 after negative results. On return, the *Badger* was dispatched to fuel with TG 27.8. At 1054 Lieutenant Commander Counihan from the USS *Core* (CVE 13) came aboard the *Bogue* in Avenger #2 to deliver special equipment. Due to bad weather, the *Badger* was unable to refuel and returned to the screen. Counihan was returned at 1340 to the *Core*. A convoy was seen on radar and was passed at 15,000 yards at 1930 bearing 045°T.

ASW searches were conducted all day on December 16. At 0800 Task Group 21.13 was located at 33° 58' N, 30° 40' W. The *Du Pont* completed fueling at 0930. Depth charges were transferred to the *Bogue* at 1012 to be later transferred to the *Badger*. At 1130 German prisoners Captain Hoffman and Executive Officer Coreth were transferred from the *Ingram* to the *Bogue*. The fueling of the *Ingram* was completed at 1205, and the ship rejoined the screen. The *Badger* transferred 15 prisoners to the *Bogue*, followed by moving five prisoners from the *Clemson* at 1507. At 1436 the *Badger* completed fueling and rejoined the screen. The *Clemson* was fueled by 1636, and then went on to the screen. All planes were recovered by 1650. The next three days, the *Bogue* maintained ASW searches during the daylight hours, with no submarine contacts detected.

Lieutenant (jg) Harold G. Bradshaw of VC-19 called it the "most dramatic of any attack we made."[15] On December 20, 1943, at 1305, during the midmorning anti-submarine patrol, Lieutenant (jg) Wallace A. LaFleur in Avenger #12 spotted the fully surfaced 1,616-ton *U-850* bearing 147°T some 70 miles from the *Bogue* (32° 54' N, 37° 01' W) and 530 miles southwest from Fayal Island, Portugal, in the Azores. The boat was on a course of 180°T, bearing 180° at a range of six miles. *U-850* was en route to the Indian Ocean as part of the 2nd Monsoon Group.

LaFleur commenced an attack run-in with depth charges while making a contact report via radio to the *Bogue*. The lookouts of Kapitanleutnant Klaus Ewerth were surprised by the Avenger. LaFleur's run-in was unsuccessful because the depth bombs would not release. Thankfully *U-850* did not react fast enough to fire at him.

9. Seventh War Cruise

He decided to go around again for a second run. The submarine had turned around from 180° to 360° by making a port turn at 15 knots. LaFleur approached at 335°T at 240 knots and released two Mk. 47 depth charges at 1310 from 300 feet. The drop was too short as the explosion was some 200 feet on the boat's starboard quarter. The Avenger received heavy antiaircraft fire on this run.

Because of a short circuit on the cockpit control box in LaFleur's plane, the Avenger did not receive an acknowledgment of his contact report. As LaFleur circled the U-boat, he continued to attempt to contact the *Bogue* on radio. He was unable to contact the *Bogue*, but in fact the carrier had received his contact message and catapulted the following planes to the scene: Lieutenant H.G. Bradshaw's Avenger #18 (at 1311), Ensign G. Goodwin's Avenger #19 (at 1312), Lieutenant (jg) T.C. Cockroft in FM #6 (at 1314), and Lieutenant (jg) K.P. Hance in FM #2 (at 1315).

These four planes arrived at 1330 but were not initially seen by the deck crew. *U-850* had changed course to 270°T and was focused on firing at LaFleur until the fighters attacked. On a course of 135°T, Hance's FM fighter #2 came in first, followed by Cockroft's Avenger #6 and Goodwin's Avenger #19. The boat changed course to 315° with its bow on to them. The AA fire from the boat became extremely heavy as the planes approached. The fighters strafed the decks, which halted all but the two guns, as Goodwin dropped four Mk. 47 depth charges from 150 feet at speed 240 knots with the boat speed at 15 knots on course. The drops were made at 1335 with the first bomb exploding 10 feet off the starboard bow and the second landing near the conning tower. The third bomb exploded about 15 feet off the port beam and the fourth exploded about 40 feet off the port quarter.

U-850 was covered with ocean spray and when it cleared it, it was observed to be on the same course trailing a large amount of oil. After the planes competed their first runs, Lieutenant H.G. Bradshaw's Avenger #18 commenced its depth charge run on the boat's starboard quarter and at 1336 he dropped two Mk. 47 depth charges from 75 feet at 230 knots as the *U-850* continued on course 315°T, still at 15 knots. Seven seconds later the depth charges landed 200 feet off the submarine's port bow and exploded.

While Bradshaw was completing his run, Lieutenant (jg) Cockroft's FM #6 and Lieutenant (jg) Hance's FM #2 strafed the starboard quarter. Cockroft saw his tracers strike the base of the conning tower aft and saw a bright flash of flame shoot from the impact area, which he

USS *Bogue*

supposed was caused by a hit in the ammunition locker. As the fighters turned back for a third strafing run, the submarine crash-dived and was totally submerged at 1337 as they flew into attack. AA fire was coming up from the guns until the boat was down, which led the pilots to believe that they had remotely controlled some of the guns (since they never saw gun crews on the deck at that time).

As the submarine had dived while turning to port, Lieutenant H.G. Bradshaw's Avenger #18 and Lieutenant (jg) Wallace A. LaFleur in Avenger #12 commenced runs using their 680-pound Mk. 24 Fido homing torpedoes. Bradshaw approached from up-track and dropped his Fido from 130 feet at speed 105 knots. It hit the water at 1337 some 200 feet ahead of the swirl of the boat and 100 feet to the right of the track.

LaFleur dropped his Fido after making his approach from the starboard quarter with an altitude of 150 feet and speed of 130 knots. The Fido struck the water about 250 feet ahead of the swirl and 125 feet to the right of the track. As the Fidos were being launched, the bow of *U-850* began to break the surface, coming up at a sharp angle. As the second Fido hit the water, the submarine came up some 280 feet ahead of the swirl and slightly to the left of its original course. Then Bradshaw's Fido struck the starboard side midway between the conning tower and the stern. The two explosions merged into one severe blast, which threw the stern high in the air, scattering debris and dirty water in all directions. The explosion was estimated to have come 150 feet above the surface. The stern disintegrated under the blast and *U-850* sank bow upward at a vertical angle. The two fighters came in during and after the explosions.

The *Badger* and *Du Pont* were ordered to the scene to pick up debris. Two and a half hours after the attack, the escorts reported picking up "dismembered bodies, pieces of clothing, life-jackets, and broken pieces of wood" and "a shoe with a foot in it, lung tissue and kidneys." This was hard evidence that *U-850* was no more.[16]

At 1745 in the evening, the *Bogue* recovered the four Avengers on search patrol. At 1810 the *Badger* and *Du Pont* rejoined the screen with Task Group 21.13, having completed picking up all visible debris at the scene of the sinking. At 2000 the task group was at 32° 50' N, 37° 41' W, en route to Bermuda.[17]

The Task Group 21.13 steamed en route to Bermuda through December 24, maintaining ASW patrols. On Christmas Day at 1140, they entered the swept channel into Bermuda. The *Bogue* anchored at

9. Seventh War Cruise

1324 in Port Royal Bay South with the Naval Operating Base providing air coverage.

On December 26, Task Group 21.13 took departure from Entrance Buoy on an easterly course at 1335. The next day, the *Bogue* received dispatch 271455 from CINCLANT as they steamed en route to Norfolk.

On December 28, the *Bogue* received dispatch 280303 from COMEASTSEAFRON. The morning ASW patrol was launched at 0747 with four Avengers, but one returned to make an emergency landing at 0801. Between 0908 and 1148, *U-172* prisoners from the escorts were transferred to the *Bogue* from the *Badger* (seven), *Ingram* (six), and *Clemson* (10). The carrier received another dispatch, 290329, from COMEASTSEAFRON.

On December 29, the Task Group 21.13 entered the swept channel at Norfolk at 1050. Squadron VC-19 launched 11 Avengers and eight FMs to NAS Norfolk at 1417. The *Bogue* was moored at Pier 7 NOB Norfolk at berth 75 at 1649. The 46 German prisoners were transferred to the Commander of the 5th Naval District from the *Bogue* at 1800.

The next day at noon, the *Bogue* was moved to the Norfolk Navy Yard at Portsmouth to moor on the port side of Pier 5, in berth 35 later. The *Bogue* and Task Group 21.13 ended the year of 1943 and a most successful seventh war cruise the next day.[18]

10

Eighth War Cruise

"The storm turned us every which way but loose."

The *Bogue* remained at the Norfolk Navy Yard from January 1, 1944, through the 9th. At 0910 on the 10th, the carrier moved to the NOB Norfolk and moored at 1035 on the starboard side of Pier 7 in berth 76. On the 12th, the *Bogue* steamed to anchor in Chesapeake Bay at 37° 14' N, 76° 06' W for HF/DF calibration. After calibration work was completed the next day, at 0925 the *Bogue* steamed on a northeasterly course en route to New York in compliance of CINCLANT order 071637 of January 1944. The carrier was escorted by the USS *Hobson* and the USS *Endicott*.

The *Bogue* and escorts entered the channel at New York, with the *Hobson* detached at the outer channel at 0725 and the *Endicott* leaving at the entrance of Ambrose channel two hours later. The carrier was moored at 1136 to Pier 14, berth 43 at Staten Island, and soon began to load P-47s aboard for ferrying to Glasgow, Scotland. The *Bogue* would be steaming with convoy UT-7 with 24 ships (mainly carrying troops) and eight escorts.

On January 18 at 1058, the *Bogue* departed Pier 14, Staten Island, and headed out to sea, to join with the convoy UT-7 (New York station) formed at 1630 en route to Boston section. The escort commander, CTF 69, was aboard the USS *Arkansas*. On the 20th at 0930, the convoy was joined with the Boston section and steamed toward Clyde.

The trip to Scotland experienced terrible weather. There were heavy seas with waves like mountains that caused the carrier to roll to 32 degrees to port at one point. On the 27th at 2025, Division Five of the convoy with seven merchant ships and escorts USS *Doran* and USS *Eagle* detached from the convoy and were ordered to head to Bristol. At 1500 the next day, the CTF 69 Division was detached from UT-7 and continued to Clyde. At 1544 the *Bogue* entered the Firth of Clyde and anchored off Greenock at 2051.

10. Eighth War Cruise

USS *Hobson* (DD-464) off Charleston, South Carolina, March 4, 1942. She is painted in camouflage Measure 12 (Modified). This photograph has been censored to remove radar antennas atop her foremast and Mark 37 gun director. (Official U.S. Navy Photograph, from the collections of the Naval History and Heritage Command, Catalog #NH 53548.)

On January 29, the *Bogue* detached from the anchorage and steamed to moor on the starboard side to King George V Dock at Glasgow, Scotland. The carrier commenced P-47 unloading operations at 1730. On January 31, 1944, the *Bogue* departed the King George V Dock and moved out to the anchorage in berth B-5 of the Merchant Ship Anchorage in the Firth of Clyde, Scotland. The ferrying mission was complete.[1]

The sailing order for TU-7 from the Naval Control Services Officer at Clyde was received by the *Bogue* as it remained at berth B-5 on February 1 and 2. On the 3rd, the carrier got underway at the Firth of Clyde as a unit of the Clyde section of TU-7. The convoy was formed at 1015 off Oversay with the guide in the USS *Arkansas*, the commodore in the USS *Elizabeth C. Stanton*, and the *Bogue* in position 61 as vice commodore. The convoy was en route to New York.

The convoy steamed a westerly course to New York from the 3rd to the 11th in poor weather, even worse than that from the trip to Clyde. The heavy seas caused the *Bogue* at one point to roll 40 degrees to port. Ralph Hiestand, an aviation machinist mate aboard the *Bogue*, recalled that "the storm turned us every which way but loose. The foc'slr and well-deck joists and girders giving up the good fight, twisted and buckled. The forward starboard corner of the flight deck peeled up like a toboggan, and some welds on the hangar deck bulkhead seams cracked. At some time, we actually took water over the flight deck rolling down the deck like the surf at Coney Island."[2]

At 1120 on the 11th, the Boston section of UT-7 was detached to Boston with six ships and escorts USS *Cowie*, USS *Knight*, and USS *Earl*. On the 12th, the carrier, with escort USS *Rhind*, was detached from Convoy TU-7 with the *Bogue* to proceed to Hampton Roads in compliance with CINCLANT 092038. On February 14, the *Bogue* entered the swept channel at Norfolk, detaching the USS *Rhind* at the outer end of the channel at 0315. The *Bogue* settled as moored to the port side of Pier 5, berth 35 at the Norfolk Navy Yard at Portsmouth to repair damage experienced in the poor weather en route from Scotland. The ship received dispatch 152047 from CINCLANT. The carrier exited the Navy Yard on the 23rd and moved to the NOB Norfolk to moor at Pier 7, berth 75.

The next move for the *Bogue*, now designated as Commander Task Group 21.11, on February 26 was steaming to the HF/DF calibration Chesapeake Bay anchorage. The carrier left the anchorage at 0808 and joined with her new escorts USS *Hobson* (DD-464), USS *Haverfield* (DE-393) (COMCORTDIV 51*)*, USS *Swenning* (DE-394), USS *Willis* (DE-395), and USS *Janssen* (DE-396) off Cape Henry at 0930. At 1336 the task group steamed past Buoy XS on a southeasterly course to rendezvous with convoy UGS-34. The convoy had departed Hampton Roads on February 23 with 104 merchants and 24 escorts en route to Port Said, Egypt.

On the 27th, 11 Avengers and 11 FMs from the new Squadron VC-95 flew to recover aboard the *Bogue*. The task force was on a course to the southeast en route to rendezvous with convoy UGS-34. The squadron launched all the Avengers and FM fighters for refresher landing practice, as well as the routine A/S search patrol. The patrol was recovered at 1634. On the 27th and 28th, ASW patrols were maintained en route.[3]

Back on February 1, 1944, Squadron VC-95 was commissioned at one of the land planes hangars at Naval Air Station Norfolk, Virginia. While the commanding officer was named Lieutenant Commander John F. Adams, the administrative officer read out the orders creating VC-95 since Adams and the executive officer, Lieutenant Aaron Goldman, were absent. The squadron had been established quickly to meet the demand for additional anti-submarine air units in the Atlantic

10. Eighth War Cruise

USS *Haverfield* (DE-393) off the New York Navy Yard, May 1, 1944. (Courtesy of A.D. Baker III, Naval History and Heritage Command, Catalog #NH 91578.)

Campaign to fight U-boats. The personnel for the new squadron were drawn from Air Group 29, which had significant experience aboard the USS *Santee* (CVE-29). Most of the aircrew, including the pilots, had made two to five war cruises.

On the date of the commissioning, the Avenger pilots were at ASDEVLANT, Quonset Point, Rhode Island, undergoing training in firing rockets. Interestingly, VC-95 was rated the highest score of any squadron in the use of rockets to that date. On February 8, the VT (Avengers) planes moved to NAS Quonset Point after completing rocket training. Refresher training on landing operations was held aboard the USS *Charger* for all pilots. When VC-95 reported aboard the *Bogue* on the February 24, 1944, the squadron was ready for action.[4]

Lieutenant Commander John F. "Jack" Adams was born October 27, 1913, in Arlington, Massachusetts, the son of Frank A. and Eleanor O. Adams. He claimed Dixfield, Maine, as his hometown. He attended the University of North Carolina at Chapel Hill, majoring in mathematics and physics, and then enlisted in the Naval Reserve. He was designated a naval aviator in December 1937 and served in Bombing Squadron Six aboard the USS *Enterprise* and USS *Yorktown* as assistant communications officer, personnel officer, and as assistant flight officer (1/38–6/40). He served as the A&R officer and primary flight instructor for

NRAB, Squantum, Massachusetts (7/40–1/42). Next, he was the executive officer of Scouting Squadron 101 (1/42–7/42), followed by serving as commanding officer of Scouting Squadron 33 for inshore patrol in the Narragansett Area (8/42–8/43). He commissioned Torpedo Squadron 51 (9/43–11/43) and commanded Torpedo Squadron 29, which became the nucleus for VC-95 (12/43–1/44).

He was described as well-liked and affable and he "exercised a great deal of experience and executive ability in welding his squadron into a compact unit. A highly developed sense of justice and fairness have earned him the respect of his officers and men in all 'official dealings' where favorable as well as adverse criticisms are meted out. On the lighter side, he had shown himself a master at cribbage, abridge enthusiast, and an excellent shortstop on the squadron softball team. A typical 'down-east' product of Maine, his conversations are generously sprinkled with illustrations and gallicisms drawn from his beloved state."[5]

On March 1, 1944, Task Group 21.11 was en route to join convoy UGS-34. The *Hobson* at 1110 was dispatched to head for the convoy, refuel, and remain until the *Bogue* joined. The *Bogue* received CINCLANT dispatch 011618. By 2240 the TG less the *Hobson* joined the convoy in position 13,000 yards on the port quarter. The next day, the *Hobson* joined the convoy, and the *Haverfield*, *Janssen*, *Swenning*, *Willis*, and *Hobson* refueled with the oiler USS *Chepachet*.

On the 3rd through the 8th, the poor weather prevented the *Bogue's* planes from launching any ASW patrols. At 0719 on the 9th, the *Janssen* picked up a sound contact at 46° 14' N, 25° 20' W. The *Hobson* was dispatched to assist with *Janssen's* sound contact. An Avenger was launched to the site, but the two escorts and Avenger were recalled at 0846 due to negative results from the search.

At 1141 on March 10, Avenger #12, piloted by Ensign A.H. Hoines, had to make a forced landing at 48° 53' N, 27° 59' W just after having launched from the *Bogue* with three other Avengers. The plane sank, but Hoines and his crew, ARM3c J.J. McGinnis and AMM3c H.S. Williams, were rescued by the *Haverfield* at 1154. Meanwhile at the same moment, Lieutenant (jg) J.A. Connearney in his Avenger #11 reported a radar contact bearing 187°T at a distance of 15 miles at 48° 13' N, 28° 13' W with visibility zero. The radar contact disappeared, which motivated the *Bogue* to dispatch Avenger #4 and the escort *Hobson* to the scene. The *Janssen* was also sent to aid the *Hobson* on scene. After the two search escorts completed their search of the area with no results, they

10. Eighth War Cruise

USS *Swenning* (DE 394) on May 1, 1944: Brooklyn, New York, at anchor off the New York Navy Yard. She was completing a 10-day yard availability for repairs, alterations, fueling, reprovisioning, and recreation and leave for the crew. After stopping in Lower New York Bay to calibrate HF/DF and magnetic compasses, she departed, in company with *Haverfield* (DE 393), for the Naval Ammunition Depot at Yorktown, Virginia. (U.S. Naval Historical Center, Photo #L45-272.02.01 from NHHC.)

rejoined the TG screen at 1525. An hour later, the last ASW patrol was recovered aboard the *Bogue*.

At 0853 the next day, the *Janssen* reported a sound contact bearing 100°T out at 1,100 yards, but the contact did not materialize, and the escort rejoined the TG screen by 0920. Later, at 1450, Lieutenant D.A. Pattie, flying Avenger #2, saw what appeared to him to be a periscope bearing 195°T out 15 miles. The escort *Hobson* reported that a lookout saw a periscope at 45° 54' N, 26° 47' W. Avenger #4 searched the area of the *Hobson* contact, but there was no positive result. At 1935 the *Janssen* and *Hobson* rejoined the screen. The *Bogue* received a message from SBNO AZORES 110414. On the 12th, both the *Swenning* and *Hobson* reported sound contacts, but they obtained negative results. As each day came, it seemed that U-boats were obviously active in the area, even though no contacts were yielding positive results.[6]

Early on the morning of March 13, 1944, *U-575*, under the command of Oberleutnant Wolfgang Boehmer, was moving submerged when suddenly two or three depth bombs dropped from an overhead aircraft exploded over the boat. No damage was noted, but the crew was puzzled how their boat had been detected. They began to suspect that they were leaving an oil slick resulting from an air attack they had encountered the previous night. A British B-17 attacked a U-boat at 130145Z and 130215Z (reported in dispatches NSS 106 and 110) in the area adjacent to that of Task Group 21.11. At 0641 the morning search was launched with four Avengers. Nine minutes later, the *Bogue* received an HF/DF contact bearing 134°T, at 15 miles in 45° 20' N, 26° 08' W. The *Hobson* and Avenger #2 were sent to investigate the contact at 0657.

At 0710 Lieutenant Commander John F. Adams was launched in his Avenger #3 to search the area of the previous B-17 attacks on *U-575*. At 1015 Adams saw a suspicious oil slick bearing 356° distance 41 miles at 46° 27' N, 27° 36' W. He and his crew dropped four sonobuoys along the track of the slick and stayed in the area for an hour. Adams was relieved by Lieutenant (jg) D. Nichols in Avenger #5 after launching at 1136. At 1205 Nichols reported a submarine sound contact. On his report back on the *Bogue*, Adams had such a strong feeling about the presence of a U-boat that the USS *Haverfield* (DE-393) left the task group screen and was dispatched to the scene, arriving at 1400. Nineteen minutes later, the DE made her first hedgehog depth charge attacks on *U-575*.

Meanwhile, the *Bogue* sighted the HMCS *Prince Rupert* at 1230 on a northeasterly course and sent a message to her that live sonobuoys were still picking up a submarine bearing 330° at a distance of 30 miles. The *Rupert* immediately headed to the scene, arriving at 1441, and made a depth charge attack at 1516. At 1535 Lieutenant Donald A Pattie in Avenger #10 began to drop sonobuoys ahead of the progressing oil slick and continued to assist in the development of the coordinated attack. The *Hobson* was dispatched at 1455 to assist in the attack and arrived on scene at 1612.

The three surface ships using sonar and Nichols's Avenger using sonobuoys tracked the underwater *U-575* as best they could. At 1833 a coordinated attack began with *Hobson* dropping very deep depth charges and the *Haverfield* and *Prince Rupert* plotting. At 1835, *U-575* broke the surface with a 20° angle up, at six knots on a course of 165°. The three surface attackers fired continuously as Pattie fired his rockets, punching two holes completely through the submarine. The gunner stated that he was sure he saw the last two rocket heads come out the other side of the U-boat and, leaving wakes, ricochet after 50 to 75 feet of underwater travel.

10. Eighth War Cruise

The submarine's deck crew fired a few ineffectual shots at her attackers using her twin 40 mm mount aft of the conning tower or the 20 mm mounts on the bridge but stopped when the surface combatants fired unrestrained back at them. Oberleutnant Wolfgang Boehmer made one last report to U-boat Command. In a bow-on attack, Pattie dropped two depth bombs spaced 60 feet, from an altitude of 75 feet in a 20-degree dive at 190 knots, which enveloped the submarine in sea spray from the explosions. The submarine settled quickly after the explosions by the bow had raised it at an angle of 45°, and disappeared at 1843.

Thirty-eight survivors of *U-575* were taken from the water, with Captain Boehmer, another officer, and 14 men by the USS *Hobson*, seven men by the USS *Haverfield*, and one officer and 14 men aboard the HMCS *Prince Rupert*. At 1927 the *Hobson* and *Haverfield* rejoined the screen after picking up survivors. At 2135 the *Hobson* was dispatched to 46° 35' N, 23° 48' W to search for an aircrew in a dinghy and then rejoined the screen. Task Group 21.11 set a course for Casablanca.[7]

The following description of the last moments of *U-575* was gathered from the German prisoners in the *Navy Secret Report on the Interrogation of Survivors from U-575 Sunk 13 March 1944*:

> Shortly after 1800, *U-575* was at 180 meters, apparently bearing up well under her second prolonged depth charge attack in one week. Then suddenly a pattern of charges exploded so close to the U-boat that its effects were devastating. The lights were blown out, all instruments were smashed, water was leaking through the port propeller-shaft, and the U-boat was well down by the stern. The Captain felt-unjustifiably, according to some of the more experienced ratings—that all was lost and gave the order to blow tanks and run the motors at flank speed. The U-boat was by now so far down by the stern that she responded only very slowly. At last she began to rise very gradually. The motors now began to heat up rapidly and, it began to burn. When the U-boat had finally risen to a depth of about 80 meters, she suddenly shot up to the surface, breaking surface almost perpendicularly. Immediately thereafter came the order from topside to abandon ship. The crew were told to come out with their hands up over their heads in token of surrender, as the destroyers had opened fire as soon as the U-boat surfaced. Three planes were flying about and dropped five or six bombs, but were using their guns. All but about four of the crew came safely through the conning tower and jumped into the water. The Engineer officer stayed behind intending to scuttle the U-boat. All the crew who took to the water had life-preservers. No rafts or rubber boats were taken overboard. About twenty of the men were wounded and some were killed by gun fire in the brief time that they were on the deck before taking to the water or while

they were attempting to swim to safety. *U-575* stayed afloat for about ten minutes, then sank out of sight. None of the survivors realized that rockets were used to sink their U-boat.[8]

This was the 10th and last patrol of the 500-ton *U-575*, having sunk at position 46° 10' N, 27° 34' W. On the 13th, the task group had received the following dispatches: CINCWA 130335 of March 1944, FOGMA 131038, CINCWA 131126, SBNO AZORES 131402, Admiralty 131416.

On March 14, Task Group 21.11, less the *Hobson*, was en route to Casablanca operating offensively as before. The ASW patrols were maintained all day. At 1655 the *Janssen* reported a sound contact at location 42° 30' N, 26° 05' W. The next minute, the *Hobson* reported en route to the rejoin the TG after having picked up a survivor, Pilot A.W. Peterman of the Royal Canadian Air Force. Shortly the *Haverfield* was dispatched to assist *Janssen* with the sound contact as well as an Avenger. By 2200 the *Haverfield* and *Janssen* rejoined the TG and all the aircraft were back on board. The contact was not able to be located.

The next day the *Hobson* was sighted at 1756 and ordered to proceed to Casablanca with the injured pilot. The *Janssen* reported a missing man for one hour and ten minutes who was believed to be overboard. She left the screen and began searching for the missing man. At 1926 the ship was vectored by Avenger #9 to search astern for the man.

On the 16th just after midnight, the *Janssen* rejoined the screen having been unable to find the missing man. At 0745 Avenger #5 with Lieutenant (jg) E.M. Koos reported a suspicious oil slick with possible submarine sound contact bearing 107°T distance 35 miles at 36° 02' N, 17° 31' W. The *Janssen* and later the *Willis*, along with the Avenger #9, were dispatched to the contact scene. Again, the contact resulted in the negative and the two escorts rejoined the TG at 1820. The planes were recovered an hour later.

The following day, just as the previous one, an oil slick and possible sound contacts were seen and heard by Lieutenant (jg) Jansen in Avenger #10 on a bearing 240°T at 34° 15' N, 12° 16' W 35 miles away. The *Swenning* was dispatched to the oil slick contact, as well as Avenger #11 with Lieutenant (jg) D. Nichols. Another sound contact was made at 1645 bearing at 134°T out 1,300 yards by the *Haverfield*. Later the two escorts rejoined the TG screen en route to Casablanca having experienced negative results.

On March 18, Task Group 21.11 arrived at Casablanca. The *Bogue* was moored at 1145 to the Jette Delure, berth H. The men of squadron VC-95 had earned their rest ashore at Casablanca, where they shopped

10. Eighth War Cruise

and visited local points of interest, and, of course, local bars. The tension of operations at sea was soon dissipated, as the pilots came to feel they were ready for more action.

In compliance with CINCLANT 211959, the Task Group 21.11 departed Casablanca, Morocco, at 0753 on March 22, 1944, on a northwesterly course toward 38° 30' N, 16° 00' W. The *Bogue* launched a routine patrol at 1557 with three Avengers and landed them at 1809. The next day, Avenger #6 with Lieutenant (jg) R.F. Richmond sighted a British convoy bearing 334°T off 100 miles at 36° 44' N, 17° 24' W at a speed of nine knots. On the 24th at 1440, Ensign R.C. Brubaker in Avenger #10 sighted Task Group 21.12 off 115 miles at 36° 05' N, 20° 53' W.

At 2000 on March 25, the *Bogue* received CINCLANT 251658 that ordered the USS *Hobson* to detach from TG 21.11 heading to Horta, Portugal, in the Azores to refuel, then to proceed to the Boston Navy Yard for availability. TG 21.11 was en route to rendezvous with convoy UGS-36 (departed March 14, 1944, from Hampton Roads en route to Port Said with 123 merchant ships and 27 escorts—arrived April 9). They rendezvoused at 0729 the next day, and then an hour later the *Bogue* and TG 21.11 departed on a course southerly due to the inability to refuel the escorts in the heavy seas.

On March 30, TG 21.11 received an important dispatch from CINCLANT 300048 directing it to head to the area of a U-boat refueler west of the Cape Verde Islands. No submarine contacts were picked up until the next day at 1658, when the USS *Willis* reported a sound contact at 19° 43' N, 34° 47' W. The *Janssen* also received a sound contact at 1844 and was assisted by the *Haverfield*. Unfortunately, none of the three escorts was able to prosecute a submarine contact.[9]

No submarine contacts were reported until 0710 on April 3, 1944, when Lieutenant (jg) J.A. Connearney in Avenger #11 picked up a radar contact that disappeared bearing 180°T off 26 miles at 12° 44' N, 34° 58' W. The *Haverfield* and *Swenning* were ordered to search the area of the radar contact, but by 1130 the escorts called off the search and rejoined the screen. The next day a white flare was seen bearing 035°T at more than 10 miles away. The *Haverfield* and *Janssen* investigated the area.

On the 5th at 0044, the *Bogue* received a radar contact bearing 195°T at 35,700 yards on a course 090° at a speed of 14 knots. The *Willis* determined that the contact was a friendly tanker. An hour and 11 minutes later, the *Haverfield* and *Janssen* rejoined the screen from the flare search effort. Then at 2100 another flare, a green one, was seen by the *Haverfield* bearing 310°T off 10 miles. The *Janssen* was dispatched to search the flare contact area. The *Janssen* reported sighting an object resembling a conning tower, which disappeared bearing 265°T distance 10 miles at 10° 19' N, 38° 03' W. The area was searched with negative results. At 0150 on the 6th, the *Janssen* rejoined the screen after having searched the flare area with negative results.

On April 7, the *Willis* reported a sound contact at 0215 bearing 000°T out 1,000 yards, but 25 minutes later the escort rejoined the screen. At 0708 by an order of CFG 21.11 from dispatch CINCLANT 062109, the *Janssen* was detached to head to Trinidad to refuel. The next day the *Willis* reported having a sound gear casualty that could not be fixed at sea. She was ordered to take a position 1,000 yards astern of the *Bogue*.[10]

The results of daily activities on the crews of VC-95 were revealed in the *Composite Squadron 95 Narrative* as follows:

> Through 11 April [44] flight operations were continued without a break. The mere report of 'so many' searches and 'so many' flights with no success cannot begin to portray the arduous and dangerous work that is the life of a squadron engaged in anti-submarine warfare aboard a CVE in the Atlantic. A routine day aboard such a CVE would start with the dawn hop-4 pairs of planes (VT and VF) doing relative sector searches on a radius of up to 80 miles from the carrier, duration 4 hours. The forenoon and afternoon hops repeating the process. The sunset hop normally is composed of 3 VT planes doing geographic 'barrier' searches with roughly the same length of legs. Depending on the proximity of the probability of an enemy submarine in the area, hops will continue throughout the night, ending with the pre-dawn hop-thus affording continuous 24 hour operations until a kill is produced or until search for a particular U/Boat is abandoned. This writer knows of no aviation activity more exacting or more fatiguing for flying personal than that engaged in by the VC-Squadrons based in the Atlantic aboard the Escort Carriers. Long hours of monotonous and difficult patrol in all kinds of weather, normally with no tangible result for their efforts-some pilots will spend as much as much as 24 months at sea without sighting a submarine-is a heartbreaking, thankless job that seasons and ages pilots as no other activity can. When opportunity for action comes, these pilots must have considered judgement, ability to make the correct tactical decisions, and above all to act quickly. Since it takes but 30 seconds for a submarine to submerge, and another 30 seconds to get beyond lethal range, every second is precious. Their skills have to be varied. In addition to flying their planes, they must be superlatively proficient in glide bombing, low-level bombing, rocket firing, searchlight runs, strafing, and in other anti-submarine warfare skills such as the use of the sono buoy-this last of itself a sufficient field for a normal person.... Small wonder, therefore, that pilots of Composite Squadrons are a breed known only to the United States Navy.[11]

10. Eighth War Cruise

At 0630 on the 12th, TG 21.11 less the *Janssen* entered the swept channel of the Gulf of Paris, Trinidad, British West Indies. The *Bogue* anchored in the Gulf at 0726. The next day, at 1150, Task Group 21.11 got underway from the Gulf of Paris at Trinidad en route to Norfolk in compliance with CINCLANT 062109. En route on the 16th, the TG was ordered by CINCLANT to coordinate operations with CTU 27.6.6 and *Asheville* and *PC 1184* while in the area 30° 00' N, 75° 00' W off Hatteras.

Task Group 21.11 entered the swept channel at Norfolk at 0213 on April 19, 1944. VC-95 with 11 Avenger and eight FMs launched at 0632 and flew to NAS Norfolk. In compliance with CINCLANT 161439, the escorts *Haverfield*, *Janssen*, *Swenning*, and *Willis* detached en route to New York. At 0951 the *Bogue* was moored on the port side to Pier 5, berth 56 at the NOB, Norfolk. The next day, April 20, the *Bogue* moved to the Norfolk Navy Yard at Portsmouth, mooring at 1134 to Pier 5, berth 33. The Squadron VC-95 was detached from the carrier and reported in at NAS, Norfolk. On April 24, the squadron moved to NAAS, Creeds, Virginia, where training and rest was to occupy the squadron for the next six weeks.

The *Bogue* remained there until April 30, 1944, when she moved back to the Norfolk NOB mooring at 1215 at Pier 7, berth 72.[12] This was the end of the eighth war cruise for the *Bogue*.

11

Ninth War Cruise

"The sound of a tin can crushed."

Seventeen days after VC-69 had disembarked from their cruise aboard the escort carrier USS *Wake Island* at Norfolk on January 26, 1944, the squadron was ordered to NAS Quonset Point, R.I., to attend the specialized anti-submarine training program held by the ASW Development Unit Atlantic. They completed the two-month training on April 26 and returned to Norfolk to embark aboard the USS *Bogue* on May 2. The VC-69 commanding officer was Lieutenant Commander Jesse Dean Taylor. The squadron landed aboard with its 12 TBMs (a TBF version manufactured by General Motors Corporation, Eastern Aircraft Division at Linden, New Jersey) and nine FM-2s (an improved version of the F4F-4 Wildcat built by the Eastern Aircraft Division of General Motors at Linden, New Jersey).

The *Bogue* detached on this war cruise with a new commanding officer, Captain Aurelius B. "Abe" Vosseller, replacing Captain Joseph Brantley Dunn on April 23, 1944. Aurelius Bartlett Vosseller was born in Jacksonville, Illinois, on January 25, 1903, son of James Oliver and Hattie (Bartlett) Vosseller. He attended public schools of Jacksonville, Whipple Academy, and Illinois College there, before entering the U.S. Naval Academy in 1920 on the appointment of Joseph Medill McCormick, senator from Illinois. As a midshipman, he was a member of class boxing and lacrosse teams, the Class Crest Committee, and assistant editor of *The Log*. He graduated and was commissioned ensign on June 4, 1924.

After graduation he had sea duty for six years, serving on the USS *Mississippi*, operating with Battleship Division 4, Battle Fleet; as assistant communication officer on the staff of Commander, Battleships; as gunnery and torpedo officer of USS *Reno*; and on the staff of Commander Destroyers, Battle Force (USS *Omaha*), as assistant gunnery officer. In May 1930 he returned to the United States for flight

11. Ninth War Cruise

instruction at the Naval Air Station, Pensacola, Florida, being designated naval aviator on March 2, 1931. Shortly thereafter he was assigned to Carrier Division 2, U.S. Fleet (USS *Saratoga*), and later joined Fighting Squadron 5, based on USS *Lexington*.

Early in 1932 he had temporary duty with Aircraft, Scouting Force, aboard the USS *Wright*, and in June of that year returned to Annapolis for instruction in aeronautical engineering at the Post-graduate School. He continued instruction at places including the Naval Air Station, San Diego, California, and the California Institute of Technology, Pasadena, and received the degree of master of science from the latter in 1934.

He next had successive tours with Fleet Air Detachment in Observation Squadron 2, attached to the battleship *Arizona*; aboard the aircraft carrier *Ranger*; and with Fighting Squadron 2 based on USS *Lexington*. He reported on June 21, 1937, to the Bureau of Aeronautics, Navy Department, Washington, D.C., and until July 8, 1940, had duty in the Plans Division of that bureau. For services during that period in the development of an oxygen mask for aircraft use in high-altitude work, he received a letter of commendation from the secretary of the Navy.

He served with Patrol Wing Five from August 1940 until August 1941, when he took command of Patrol Squadron 55, later redesignated Patrol Squadron 74, until February 19, 1942. For services in that assignment, he was awarded the Bronze Star Medal with Combat "V" and the Air Medal. The citations follow in part:

Bronze Star Medal: "For meritorious service as Commander of an Air Squadron during operations in the Atlantic Area from August 1941 to January 1942. Undaunted by hazardous weather conditions while leading his squadron from Argentia to Iceland in August 1941, (he) skillfully completed the pioneer mission despite meager and inaccurate weather information and the lack of air navigational aids, carried out reconnaissance flights against enemy submarines and escorted convoys until January 1942, and in addition, enabled the planning for and construction of a vitally needed Naval Air Station in Iceland."

Air Medal: "For meritorious achievement in aerial flight as Pilot of a Naval Aircraft in operations against enemy forces in the North Atlantic War Area during the winter of 1941 and 1942. Completing numerous anti-submarine and convoy coverage flights in the face of constant hazards of ice, low visibility, blizzards, and high winds (he) contributed materially to the success of his squadron in providing protection to valuable convoys traversing that area."

From February to December 1942, he served with the Anti-

USS *Bogue*

Submarine Warfare Unit, Atlantic Fleet. He then had fitting-out duty in USS *Bunker Hill*, then building at the Bethlehem Steel Company's Shipbuilding Division at Quincy, Massachusetts. Before the commissioning of that carrier in May 1943, he was ordered to organize and establish the Aircraft Submarine Warfare Development Detachment, Quonset Point, Rhode Island, and retained command of that unit until April 1944. For outstanding service in that command, he was awarded the Legion of Merit. The citation states in part:

"For exceptionally meritorious conduct ... as Commander Antisubmarine Development Detachment from the early part of April 1943, until late March 1944 ... Captain Vosseller was directly responsible for the evolution of effective technique and tactics employed by aircraft in combat against enemy U-boats, the development of new methods of training and the use of new projectiles and detention devices, countermeasures against new German torpedoes and many other weapons and methods."[1]

Vosseller was designated as commander of Task Group 22.2 aboard the *Bogue*, which included CORTDIV 51 (Commander Theodore S. Lank) with the USS *Haverfield*, USS *Swenning*, USS *Willis*, USS *Janssen*, and the USS *Frances M. Robinson* (DE-220).

The *Bogue* departed from NOB Norfolk at 1400 on May 4, 1944, and headed to the HF/DF calibration area in the Chesapeake Bay at 37° 14' N, 76° 07' W, anchoring at 1718. The movement was in compliance with CINCLANT 041523 of May. The *Bogue* was ordered to operate against U-boats west of the Cape Verde Islands. At 0605 on May 5, TG 22.2 got underway on a southeasterly course, and later between 1311 and 1813 landed and recovered 21 TBMs and 11 FM-2s. At 2115 the *Swenning* reported a sound contact bearing 330°T off 900 yards at 35° 48' N, 73° 35' W. The *Haverfield* assisted, but the two escorts did not develop the contact, and returned to the screen by 2240.

From May 6 through the 11th, the *Bogue* maintained ASW patrols every day, but no contacts were discovered. On the 10th, the *Bogue* refueled all five of the escorts and altered course to pass through 23° 00' N, 35° 00' W at 2124 in compliance with CINCLANT 102151. On the 12th, at 1300, the *Janssen* reported a sound contact bearing 156°T out 1,000 yards at 22° 16' N, 35° 35' W, but had negative results in prosecuting. At 1527 the *Willis* had a sound contact bearing 070°T distance 1,000 yards at 21° 50' N, 35° 12' W, but could not finalize.

On May 13, CTG 22.2 established an 0800 rendezvous with the CVE USS *Block Island's* Task Group 21.11 to answer a request for

11. Ninth War Cruise

Starboard quarter view of the destroyer escort USS *Francis M. Robinson* (DE 220) on December 6, 1950. (U.S. Navy photo #L45–102.03.03 from the Naval History and Heritage Command.)

refueling its escorts at 19° 45' N, 34° 00' W. The *Bogue* refueled the USS *Ahrens* and USS *Barr* using 86,000 gallons of fuel oil. TG 21.11 then proceeded to Casablanca.

Approaching dusk at 1831 some 500 miles west of the Cape Verde Islands, the USS *Robinson* was making 17 knots heading 200°T when the sonar operator reported a sound contact bearing 270°T distance at 3,000 yards at 18° 09' N, 33° 12' W. The *Bogue* immediately turned away, while the captain of the *Robinson*, Lieutenant Commander John E. Johansen, ordered general quarters, deployed a "Foxer" (noisemaker to decoy any possible acoustic tracking torpedo that a submarine may have fired), and moved quickly directly toward the contact.[2]

The escort fired 24 ahead-thrown Mk 10 Hedgehog projector charges, followed by five salvos of Mk 8 magnetic influence depth charges. Four underwater explosions were heard and recorded. Johansen lost any contact with the submarine, as all evidence pointed to a sinking. In fact, later evidence confirmed that the 1,120-ton *RO-501* had been sunk at 18° 07' 59" N, 33° 12' 59" W in 2,900 feet of water. It was the ex-German *U-1224* handed over to the Japanese and was on its journey from Kiel, Germany, to Penang, Malaysia. The *RO-501* carried precious metals, uncut optical glass, models, and blueprints (necessary to construct a Type IX U-boat) in addition to motors and blueprints for the

Messerschmitt Me-163 "Komet" rocket fighter airplane. The idea was that the trained Japanese sailors would pass along their expertise. The route to Malaysia took *RO-501* to the Azores for refueling, and then was expected to go around the Horn of Africa.[3]

That same day at 2041 the carrier recovered three TBM Avengers and four FM-2s. The TBM Avenger #18, piloted by Ensign A.D. Bohlen, was unable to get its wheels down because of a hydraulic failure and was ordered to conduct a water landing on the port side of the *Bogue*. The *Willis* successfully picked up the crew of Ensign Bohlen, AMM3c D.E. Locke, and ARM3c R.H. Cousins. At 2250 the escorts *Haverfield* and *Robinson* rejoined the screen.

On the 14th, the ASW patrols were maintained all day. At 1901 *Robinson* reported a sound contact bearing 160°T at 1,000 yards at 14° 23' N, 33° 28' W. With negative results, the escort rejoined the screen at 1920. Avenger #20 with Lieutenant D.G. Sprague reported at 2211 a radar contact that disappeared bearing 158°T out 15 miles. The *Robinson* and *Swenning* were dispatched to search the area. The next morning at sunrise, Task Group 22.2 returned to the radar contact. No contacts were reported that day.[4]

Since so many U-boats had been lost during the daytime, often seen cruising on the surface, the only solution left to them was to search the Allied shipping at night. For the ASW escort carriers like the *Bogue*, there were radar and sound contacts from submarines at night that needed to be prosecuted. This *Bogue* cruise was the start of a concentrated effort by the VC-69 skipper, Lieutenant Commander Jesse D. Taylor, to conduct night flights to make attacks against U-boats from the carrier. This had been done before, but not to the extent that the *Bogue* squadron had utilized. Of the total 3,230.2 flight hours flown during this ninth cruise, there were 892.8 hours logged on night flights.

This was a new skill and tactical method of attack that had to be enabled for the pilots in order to take advantage of it. The key issue was obtaining the best illumination of the target U-boats that were detected by radar or sound contacts. This came first with parachute flares that were difficult to deploy. Since there were no flare tubes on the Avenger, in order to launch a flare, either the gunner or radioman had to open the entrance hatch and, once given the command, throw a flare out. This process interfered with the duties of these crewmen at an inopportune time. This was just something VC-69 had to deal with until they had a chance to have the planes modified back in the States.[5]

11. Ninth War Cruise

During the period from May 16 to the 29th, there were a few Avenger radar contacts, which prompted escorts being dispatched to investigate. These occurred on the 17th with Lieutenant G.L. Nelson at 0340 in Avenger #15, and on the 22nd at 0634 with Ensign W.D. Gordon in Avenger #14. None of the contacts resulted in actionable events against U-boats. On the 20th, the task group received orders in CINCLANT 201814 to head to Casablanca. On the 29th, the TG entered the swept channel at Casablanca, and the *Bogue* ended up moored to the Jettee Delure, in berth I. On May 30 upon hearing the news regarding the sinking of the USS *Block Island*, the USS *Haverfield* was dispatched to assist the USS *Barr* at the request of Commander Moroccan Sea Frontier (COMMORSEAFRON) 302135B.[6]

About 300 miles west-northwest of the Canary Islands on May 29, *U-549* was able to slip undetected through the screen of escorts around the USS *Block Island* (CVE-21). At approximately 2013, a German torpedo hit on the starboard bow, followed by a second one on the port side aft approximately 10 seconds later. With the carrier severely damaged, the captain of the *Block Island* made the decision at about 2040 to abandon ship on the starboard side forward, this being the windward side. The carrier carried out an orderly abandonment as the USS *Ahrens* (DE-575) and the USS *Robert I. Paine* (DE-578) moved in to pick up the survivors. A third torpedo hit about eight minutes later on the port side and caused the carrier to sink at 2155. The *Ahrens* then picked up 674 survivors from the carrier, and 277 other survivors were rescued by the *Paine*. Thankfully, the *Block Island* lost only six men.

At 2030 the USS *Barr* (DE 576) was attacked by *U-549* and damaged by a GNAT (passive German Naval Acoustic Torpedo) in the stern. She had unfortunately not deployed her "Foxer" decoy gear. Twelve died aboard the DE and 16 were wounded. While the escorts *Ahrens* and *Paine* were engaged in recovering survivors, the USS *Eugene E. Elmore* (DE 686) was the only escort available to find and attack *U-549*. Several minutes after the *Barr* had been hit by the GNAT, a second GNAT just missed the USS *Eugene E. Elmore*.

At 2102 the *Ahrens* gained a sonar contact on a target off 1,700 yards, but since she was engaged in the rescue, the contact information was passed to the *Elmore*. At 2113 the *Elmore* conducted a hedgehog attack on the U-boat contact, but no results were visible. A second hedgehog attack was delivered. Twelve seconds later there were three major explosions. A few minutes passed when a heavy crumbling explosion reverberated in the sea. *U-549* had been destroyed southwest of

Madeira, Portugal, at 31° 13' N, 23° 03' W, killing all 57 hands aboard, including Kapitänleutnant Detlev Krankenhagen.

After the three escorts searched the area along with two shore-based bombers the following day, the remaining ships of Task Group 21.11 steamed at 0930 toward Casablanca, with the *Elmore* towing the *Barr*. The ships arrived on June 2. The *Block Island* was the only U.S. carrier lost in the Atlantic in World War II.

Six Wildcat fighters from VC-55 were in the air when USS *Block Island* was torpedoed, and this left them with no place to land. They headed for the Canary Islands, but all aircraft had to ditch at night after running out of fuel and only two of the six pilots were rescued. These pilots were picked up by the *Haverfield* near Las Palmas and returned to Casablanca.[7]

At 0900 on June 2, 1944, the *Haverfield* returned from its mission and moored to the fuel dock at Casablanca. Just after noon, the *Janssen* and *Willis* departed Casablanca to conduct A/S search until the time to join Task Group 22.2 at Buoy A in compliance of COMMORSEAFRON 011820 of June. The TG departed Casablanca less the *Haverfield* at 1640 from Buoy A on a course to the northwest in compliance with CINCLANT 302044 of May to hunt for U-boats between the Azores and Northwest Africa. The next day, the *Haverfield* joined the task group at 0745 as daily A/S search patrols were maintained. There were no contacts picked up until June 5, when both Lieutenant (jg) W.C. Hirsch in Avenger #11 and Lieutenant (jg) A.L. Hirsbrunner in Avenger #13 had reported radar contacts from the same source. Hirsbrunner heard definite propeller noises on his sonobuoys. The *Haverfield, Janssen, Willis*, and *Swenning* were dispatched to investigate, while the *Bogue* and *Robinson* stayed off 10 miles away from the contact. No submarine was prosecuted.

On June 7 at 1415, CTG 22.2 dispatched the USS *Swenning* to 43° 23' N, 17° 17' W to pick up an aircrew in a dinghy. The escort picked up eight survivors (two officers and six sergeants) of a Royal Air Force Halifax four-engine heavy bomber, aircraft K of RAF Squadron 517 that had been forced down to ditch at sea. The next day, a sonar contact was reported at 1624 by the *Willis* bearing 230 T, distance 5,000 yards. The *Willis* rejoined the screen at 1904 having developed the contact with negative results.

On the 9th, the *Swenning* rejoined the task group at 0245 and took station 2,000 yards astern of the *Bogue*. At 0745 the FM #9 with Lieutenant (jg) R.K. Lohman reported seeing what looked like a swirl

11. Ninth War Cruise

bearing 139°T off 40 miles at 41° 54' N, 20° 46' W. The *Bogue* launched Avenger #11 to assist in the investigation but found no indication of a submarine on his sonobuoys. The *Robinson* and *Swenning* were refueled that day. The next day, Lieutenant Commander Taylor in Avenger #14 reported a disappearing radar contact, but the sonobuoys did not pick up an indication.

On the 11th at 0811, Lieutenant (jg) D.G. Sprague in Avenger #13 reported seeing a periscope bearing 025°T off 7.5 miles at 46° 54' N, 20° 35' W. The weather was poor with visibility one-quarter to one-half mile and ceilings to 300 feet in the area of the sighting. The pilot found it difficult returning to the sighting due to an error in his navigation system. Sonobuoy search proved to be negative. The *Haverfield* and *Robinson* were dispatched to the area with negative results. The *Swenning*, later assisted by the *Janssen*, also gained a sonar contact at 1442, but also showed no results. No contacts were reported the next day.

On June 13, the Task Group 22.2 was en route to Norfolk in compliance with CINCLANT 122218. The *Haverfield* was refueled. At 1016 the *Robinson* reported a sonar contact bearing 000°T off 1,000 yards. Eight minutes later, *Haverfield* reported the same contact. The *Swenning* came to aid the two escorts, but the sonar contact was not developed. Next the *Janssen* and *Willis* were refueled. No contacts were reported on the 14th.[8]

On June 15, Task Group 22.2 became part of a fascinating operation associated with a dramatic attack on a Japanese submarine. The Japanese *I-52* was commissioned in December 1943. It was built by the Mitsubishi Corporation as an underwater blockade runner with a length of 357 feet and a crew of 94, able to cruise at 12 knots. Under the command of Commander Kanmeo Uno, its mission was to run an exchange trip to the Kanomon Submarine Base at Lorient, France, on the south coast of Brittany. Before departing, *I-52* was loaded with two tons of gold in 147 bars, which was packed in 49 metal boxes from the Osaka branch of the Bank of Japan. It was intended to be the payment for the drawing and samples of advance German weapons.

The *I-52* sailed from Kure to Singapore on March 10, 1944, with 14 passengers and technicians from Nihon Kogaku KK (to study German AA gun sights) and from Mitsubishi Electric and their Instrument Company (to review HA directors). Another engineer aboard was assigned to study Daimler Benz's techniques for building torpedo boat engines. At Singapore the ship was loaded with 120 tons of tin in ingots, 102 tons of tungsten, 54 tons of raw rubber (caoutchouc) in bales, 9.8

tons of molybdenum, 11 tons of tungsten, 3.3 tons of quinine, 2.88 tons of opium, and 58 kg of caffeine. On April 23, the *I-52* sailed from Singapore across the Indian Ocean and around the Cape of Good Hope and into the south Atlantic on May 15.

From the day the *I-52* was commissioned, the Allies had been tracking her through radio intercepts. On June 6, 1944, the Japanese Naval Attaché in Berlin sent a radio transmission to the *I-52* with instructions to rendezvous with a U-boat on June 22 at 2115 (GMT) at 15° N, 40° W. This transmission was picked up, decoded, and passed by Ultra signals to the 10th Fleet.[9]

Back on June 15, as a response to 10th Fleet information, Task Group 22.2 was directed by CINCLANT 150344 to proceed to area 21° 00' N, 40° 00' W to intercept the *I-52* and U-boat. The next sonar contact was reported by the *Swenning* at 0235 on June 17, but results were negative. The 18th yielded the same negative results from several radar contacts that day. On the 20th at 2242, Lieutenant G.L. Nelson in Avenger #21 crashed in the sea on the port side of the *Bogue* while attempting to land. Another Avenger (#16) with Lieutenant R.D. Morrison crashed into the sea. Both Avenger pilots and crews were picked up by escorts. On the 21st, the *Haverfield* and *Robinson* transferred their rescued Avenger crews to the *Bogue*.[10]

At 2115 on the evening of June 22, some 850 miles from the Cape Verde Islands (approximately 15N, 40W), Kapitanleutnant Kurt Lange's *U-530* met with the Japanese Commander Kanmeo Uno aboard the *I-52*. The *I-52* embarked a German officer (Commander Alfred Schafer to help navigate the end leg to Lorient), two radio operators (Petty Officers Kurt Schulze and Rolf Behrendt), a Naxof FuMB7 radar, and an Enigma coding machine. The *U-530* departed the scene en route to Trinidad while the *I-52* moved toward Lorient.[11]

At 2203 the following day, June 23, 1944, the CO of VC-69, Lieutenant Commander Taylor, with his crew of two in his Avenger #20 took off from the USS *Bogue* on his sector search between 180° to 270° out to 75 miles on a routine anti-submarine patrol mission. At 2339 on the first leg of the second 30° sector while flying on a course of 220° at 1,500 feet, speed 145 knots, the radioman, ART1c Edward A. Whitlock, reported an indication of a vessel on his radar scope on the starboard bearing about 55° relative out 10 miles.

When Taylor's Avenger was a mile from the contact at 2344, he dropped a full pattern of sonobuoys—a newly developed underwater microphone that floated on the surface and picked up underwater

11. Ninth War Cruise

sounds and transmitted them to the aircraft, usually dropped in packs of five, code-named purple, orange, blue, red, and yellow (POBRY). He also dropped two smoke lights. The sonobuoy immediately picked up submarine noises as the plane continued to close. When the Avenger was only a half mile from the contact, Taylor directed the gunner to launch a Mark VI instantaneous flare. Just before the flare was released, Taylor was able to see the stern of a surfaced vessel, and when the flare was illuminated, he saw a large submarine fully surfaced making 10 to 15 knots. Taylor turned right, and then moved back left to attack, dropping to 300 feet altitude, in a glide angle of 10° with a speed of 175 knots. He dropped two Mark 54 depth bombs set to 25 feet. Taylor looked over his left shoulder and saw the first bomb explode close aboard on the starboard side of the *I-52*, while the second was about 75 feet abeam.

The flare was still at 600 feet above the water on the plane's port beam. Taylor and the gunner noted that the submarine was submerging, but the conning tower and the stern were above the surface. Taylor made a 360° tight turn and came around at 2350 to drop a Fido (an acoustic ASW torpedo) from 250 feet. A loud explosion was heard on the orange sonobuoy that seemed to last about a minute. Taylor called the noise "the sound of a tin can crushed" while the radioman thought it sounded like "the breaking of twigs or crumpling of paper but heavier and deeper in tone." The gunner compared it to "the sound of a pile of small brittle twigs being stepped on or like paper being crumpled into a ball."[12]

Taylor was absolutely sure he had sunk the *I-52*, but as Taylor's patrol ended, he was relieved by Lieutenant (jg) William "Flash" Gordon in Avenger #17, accompanied by civilian underwater sound expert Price Fish. They arrived on the scene just after midnight and circled with Taylor for some time. At about 0100 on the next morning of June 24, Fish reported hearing some faint propeller noise in the area. Captain Vosseller wanted to make sure of the sinking and ordered a second attack. Taylor departed the area at 0115 after confirming the original location to Gordon at 15° 16' N, 39° 55' W. Gordon dropped another Fido at 0154 and 18 minutes later a loud rolling explosion was heard. Propeller beats were heard for a few minutes but faded into silence. Though it was thought that perhaps Gordon had hit another U-boat, it was later determined that the explosion was probably the results of remnants of the *I-52*.

At 1300 the *Haverfield* reported picking up debris from the oil slick that included several bales of crude rubber, a rubber sandal with a

USS *Bogue*

Japanese inscription on it, fragments of silk, lumber thought to be Philippine mahogany, and a large piece of human flesh. The *Janssen* noted considerable debris as it passed through the 15-square-mile oil slick, and at 1705 it was ordered to pick up debris including 65 bales of crude rubber, pieces of wood with paper on them stamped with Japanese and Chinese characters, small pieces of rubber with human hair and pieces of metal imbedded, and a rubber blanket with small rubber shoe attached. At 2340 the *Bogue*, with escorts except *Janssen*, was ordered to alter course to transfer two Avengers to Task Group 22.6 with the USS *Wake Forest* CVE, for further transfer to TG 22.6 with the USS *Croatan* CVE in compliance with CINCLANT 242124.[13]

The *Bogue* refueled the *Robinson*, *Swenning*, *Haverfield*, and *Willis* on June 25. A sonar contact was reported by the *Roberson* at 1344 bearing 270°T at 800 yards in 18° 27' N, 40° 41' W. Negative results were later determined. At 1443 the *Bogue* launched Avengers #10 and #19 to be ferried to TG 22.6 to be later ferried to TG 22.5, which complied with CINCAIRLANT 250144. At 1654 Avenger #32 landed with the pilots of the ferried planes to TG 22.6. The plane was launched 1717 back to TG 22.6.

After sighting TG 22.6 at 1723, TG 22.2 altered course toward Bermuda. On June 30, 1944, Task Group 22.2 entered the swept channel at Bermuda, and at 1456 the *Bogue* was anchored in Port Royal Bay South.[14]

The next day, July 1, 1944, at 0813 the *Bogue* and Task Group 22.2 escorts departed Bermuda en route to Norfolk in compliance to CINCLANT 012553 of July. On July 3 at 0100, TG 22.2 entered the swept channel at Norfolk. Later, at 0526, the *Bogue* launched six Avengers and eight FMs from VC-69 to NAS Norfolk. At 0630 the CTG 22.2 detached the escorts *Haverfield*, *Janssen*, *Willis*, *Swenning*, and *Robinson* to proceed to New York in compliance with CINCLANT 301502. The *Bogue* anchored in berth 3, Hampton Roads at 0748 and then got underway for the NOB at Norfolk to moor portside to Pier 7, berth 75 at 0950.

The USS *Bogue* had ended its ninth war cruise and Task Group 22.2 was dissolved.

The results of the war cruise had been good for Captain Vosseller's first command of a CVE. He had a number of recommendations based on what he saw. He had come to the carrier as the former head of the ASDEVLANT command, so suggestions were surely appropriate. A few of such recommendations were expressed as follows: "In predominately night operations, to which present indications point, the attrition of aircraft can be expected to be greater than the past. At the same time fighters cannot be used for their principal function of strafing and

11. Ninth War Cruise

in addition their rendezvous with the torpedo planes at night is out of the question unless all planes turn on running lights which is unacceptable in submarine waters. It is further submitted that the need for fighters for strafing is now reduced due to the installation of rockets on VTB aircraft. It is therefore considered that the allowance of fighters might logically be reduced to five."[15]

In covering the issue that aircraft made only one visual sighting, Vosseller noted: "It might very well be that the very unsatisfactory illumination provided by flares prevented additional sightings at night but in any event it is considered that another change in enemy submarine tactics is now established and that retention of an effective offensive is contingent upon general use of searchlight equipped aircraft from CVEs."[16] Admiral Ingersoll and other ASW units under his command took the recommendations from these CVE captains and squadron commanders seriously, and before long significant changes in aircraft composition for escort carriers were made.

The mission operations at night were decidedly increased with this cruise aboard the *Bogue*. Of the 3230.2 hours flown during the cruise, 892.8 hours were logged at night even in good and bad weather. This focus on night operations led to the first successful night attack by a carrier plane.[17]

In his War Diary comments regarding the cruise just past, the Commander of CORTDIV 51, Commander Theodore S. Lark, presented important and rather interesting observations about his escorts supporting the *Bogue*: "Escorts had no positive contacts during entire cruise beginning 4 May 1944. All the contacts obtained were definitely determined to be fish or other disturbance in the water. In most cases several contacts, giving good traces and solid echoes, were obtained in same area as original contact. The characteristics upon careful examination were those of fish—little or no target movement or erratic target movement, wide target, no doppler, gradual dispersal of target at short ranges, target lost when in excess of six or seven hundred yards. When charges dropped to confirm opinion, fish were later found in the water."[18]

12

10th War Cruise

"On this ship you have the dramatic evidence [the POWs] of your success."

On July 4, 1944, the *Bogue* moved from the NOB Norfolk to the Norfolk Navy Yard at Portsmouth. The *Bogue* remained at the Navy Yard undergoing repairs and installations from July 5 to the 18th.

On the 19th, the *Bogue* got underway for a post-repair trial run and returned to the yard to berth at #7 and #8 at 1905. On the 21st, the carrier departed the Norfolk Navy Yard on another post-repair run en route to the NOB Norfolk to moor beside Pier 5 at berth 55 at 0940.[1]

The new composite squadron to replace VC-69 was to be VC-42. The squadron was formed on April 15 of 1943 in hangar 22 at Alameda Naval Air Squadron with six pilots, including the commanding officer, Lieutenant Commander Stuart Stephens from Newport, Arkansas. These officers started building a squadron by meeting assigned officers and men as they reported aboard. Aircraft was arriving along with equipment and supplies required by a new squadron. The squadron was getting organized and by June the personnel quota of 26 officers, five chief petty officers, and 168 men were aboard.

Training was the real mission of the squadron for many months, in both air operations and ground classes. From the beginning, the squadron was training for action in the Pacific. Unfortunately, in early May the squadron discovered that they were going to be assigned to the Atlantic Fleet for anti-submarine warfare operations. Their authorized complement of planes was changed from 12 fighters and nine torpedo bombers to nine fighters and 12 torpedo bombers. Thus, three fighter pilots were transferred without replacements. The skipper, Lieutenant Commander Stephens, who had been a fighter pilot in the South Pacific, was quite disappointed when he was ordered by COMFAIRWC to fly Torpedo planes instead of fighters, but he carried on leading flights of both aircraft types.

12. 10th War Cruise

The squadron had experienced its share of flight accidents so far, but the first death occurred on May 10 when Ensign L.L. Stout was flying low over the San Joaquin River at a location some five miles northeast of the auxiliary field at Vernalles when he hit some high-tension wires, crashed in a swampy area, and was killed instantly. The second and more shocking tragedy occurred on July 16 when VC-42 skipper Stephens was killed when his torpedo plane was struck by his wingman, went out of control, and crashed into Monterey Bay. His radioman, S1c A.D. Gilder, Jr., and gunner, AM3c A.C. DeWeber, were also killed. Only Stephens's body was recovered. Twelve days later, Ensign Head failed to pull out of a routine glide bombing dive and crashed at 300 knots in Monterey Bay (near the skipper's crash location). The crash instantly killed the pilot Head and crew of ARM3c W.S Brillhart and AOM3c J. Flinn. The commanding officer's replacement was Lieutenant Commander Jesse T. Yavorsky, who took command of VC-42 on July 30, 1943.[2]

VC-42 was loaded aboard the USS *Guadalcanal* (CVE-60) on October 31, 1943. The squadron's first ASW cruise in the Atlantic began when they boarded the USS *Croatan* (CVE-25) beginning March 25, 1944. When the squadron detached from the carrier docked at Pier 7 at the Naval Operational Base at Norfolk on May 11, it was stationed at East Field under CASU-21. CINCLANT authorized the skipper to grant leave for all officers and men for seven days in two leave periods. The first leave group returned on May 21, at which point the second leave group headed out for leave.

Four days afterward, VC-42 was moved to Naval Auxiliary Air Station (NAAS) Creeds, Virginia, which was some 30 miles south of Norfolk. On the same date, six VT pilots and their radiomen were detached to Vero Beach for a Smoke Bomb Experimental Project. The pilots were directed by Navy Lieutenant Pierce and Captain Day of the Army Chemical Warfare Service to develop basic doctrine for aerial smoke screen coverage support of group troops in amphibious landings. This small detachment of 12 men returned to NAAS Creeds on June 10.

During this period between cruises, six pilots and three other officers were transferred out of the squadron while eight new pilots reported aboard. Refresher training began in earnest during this time. The torpedo pilots were active in rocket practice at Manteo, North Carolina, glide angle calibration, anti-submarine bombing, and night flare illumination. The fighter pilots worked on strafing, fixed gunnery of towed sleeves, and day and night division tactics. Each pilot flew navigation flights and bounce drills in daylight and at night. The social life was built around the schedule of day or night training. Monday, Tuesday, and Wednesday for night training were from 1500 to midnight, while the other days were regular hours from 0800 to 1700 for day training. Half of the personnel had Saturday and half of Sunday off, while the other had Sunday off and Saturday afternoon off and until 1500 Monday to report from liberty.

The squadron had one all-squadron party at Pungo Beach with swimming, softball, hot dogs, and cases of beer. On July 14, the squadron moved back to East Field. Before leaving Norfolk, the officers held a farewell party at Thalia Acres, a nightclub between Norfolk and Virginia Beach, while the enlisted men held their party at Ocean View.

COMAIRLANT assigned VC-42 to the USS *Bogue*. For this cruise, Captain Vosseller wanted some TBM-1D Avengers, which were equipped with ASD microwave radar and an L-8H searchlight. He was able to obtain two each TBM-1D Avengers with four combat teams from VC-19 and VC-13 in trade for two each TBM-1Cs and four combat teams from VC-42. VC-42 also received two civilian technicians to maintain the efficiency of the new radar equipment and searchlight installations.

On July 23, the VC-42 personnel and material were loaded aboard. The pilots had bounced at Monogram Field and all ensigns who had not landed aboard for three months had qualified on the USS *Prince William* (CVE-31). Two guests of Captain Vosseller, navy Captain Collins and an Army lieutenant colonel, were attached to the *Bogue* for half of the cruise to observe the flight operations and tactics.[3] Also onboard were five fighter director officers. Vosseller expressed his displeasure later when he said, "The training these officers had received may be and probably is excellent from the standpoint of air-to-air work. However, not one of them had the slightest conception of the operations in which this ship is currently engaged and it has been necessary to train them practically from the ground up.... It is submitted that there should be a course in at least one of the Navy's fighter director schools which fits officers in this classification for duty in the Combat Information Center aboard ships engaged in ASW operations as well as strict fighter direction work."[4]

On the 24th at 1031, the *Bogue* departed the NOB Norfolk en route to the calibration area anchoring in the Chesapeake Bay at 1527. At 1545 HF/DF calibration commenced. After calibration was completed at 0314 on July 25, 1944, the new Task Group 22.3 departed the anchorage and moved out into the channel. The TG included the *Bogue* and

12. 10th War Cruise

escorts *Haverfield*, *Janssen*, *Willis*, *Wilhoite*, and *Swenning*. The TG joined up off Cape Henry and set a course en route to conduct simulated air attacks on UGS-49 and to conduct anti-submarine exercises in the vicinity of Bermuda in compliance of CINCLANT 160055 of July 1944. At 1757 the *Bogue* completed 20 Avenger and 14 FM refresher landings.

Captain Vosseller wanted to make more use of the fighter pilots by having the most experienced FM pilots qualify in the Avenger to support daytime search efforts and free up more Avengers for night operations. Unfortunately, this idea met a quick reversal when at 0930 on the 26th, Lieutenant (jg) Johnny Sutton, Jr., made his first Avenger landing. He was approaching for a normal landing when he descended slightly too low, and his hook struck the guard rail of the ramp, which weakened the arresting device. Though the hook did not break, it caught the number 7 wire while the barrier operators lowered their barriers. The hook

Port bow view of radar picket escort ship USS *Wilhoite* (DER-397) underway off the coast of Oahu, Hawaii. (Accession #: Naval Subjects Collection, Catalog #L45–307.03.01.)

did not hold and passed through the first two barriers, then through the third and final one.

Then the right wing of Sutton's plane struck the top of the tail and the folded left wing of the second Avenger piloted by Lieutenant Watson that had just landed. Alert Watson ducked his head when Sutton's wing passed over him. The wayward Avenger continued to move to the right, hitting the tails of two parked Avengers positioned side by side on the starboard bow. Three men (C.H. Wilson of the A.C.G., AEM2c G.K. Lynch, and ART3c R.B. Donnelly) who were making a post-flight inspection were pushed overboard along with the outboard plane. The inboard plane was pushed from the flight deck down into the forecastle. As fate would have it, the three men in the water, suffering only some bruises, were picked up by the *Haverfield*. Sutton's Avenger ended up standing at the corner of the flight deck on its nose with its wheels at the edge with the fuselage at a 70-degree angle from the horizontal.

Sutton was able to crawl out of his plane unhurt. Thankfully, all the flight deck staff were able to keep clear of the Avenger's path too. No one was a casualty, but the two planes that were lost (one overboard and one wrecked beyond repair) were the special Avenger TBM-1D planes with the searchlights. Now there were only two searchlight Avengers left on board. By 1600 that day, the flight deck was cleared, and training operations were recommenced in the afternoon and evening.

The convoy UGS-49 transiting en route to the Mediterranean near TG 22.3 wanted to test the smoke screen defensive tactics against aerial assault. At 1624 two Avengers launched to find the convoy, and it was sighted at 1744 some 66 miles from the *Bogue*. Two hours later, three Avengers and two FMs were launched to "attack" the convoy. As the planes approached, all the convoy ships began laying a smoke screen. The attacking planes had little interference with the smoke screens as they performed their coordinated attack simulation runs.[5]

From July 27 to the 29th, Task Group 22.3 worked with the submarine USS *R6* based in Bermuda. This training gave the TG an opportunity to see a submarine in operation. Each day, *R6* would surface at a specific location within the radius of the ASW search area of VC-42. The sub would crash-dive immediately to practice deploying and using sonobuoys to gain a contact. At other times the sub would remain on the surface while FMs and Avengers coordinated simulated strafing and depth bomb runs. Night practice sessions were conducted to gain searchlight attack experience.

On July 29 at 0435, Lieutenant C.E. Lair gained a radar contact on

12. 10th War Cruise

R6 and attacked using searchlight and depth bomb action. This realistic training was deemed invaluable to all those engaged in the simulations. The TG escorts were also part of the training exercises to hone their skill. The training was concluded at 1047 that day as the *Bogue* and escorts proceeded to Hamilton, Bermuda, where the three wrecked Avengers were transferred to a barge and four replacement Avengers were loaded via hoist in compliance to CINCLANT 262133. The *Bogue* anchored off NAS Bermuda in Port Royal Bay, South Bermuda, at 1730. After one day of liberty, on July 31 TG 22.3 with the *Bogue* moved to Murrays Anchorage to anchor.[6]

At 0613 of August 1, 1944, the *Bogue* departed Murrays Anchorage, Bermuda, with Task Group 22.3 escorts en route to 46° 10' N, 21° 15' W, as specified by 10th Fleet information that a U-boat was heading west from the estimated position. The order was conveyed via CINCLANT 290214. The following day, Task Group 22.6 lost the USS *Friske* (DE-143) to a torpedo at 47° 10' N, 32° 40' W. The flagship of TG 22.6 with the USS *Wake Island* was already affected by a shortage of planes. CTG 22.6, therefore, requested the Task Group 22.3 expedite its arrival.

On the 5th at 0615, Ensign Larson in his Avenger (a TBM-1C) sighted the *Wake Island*. The carrier was 100 miles from the *Bogue* on bearing 053°, so TG 22.6 was relieved and departed for Norfolk. From August 5 through August 13, the *Bogue's* planes and escorts conducted a thorough search of the assigned area from CINCLANT, reporting seven radar and sonar contacts but nothing to show from investigation except negative results.

During the time from 1400 on August 14 until 0323 August 15, the *Bogue* was hampered by fog banks moving throughout the North Atlantic, leaving problems for nearly every flight. At 1410 on the 14th, four Avengers and four FMs were launched. As Lieutenant (jg) Mabry catapulted from the *Bogue*, his radioman, ARM2c D.A. Bardon, suffered a severe cut on his hand when the radio receiver was dislodged. With Bardon's hand bleeding, Mabry returned to land aboard the carrier. At 1747 he was able to launch again with another radioman.

A launch of two Avengers occurred at 2203, but 25 minutes later Lieutenant (jg) Revenaugh in Avenger #20 made a forced landing with his engine losing power and his radio out. He was replaced by Lieutenant Q.O. Keinholz and Lieutenant (jg) Wayne A. Dixon in "Baker" radar planes. Lieutenant (jg) Dixon in Avenger #17 reported a contact at 0300 on the early morning of August 15, which was acknowledged by the carrier. This contact was *U-802* on its way to the Gulf of St.

Lawrence. Dixon lost his communications with the ship and radio contact was never reestablished. Dixon and his crew, ARM3c C.G. Melton and AOM3c D.J. Scinio, were never seen again. The cause of the loss was never confirmed.

During the rest of the night, VF-42s planes obtained three contacts: two by Lieutenant F.B. Underman at 1454 and 0555 and one by Lieutenant (jg) M.B. Wheeler at 0526. All contacts were deemed negative after investigation. Air patrols the next day, August 16, reported no contacts. The *Bogue* had unknowingly crossed paths that day with *U-802* and had zigged out of range of a torpedo before the submarine's location was firm. At 1440 the *Janssen* picked up a sonar contact, and an attack with depth charges was made at 1527 by the *Swenning*. But there was no indication of damage found and the contact was lost. Searches that night and the next day found no additional information.

On August 19 at 0030, Lieutenant Carl E. Lair's radioman, ARM3c H.W. Iwanicki, saw a radar blip of *U-802* from their Avenger #11 (a TBM-1D version) showing out 20 miles away. Lieutenant Lair moved lower to 150 feet, and, at three-quarters of a mile from the target, the searchlight was turned on by AMM2c C.E. Paris, revealing a fully surfaced submarine dead ahead. Paris saw one man on the bridge. The pilot began a depth charge attack at 0040 from 75 feet at 140 knots, dropping three MK XI British 250-pound depth bombs at a 120° angle. The searchlight operator in his debrief noted that the depth charge plumbs covered the forward part of the U-boat and that the MK 2 markers (attached to each depth bomb) were seen astride the wake. Before Lair could get around for another attack, the U-boat was totally submerged. He dropped a sonobuoy pattern but did not pick up any submarine noises. At 0140 Lieutenant Lair was relieved by Lieutenant (jg) R.L. Revenaugh, who regained Lair's sonobuoy channels and then decided to lay his own sonobuoys with no contact.

At 0640 Lieutenant (jg) Wheeler's radioman picked up a radar blip, but it disappeared as he approached. At dawn a large oil slick was visible, proving some evidence of U-boat damage. The commander of TG 22.3 knew of an approaching bad front that was a promise of bad weather coming and decided to take the *Bogue* and two of his escorts to the southeast to expediate passage through the front. Three escorts were left with the estimated courses of the U-boat. Six Canadian frigates (EG-16) were assigned to aid Captain Vosseller. The USS *Card* flagship of TG 22.1 offered to give Vosseller support, but it was not needed.[7]

The front had passed by daylight of August 20 as the *Bogue* and her

12. 10th War Cruise

escorts were again heading north on the way to a location that the aerologist indicated would be clear of fog. Four Avengers were launched at 0630 with no contacts encountered. At 1035 Lieutenant (jg) A.X. Brokas (in #19), Lieutenant (jg) Mabry (in #12), Lieutenant (jg) R.B. Law (in #10), and Lieutenant (jg) B.C. Sissler (in #16) all took off in TBM-1Cs. On patrol at 1227, Brokas's radioman, ARM2c H.A. Ermer, saw a radar blip on his scope out five miles. Just 30 seconds later, Brokas sighted a fully surfaced submarine four miles off the starboard bow. He increased speed getting ready to attack. Reaching three miles from the U-boat, it began to fire at them, but thankfully their antiaircraft fire was not effective, and they received no hits.

When Brokas reached 1200 yards from the target, he started to fire his MK.5, 3.5-inch, forward-firing aircraft rockets in four salvos of two rockets each spaced 200 yards apart. The first three salvos were too short, but the fourth hit the water close by the sub. The submarine was turning to the left, which caused the last rockets to reach the stern at an oblique angle. After firing his rockets, he released two MK.54 torpex-filled depth bombs at 100 feet at an incline of 150 degrees at 240 knots. The bombs (fused at 25-foot depth) hit close aboard the port side, sending water skyward as the explosions helped obscure the submarine. One AA gun and a few deck crewmen were blown overboard by the explosions.

The U-boat continued forward and turned 360° to the right, followed by another turn to the left. Brokas dropped a sonobuoy pattern some 15 seconds later as the U-boat submerged, as Brokas and his radioman listened. Engine cavitations lasted for 55 seconds. An oil slick appeared for a half mile from the submarine's dive location, as Brokas laid a second sonobuoy pattern, which yielded no indications. A smoke float was dropped to mark the contact spot.

Though Lieutenant (jg) Brokas and his crew were operating well, additional planes were on the way to support the action. At this time, the other three Avengers that had launched with Brokas were near. A "killer" group of two more Avengers (Lieutenant [jg] M.J. Sherbring in #21 and Lieutenant [jg] W.S. Porter in #18) and two FMs (Lieutenant J.B. Watson in #7 and Lieutenant [jg] J. Sulton in #9) were launched and vectored to the scene. Because there was little wind in the afternoon, the rockets were removed from the two "killer" group Avengers to reduce the weight for launching.

The first plane to arrive on scene at 1336 was Lieutenant (jg) Mabry, who was ordered to climb to 7,000 feet to allow the carrier to determine the exact position of the contact using the Racon (YJ) and to aid in communications. When all six planes had reached the contact position by 1355, Brokas was relieved, giving tactical command to Lieutenant (jg) Porter. More sonobuoys were dropped, but no contact was made. Lieutenant Watson sighted the U-boat just below the surface at one end of the oil slick at 1421, and alerted the other planes. Nine minutes later, two periscopes and Schnorchel gear appeared. Sherbring and Sissler dropped depth bombs on the submarine, but they fell short. When the boat slowly surfaced, Sissler made a rocket attack. Seven rockets appeared to hit the target squarely, but the eighth hung up on the Sissler's Avenger wing.

From the time the boat had been sighted, Lieutenant Watson had continued to strafe the target. His fellow attackers joined in the action to strafe as they made their runs. By 1434 the U-boat was fully surfaced as members of the crew appeared wearing life belts and jackets on the conning tower and the deck. A minute later, they began to abandon the submarine, and the strafing stopped, though six bodies were later found by the escorts.

At 1440 an explosion occurred that "rocked" the boat and it began to sink. A few minutes later, only the conning tower was above the surface when the stern rose and the bow nosed down at a steep angle and slid below the waves. A few seconds later, a second explosion occurred,

Air attack on German submarine *U-1229* by Lieutenant (jg) M.J. Sherbring, VC-42 plane from USS *Bogue* (CVE-9), incident #6972. The submarine was sunk, 17 crew members died, and 41 individuals survived. (U.S. Navy Photo, August 20, 1944, #80-G-244761, in the collections of the National Archives.)

12. 10th War Cruise

which destroyed the boat, sending debris and water up to 100 feet high.[8]

At 1545 the *Janssen* picked up 42 U-boat survivors—two regular German naval officers, 39 enlisted men, and one special-guest officer. Among the survivors was Leutnant Oskar Mantel (Propagandamann), a well-trained and experienced Abwehr agent (Abwehr was the primary German organization responsible for obtaining secret military intelligence and covert operations during World War II) who had successfully completed assignments in Spain and France. Before World War II, he had lived in New York City for 12 years.

The paper on the survivors confirmed that the submarine that had been sunk was the *U-1229* commanded by Korvettenkapitän Armin Zinke. Zinke left from Trondheim on July 26, 1944, on his first, and ultimately his last, war cruise under orders to put Mantel ashore along the Maine coast to carry out sabotage operations. Zinke died from strafing fire when surfacing to abandon the boat. Another officer died on the boat. One of the rescued men died on the night of the 20th. "Stabs Ober Steuermann Fritz Beer expired due to immersion and shock despite all efforts of the Medical Officer and those assisting him. Artificial respiration, adrenalin and oxygen were applied with negative results. After his demise he was buried at sea in accordance with the traditions of the Navy and in the presence of the Senior surviving officer."[9]

After Beer died, this left only one regular German naval officer, Oberleutnant (Ing.) Willy Büttner, an engineer, surviving. Five prisoners had minor bullet wounds. The prisoners were transferred to the *Bogue* the next day at 0905.

The *U-1229* sank at position 42° 20' N, 51° 39' W in the Grand Banks of Newfoundland, about 300 miles southeast of Cape Race. It was a 750-ton, Type IX-C submarine built by Deutsche Werft, Finkenwerder and commissioned on January 13, 1944. It had a maximum depth of 200 meters and could crash-dive in 30–38 seconds. On the deck/conning tower, it had two twin 20 mm cannons on platform I and an automatic 37 mm mounted on platform II. It carried 14 torpedoes, with four tubes forward and two aft. It was driven by two nine-cylinder M.A.N. Diesels, with Büchi superchargers. It was not fitted with radar, due to a shortage at the base.[10]

In the CNO's *Final Report on the Interrogation of Survivors from U-1229*, the following was revealed about the crew:

"General—U-1229's complement was 57, consisting of four officers, five chief petty officers, thirteen petty officers, and thirty-five men.

USS *Bogue*

Air attack on German submarine *U-1229* by Lieutenant (jg) B.C. Sissler, VC-42 plane from USS *Bogue* (CVE-9), incident #6972. The submarine was sunk, 17 crew members died, and 41 individuals survived. (Photo, August 20, 1944. U.S. Navy Photo #80-G-244769 in the collections of the National Archives.)

Although a considerable number had had no previous U-boat experience, the crew was of superior caliber compared with others recently encountered. The engineer[ing] officer himself said they had developed well and had become an excellent crew. Prisoners were not unduly secure and several needed no urging at all to tell all they knew. This is thought to be partly due to events on the fighting fronts in the past weeks, plus a high incidence of men genuinely anti–Nazi who wanted to get the whole business over as soon as possible. It is also undoubtedly true that the unpopularity and inefficiency of their captain did much to ruin the morale of a good crew.

"Officers—Although little is known of the early career of Korvettenkapitän Armin Zinke, it is apparent that he ranks high among the

12. 10th War Cruise

more inept German U-boat commanders encountered in this war. His crew did not have a good word to say about him. During *U-1229*'s working up period and trials, Zinke was drunk a good deal of the time. At all times he was morose and uncommunicative both with the officers and the men, and it was seldom that he allowed anyone to address him, except in compliance with an order. His faults as a man might have been overlooked, but survivors held him directly responsible for the loss of their boat due to his practice during the last few days of the patrol of remaining continually on the surface during daylight. Zinke belonged to the 1930 Naval Term and wore the minesweeper badge. It is believed that this was his first and last patrol on a U-boat.

"Leutnant zur See Quertin [deceased], the first watch officer, was formerly quartermaster on *U-504* under Poske. He was popular with the crew, particularly as he couldn't get along with the captain. He wore the Iron Cross 1st class. Nothing is known of Uhlenbrück [deceased], the second watch officer. He joined the boat as a midshipman in Hamburg and wore the minesweeper badge.

"Büttner, the engineer and only officer survivor, was also a lower deck promotion. In peacetime he served on the *Grille*, Adolf Hitler's yacht, which was also used as an experimental ship for steam turbines. Büttner later served on a destroyer and then commissioned *U-561* under Bartels. When he left her early in 1943, he was a machinist. He attended the Marineschule at Flensburg before receiving his commission. Büttner was popular with his men and was probably a competent engineer officer. He was an ardent National Socialist, although quite ready to admit that the war, and particularly the U-boat war, was lost, and he was full of the kind of 'crocodile tears' emotion so often encountered in certain types of Germans. Büttner, in addition, was extremely proud of his attainments as a U-boat engineer and frequently his vanity outran his security.

"Men—The 'greenness' of many of the crew was offset by the experience and ability of several of the petty officers. One, a coxswain who did not survive the sinking, had celebrated his 500th day at sea on U-boats in this war a few days before he lost his life. In conclusion, it is worthy of note that the pharmacist's mate, who was lost in the final action, was killed at his regular action station on the 20-mm. cannon!"[11]

Of significant interest to Naval Intelligence was the German Schnorchel now being deployed on most U-boats. On *U-1229* the Schnorchel was installed at Oderwerke, Stettin, Germany, during its final overhaul (about May 8 to June 20, 1944). It was fitted on the starboard side forward of the conning tower. When the mast was raised, its top was one to two feet lower than the tops of the extended periscopes. It was usually raised or lowered when the boat was at a depth of 20 meters, though *U-1229* maintained a depth of 13 meters at speed of about five knots. When the top of the Schnorchel undercut a wave, the floater valve was actuated, cutting off the air supply and greatly reducing the pressure within the boat.

Unfortunately for the Allied cause, the Schnorchel would become of outstanding use in reducing detection. *U-1229* cruised submerged on Schnorchel from about July 28 to August 14, surfacing for only a few minutes to take navigational sun fixes. The prisoners stated that the longest period spent at Schnorchel depth without coming to the surface was 36 hours.[12]

A dispatch from CINCLANT 202353 in response to the communications about the sinking of *U-1229* read: "Good work. Get U-boat reported at present in area of Flemish Cap."[13] But on August 22, CINCLANT 222154 ordered the Task Group 22.3 to head to Argentia, Newfoundland. On August 24, the task group entered the swept channel, and at 0904 the *Bogue* was moored on the starboard side to berth F and G at the Naval Operating Base (NOB) Argentia.[14]

On that afternoon, Admiral R.J. Ingersoll, the commander in chief of CINCLANT, and his staff came aboard the *Bogue* to honor VC-42 pilot Lieutenant Lair and his crew, and those involved in the sinking of *U-1229*. The entire ship's company was lined up at attention on the hangar deck as the admiral was piped aboard. The VC-42 squadron officers were formed forward of the elevator pit, with the men along the starboard bulkhead as the admiral and his staff stepped on the deck and received the salutes of Captain Vosseller and others.

Admiral Ingersoll stepped up to the microphone and made a brief congratulatory address: "It is not often that I am so fortunate as to be able to make awards for successful action against the enemy so promptly and under such suspicious circumstances. Here on this ship you have the dramatic evidence [the POWs] of your success. Just prior to this present cruise, I recommended the *Bogue* for the Presidential Unit Citation because of her outstanding record in anti-submarine warfare. I am now going to repeat the recommendation so as to include Squadron VC-42. This latest success should certainly assure approval of the citation."[15]

The admiral presented, personally, decorations to 20 officers and men of VC-42. He called each name of the recipients and pinned the

12. 10th War Cruise

medal or ribbon on his breast. The decorations included two Distinguished Flying Crosses (Lieutenant Lair and Lieutenant [jg] Brokas), 10 Air Medals and eight Letters of Commendation. Lieutenant Lair's crew of Iwanicki and Paris received Air Medals for their searchlight attack on August 19. Lieutenant (jg) Brokas's crewmen, Ermer and Graves, also received Air Medals. For the *U-1229* effort, the pilots received Air Medals while their crewmen received Letters of Commendation. On the recommendation of Captain Vosseller, the admiral presented Aerologist I.I. Wilkinson, USN, with a Letter of Commendation for his prediction of the hole in the fog that allowed Brokas to sight *U-1229*.

In the evening of August 24, a victory celebration was held at the officers' club at the Naval Air Station Argentia. The ship's company and all squadron officers were present. During the next several days, there was a formal *Bogue* victory cocktail party attended by some women from the Civil Service employees of the Air Station and two excursions to St. John's (the capital of Newfoundland and a town of 25,000 population located some 85 miles from Argentia).[16]

On August 28, 1944, Task Group 22.3, with the *Bogue* and escorts *Haverfield*, *Janssen*, *Willis*, *Wilhoite*, and *Swenning*, departed NOB Argentia at 1050. They steamed past Cape St. Mary abeam en route to a new 10th Fleet U-boat location of 44° 30' N, 45° 30' W in compliance with CINCLANT 271952.

From August 29 to September 7, there were a limited number of flights because the weather was bad. On September 8 at 1637, Lieutenant (jg) W.S. Porter and crew in Avenger #16 sighted a submarine periscope bearing 347°T distance 72 miles at 43° 43' N, 52° 18' W and immediately attacked but had no visible results. Five other Avenger pilots (Lieutenant Commander Yavorsky, Lieutenant Lair, Lieutenant [jg] Revenaugh, Lieutenant [jg] McGusty, and Lieutenant [jg] Sherbring) were vectored to the scene to hear the sonobuoy submarine noise and made attacks, but with no results.

At 2030 the *Haverfield* arrived and heard sonar indications at a depth of 300 feet. She made a hedgehog attack, but there were no results, and the contact was not regained. She was joined by *Janssen*, *Wilhoite*, and *Swenning*, which also made sonar contact. Task Group 22.4, with escorts *Sloat*, *Keith*, and *Ottersetter*, was en route to join TG 22.3 in searching the area for contacts as requested from Vosseller. The *Bogue* and *Willis* remained in the general vicinity of the contact.

During the period from September 9 through September 14, there were 13 radar and sonar contacts from planes and surface vessels. There were also two Schnorchels seen by pilots. Three more attacks were made, with two from VC-42 planes (September 9 by Lieutenant Nelson and September 13 by Lieutenant [jg] Wheeler) and one by escort *Wilhoite* on September 13.

At 0027 on September 15, two searchlight Avengers were landing aboard the *Bogue* when Avenger #20 caught the #2 pendant and its tail hook pulled out, causing a crash into the barrier and island structure. The Avenger was wrecked beyond repair onboard, which left only one Searchlight version plane left.

The end of the hurricane that had passed along the eastern seaboard in mid–September caused problems for VC-42 pilots on the 16th. That day at 0134, three Avengers were launched on a sector search out to 70 miles. In Avenger #18, Ensign Schroeder at 0540 for some reason had not checked in on schedule and advised using his VHF that he could not give his ETA since his plane had been pushed far out of position by the heavy winds. He was directed to orbit, turn his ABK (aircraft radio receiving equipment) on to "emergency," and climb until the carrier picked him up on radar. Unfortunately, the ABK was not working and the *Bogue* or any other escort could not locate him. He was then directed to key MOs on channel 3665 so the ships could get a bearing by RDF. His approximate bearings were gained by different ships in the TG to allow them to vector his on 250°T. At 0740 after he was flying for 50 minutes, the *Bogue's* SK radar picked him up on bearing 066° at 49 miles away. Three minutes after, Schroeder picked up the *Bogue's* YE. Then he was ordered to lower altitude to reduce head winds and two Avengers, flown by Lieutenant (jg) Law and Lieutenant (jg) Porter, were vectored to bring Schroeder in. Unfortunately, Schroeder had only eight gallons of gasoline left and he was forced to make a water landing. At 0905 the *Wilhoite* picked up Schroeder and his crew uninjured.

The problems were not over. At 1353 on September 18, Lieutenant (jg) McGusty approached the carrier experiencing a violent pitching and yawing deck. With oil having accumulated on his windshield, he could barely see the LSO (landing signal officer). McGusty lined up to the port of the center line, and appropriately the LSO waved him off to go around for another try. McGusty misinterpreted the signal and took it as a cut (cut the engines and land). McGusty landed in a skid with his plane hitting on its right wheel, shearing off the main right oleo strut and wheel. The plane bounded high in the air over the first two barriers. The tail hook caught barrier three, which snapped the plane down to the deck violently. McGusty's plane landed on two planes (#17 and #13)

12. 10th War Cruise

parked forward of the barriers. One was damaged beyond repair, and his Avenger was destroyed. Thankfully, no one was injured in the accident. The next day, CINCLANT message 192012 ordered Task Group 22.3 to return to Norfolk.

On the 20th at 1445, the *Wilhoite* came alongside the *Bogue* to transfer Ensign Schroeder and his crew of Avenger #18 that had been recovered from the sea on the 16th. On the 23rd at 0829, the *Haverfield* came alongside the *Bogue* to transfer official mail and cruise reports. VC-42 launched its eight Avengers and nine FMs to NAS Norfolk. Task Units 22.3.1 and 22.3.2 were dissolved by CINCLANT 211853.

At 0234 on the 24th, the *Bogue* entered the swept channel at Norfolk. Twenty-four minutes later, the escorts *Haverfield, Janssen, Willis, Wilhoite,* and *Swenning* were detached to proceed to New York in compliance with CINCLANT 192012. The *Bogue* moored at 0930 on the starboard side of Pier 5, in berth 53 and 55 at NOB Norfolk. The next day, the *Bogue* moved to the Norfolk Navy Yard at Portsmouth and moored portside to Pier 4, berth 29.

During the period from September 8–19, VC-42 Air Combat Intelligence (ACI) Officer Lieutenant J.L. Blackman recorded the number of times that each pilot's sortie received radar blips against Schnorchel U-boats yielding negative results. It was a darkly humorous, yet accurate, measure of the psychological strain being inflicted upon the pilots. In this "Survival of the Blip-piest" award presentation, Lieutenant (jg) Wheeler received the leather medal with seven blips, Lieutenant Underman got the wooden medal for five blips, Lieutenant (jg) Brokas received the paper medal for two blips, and five other pilots received honorable mention with only one blip each.[17]

Back on September 23, all hands aboard the carrier took part in a celebration of the *Bogue's* second birthday. It included a movie, a play covering the "eccentricities" of the ship and the officers, and a banquet.

The 10th war cruise was unique in several ways. It made significant use of searchlights, and, in effect, made the first attack on a submarine by a searchlight-equipped carrier plane. From information gained in Lieutenant Lair's attack on *U-1229*, the *U.S. Fleet Anti-Submarine Bulletin of September 1944* noted: "Searchlights recently installed in TBM aircraft of CVE groups are already proving their worth, the first searchlight attack from a U.S. CVE having been made at 0030, 19 August by TBM-11 from the U.S.S. *Bogue*. This classic attack ... demonstrated its practicability and although possibly not immediately successful, directly led to a subsequent sinking of a submarine."[18] The combination of locating enemy submarines on the surface by using ASD (APS-3) airborne radar and the L-8H searchlight was to become a standard in the Allied ASW world. The impact of the U-boat Schnorchel was growing and would surely decrease the U-boat destructions.

The post-cruise conference on September 25, 1944, was of great interest to the senior flag officers because of the German "Schnorchel" experience and the sinking of the *U-1229*. The flag officers who attended were Vice Admiral P.N.L. Bellinger (commander Air Force, Atlantic Fleet), Rear Admiral A.C. Read (commander Fleet Air, Norfolk), and Commander Seitz (chief of staff of CINCAIRLANT). A number of captains and commanders were also in attendance, plus the Operations, Training, and Material officers from CINCLANT Norfolk, commander AIRLANT, commander 10th Fleet, ASDEVLANT, CASU, and COMFAIR Norfolk. Also included was Captain Galley of the USS *Guadalcanal*. All of these visitors made for a crowded Norfolk NAS Administration Building.

All the torpedo pilots and some of the FM fighter pilots from VC-42 participated. All aspects of the cruise were discussed in detail, with many questions asked of VC-42 skipper Lieutenant Commander Yavorsky; Lieutenant Lair, who made the first CVE searchlight attack; Lieutenant (jg) Brokas, who sank the *U-1229*; and Lieutenant Blackman, the air combat intelligence officer.

The total flight hours logged by VC-42 during the 10th war cruise totaled as follows:
Number of Fighter Hours flown in daylight=577.3, Night=0.0
Number of Avenger Hours flown in daylight=1,281.5, Night=389.2
Total Flight Hours Flown: Daylight=1,858.8, Night=389.2
Grand Total: 2,248.0 Hours.[19]

13

11th Cruise

"An appropriate time to reduce offensive sweeps of CVE support groups."

While the *Bogue* task groups and other CVE task groups were successfully searching for and sinking U-boats, the wider picture of the war in the Atlantic and Europe had been undergoing significant change. Over the first five months of 1944, U-boat losses were so heavy that by May 1944, North Atlantic operations had virtually ceased. In this period, only 25 merchant ships were lost in the North and South Atlantic at a cost of 77 U-boats from all causes. At the same time, the Allies were not so successful against them as they passed through the Bay of Biscay from French bases, the Northern Transit Area from Norway, and directly from Germany. Now equipped with 10cm radar detectors, they lost only five of their number in the Bay, but in mid–May were badly hit by RAF Coastal Command off Norway.

By then the whole complexion of the U-boat war near the shores of Europe changed with the Allied invasion of Normandy on June 6, 1944. The decreased U-boat activity before Normandy ended when the number of U-boats increased from June 5 from one submarine to 20 by June 8. The largest share of the increases was not from attempting to enter the English Channel but from setting up defensive patrols off the Biscay ports to counter potential invasion attempts.

The Allied countermeasures to protect the cross-channel and invasion areas from U-boats was impressive. On June 6, 10 escort groups with 54 ships were ready to block western approaches to the Channel and three CVEs were used to provide fighter cover for escorts close to enemy shores. These anti-submarine forces did not include the escorts and aircraft provided for convoy protection of ships running to and from France.

Only 18 ships were sunk in the Biscay-Channel area in June 1944, while 12 U-boats were sunk in the same area. With Allies applying continual pressure on U-boats operating in this area, they sank only two merchant vessels in July and six in August. The Allies sank nine U-boats in July and 12 in August. After the Allied ground forces had crossed the Cherbourg Peninsula in the first week in August, which threatened the enemy's Biscay ports, U-boats began to abandon the Biscay-Channel area by the end of August and sailed to Norwegian ports. In Norway they were more vulnerable to Allied air attacks. In addition to the difficulties associated with repair and maintenance of U-boats at the small and inadequate Norwegian ports, the major issue for German U-boats was the loss of the Biscay bases, which significantly increased the length of the voyages required to reach operating areas.

In September the German U-boat force focused primarily on getting its U-boats to Norway. Some 25 U-boats were involved in transiting that month, conducting the trip submerged and using Schnorchel. The number of U-boats at sea in September 1944 peaked in these last months of the war to 57 due to this transiting activity. Only 10 ships were sunk in the Atlantic in September, but none were sunk in the Biscay-Channel area. By the end of September, U-boats had completed their migration from the Biscay-Channel area. The average number of U-boats at sea decreased to 30 in October. October 1944 was also the first month of the war since September 1939 that not a single ship was sunk in the Atlantic.[1]

As the number of U-boats to hunt declined, Admiral King thought it was time to change the focus of CVE operations in the Atlantic. On October 23, 1944, he wrote Admiral Ingersoll the following: "Until there is a marked renewal of U-boat activity in Atlantic areas of U.S. responsibility, it is considered that the present is an appropriate time to reduce (or suspend unless the U-boat estimate shows attractive targets) offensive sweeps of CVE support groups in the interest of concentrating more time on the training and material readiness of such groups for further intensive operations."[2]

The *Bogue* remained at the Norfolk Navy Yard at Portsmouth until October 11, 1944, at 0907, when she departed for the NOB Norfolk to moor on the starboard side to Pier 5, berth 56. While the *Bogue* was preparing for the next cruise, the replacement squadron was recovering from its last CVE cruise aboard the USS *Croatan*. Back on July 22, VC-95 disembarked from the carrier and lodged at NAS Norfolk. Lieutenant S.W. Pope was recovering from a secondary infection after his appendectomy at sea. Meanwhile, the squadron personnel were taking their two-week vacations, given in two leave periods with half of

13. 11th Cruise

the crew at a time. Five pilots who had completed seven cruises in the Atlantic were given change-of-duty assignments. Lieutenant W.Z. Lane reported to the squadron as the squadron flight surgeon.

The squadron moved from NAS Norfolk to NAAS Pungo, Virginia, on July 27. For all those not on leave, daily flights commenced in anti-submarine warfare. Cross-country navigation flights were conducted for some pilots. The men took part in swimming, volleyball, softball, and the use of pneumatic life rafts.

On August 5, nine FM-2 fighters were flown to Willow Grove, Pennsylvania, for installation of rockets. Each fighter was provided six zero-length rails to give them a lethal weapon to use in anti-submarine attacks. On the 8th, the executive officer, Lieutenant Pope, reported for limited duty with the squadron.

On September 3, all the men had returned from leave as orders were received for all Avenger pilots and their aircrewmen to report to ASDEVLANT at Quonset Point, Rhode Island, for training in the use of searchlights. This meant VC-95 was fully qualified for night action in the Atlantic against U-boats. The flight surgeon, Lane, as well as Air Combat Intelligence Officer Lieutenant R.L. Colmore, accompanied the pilots to Quonset Point. While at Quonset Point, the Avenger pilots also received training in ballistic aiming for rocket firing. This was an experimental project and VC-95 was the first squadron to take the training. The training syllabus was written based on the experience gained with the squadron. The fighter pilots back at Pungo continued to receive their standard training in ASW.

On August 13, all the squadron aircraft at Pungo were evacuated to Augusta, Georgia, to avoid a hurricane threatening the area. On September 23, VC-95 moved to NAAS Manteo, North Carolina, where fighter pilots received training in rocket firing. The pilots broke all existing records for ease and speed in completing the syllabus and acquired the best score of all squadrons trained at Manteo to date.

On October 5, 1944, Captain Aurelius Bartlett Vosseller was relieved by Captain George John Dufek as captain of the USS *Bogue*. Captain Dufek was born in Rockford, Illinois. During high school, he joined the Reserve Officer Training Corps (ROTC). He was appointed to the U.S. Naval Academy in Annapolis, Maryland, in 1921. On his graduation in 1925, he was commissioned as an ensign and commenced his career aboard the battleship USS *Maryland*. He was later assigned to the submarine USS *S-39* and was promoted to lieutenant (junior grade) in 1928.

USS *Bogue*

In 1932 he entered flight training at Naval Air Station Pensacola, Florida. Upon graduation as a naval aviator in 1933, he served as navigator and executive officer on three different ships. He was promoted to lieutenant in 1935 and served aboard the aircraft carrier USS *Saratoga* in 1938. As World War II arrived, Dufek commanded a flight training squadron, served as senior naval aviator in Algeria during the invasion of North Africa, and assisted in the planning for the invasion of Sicily and Salerno. After his promotion to captain, he took part in the invasion of southern France.[3]

On October 7, VC-95 moved to NAS Norfolk, while the Avenger (VT) detachment remained at Quonset Point. At this time, the squadron received nine new FM-2s as replacements. The fighter pilots conducted bounce drills prior to requalification landings aboard the USS *Charger*. Two days later, the VT detachment returned from ASDEVLANT at Quonset Point to NAS Norfolk. The VT planes were turned in for six TBM-3s and six TBM-3Ls. On the 10th, eight new Avenger pilots who had been trained in anti-submarine warfare at NAAS Boca Chica, Florida, reported to the squadron.

On the 13th, the squadron was preparing for deploying with *Bogue*, while VT pilots were getting checked out in day and night landings aboard the USS *Charger*. On October 18, 1944, VC-95 reported aboard the *Bogue* ready to sail, but the carrier had to return to the Norfolk Navy Yard at Portsmouth to repair an engine problem. Finally, on the 21st, the *Bogue* departed NOB Norfolk, joining with the escorts of COMCORTDIV 51 at 1230 with the *Haverfield*, *Janssen*, *Willis*, *Wilhoite*, *Swenning*, and the USS *Cockrill* (DE 398). These ships were designated as Task Group 22.3. The initial course was southeasterly en route to Bermuda in compliance with CINCLANT AD COMD 182044 of October.

The next few days, the squadron conducted refresher landings aboard the *Bogue*. On the 23rd at 1046, Task Group 22.3, less the *Swenning*, entered the swept channel at Bermuda. Two hours later, the *Bogue* was anchored in Port Royal Bay, South, Bermuda.

During the next several months, Task Group 22.3 would be engaged in conducting ASW exercises with friendly submarines to maintain and increase its proficiency in searching, tracking, and attacking submarines. This was in compliance with the direction from Admiral King regarding CVE task groups as stated. There were also to be experiments with possible tactics that might improve operational results.[4]

On October 27, six TBM-3Ls with all searchlight pilots as well as with nine FM-2s and all fighter pilots were based for a temporary period

13. 11th Cruise

lasting 10 days at NAS Kindley Field, Bermuda, to test ASD Radar gear. High winds and lack of facilities limited the success of the work. On November 7, VC-95 reported back to the *Bogue* for 17 more days of ASW exercises as before.

The process for the real-world exercises was to define a location usually 50 miles off the coast of Bermuda and out to a radius around the designated location. The four submarines that participated were the USS *R-6*, the USS *R-1*, the Italian submarine *Onice*, and the Schnorchel-mock-up-equipped Italian submarine *Speri*. Their escorts were either the USS *Method* (AM 264) or the USS *PCE 847*. Both day and night exercises using aircraft searchlights were involved in the exercises, as well as full use of vectored Task Group 22.3 escorts to contacts.

The exercises continued until November 21, when Task Group 22.3 was en route to New York in compliance with CINCLANT 172012. The winds and high sea conditions forced several course changes. At 0854 on November 25, the task group entered the swept channel at New York. The *Bogue* moored on the starboard side to Pier 26, North River, New York City at 1438 for 10 days of rest and recreation.[5]

On December 4 at 1408, the *Bogue* departed Pier 26 on the North River and stood out in the channel. With the escorts except *Haverfield* and *Janssen*, Task Group 22.3 steamed at 1744 en route to 44° 00' N, 68° 00' W to operate to find an enemy submarine in compliance with CINCLANT 041851. Later, at 2230, the *Haverfield* departed to join the group. The next morning, December 5, at 0300, the *Janssen* departed New York en route to the task group. When the task group arrived on scene at 1215 under the direction of Commander Eastern Sea Frontier (CESF), COMDESRON 15 and CTU 27.1.3 reported to TG 22.3.

The *Haverfield* and *Janssen* were ordered to form a barrier patrol across the entrance to the Gulf of Maine between Phelps Bank and Georges Bank. The rest of TG 22.3 maintained an aircraft barrier between Nova Scotia and Georges Bank. DESRON 15 was patrolling east and west along a line 43° 25' N, while TU 27.1.3 patrolled southeast of Mount Desert Rock. At 0328 CTG 22.3 relieved COMDESRON 15 as OTC and DESRON 15 steamed back to base.

At 0622 Avenger #7, piloted by Lieutenant Pope, had a disappearing radar blip bearing 205°T out 60 miles. Pope picked up the contact at 23 miles and followed it to 15 miles but it disappeared. TU 27.1.3 headed toward the contact, and at 0719 the *Willis* and *Swenning* were vectored to the scene. At 0938, a MAD (magnetic anomaly detector) equipped plane was requested to assist in the contact. Thirty minutes later, Lieutenant (jg) Nelson sighted an oil slick bearing 162° distance 59 miles. A dropped sonobuoy had a no-contact sound noted. At 1115 the CESF reported a Catalina plane, and a MAD-equipped blimp was dispatched to the area of Nelson's radar contact.

The blimp arrived at 1554 to patrol the area and had some MAD indications as the escorts *Willis* and *Swenning* were dispatched to the scene. The escorts picked up a sonar contact and dropped depth charges. At 1905 the blimp's contact of 1554 was deemed a wreck and was abandoned. All aircraft were recovered aboard the *Bogue*, while the Avenger #10 with Lieutenant (jg) Brubaker was vectored to Bangor, Maine, because of the rough weather.

The next morning at 0038, the Avenger #10 with Brubacker landed at Dow Field at Bangor. The *Cockrill* had a sonar contact bearing 359°T out five miles, as the *Willis* and *Wilhoite* were vectored to assist. *Haverfield* and *Janssen* were directed to the northern edge of Georges Bank to the entrance of the Gulf of Maine between Nantucket Shoals and Georges Bank. After Avengers were sent to investigate, they and the escorts tried to develop the contact, but ended with negative results.

With no confirmed contacts yielding positive results, on December 11 Task Group 22.3 was ordered to return to Norfolk in compliance with CINCLANT 111621. TU 27.1.3 steamed to Casco Bay in compliance with CESF 112201. The wind and sea states delayed the speed of the voyage to Norfolk. Finally, at 0820 on December 15, 1944, the *Bogue* launched 12 Avengers and nine FMs to East Field, Naval Air Station, Norfolk. Task Group 22.3 entered the swept channel at Norfolk, and by 1755 the *Bogue* was moored portside to Pier 6, Berth 39 at Norfolk Navy Yard, Portsmouth.[6]

On December 16, ceremonies were held aboard the *Bogue* as the Presidential Unit Citation for meritorious action during the period April 20, 1943, through July 3, 1944, was awarded. All VC-95 personnel aboard the carrier from February 24, 1944, through April 20, 1944, were included in the citation. Letters of Commendation and the Commendation Ribbon were also awarded to Lieutenant (jg) W.H. Schlanker, Lieutenant (jg) G.C. Benoit, Lieutenant (jg) W.P. Hughes, and Ensign E.L. Valeich for meritorious conduct in attacking of enemy submarines.

On the 17th, VC-95 spent the next 10 days for additional training in night flying, using sonobuoys and radar maintenance and use, as well as doing a major checkup on all the planes. On the 21st, at 1150 the *Bogue* headed to the calibration area departing the Norfolk Navy Yard. As 1500 came, six Avengers took off from East Field NAS heading to the

13. 11th Cruise

Bogue. At 1600 the escorts *Willis* and *Janssen* rendezvoused at the north end of York Spit channel. At 1652 five Avengers landed aboard, while Avenger #3 returned to East Field. The *Bogue* was anchored at 1835 in 37° 13.5' N, 76° 06' W.

That day VF fighter pilots Lieutenant V.J. Goletti, Lieutenant (jg) A.H. Chaney, and Lieutenant (jg) D.W. Hazelton were detached from VC-95 and assigned to a new Pacific Air Group being formed. This was an opportunity for these three fighter guys to exercise their combat skills better than was possible in a composite squadron in the Atlantic. At this point, VC-95 had 10 VF pilots for the nine FM-3s assigned.

On the 22nd at 1100, HF/DF calibration commenced. At 1600 five Avengers flew to East Field NAS Norfolk. The *Willis* and *Janssen* were released to proceed to the NOB, Norfolk. At 0245 the following day, HF/DF calibration was completed. Later, at 0650, the *Bogue* departed from the anchorage en route to the NOB Norfolk. At 1008 the carrier was anchored at Hampton Roads. Then at 1147 the *Bogue* headed to NOB, Norfolk, and was moored on the starboard side to Pier 5, berth 51 an hour later.

On December 26, 1944, at 1310, the *Bogue* (CTG 22.3), with VC-95 embarked, departed NOB Norfolk and stood out the channel. The escorts *Haverfield, Janssen, Willis, Wilhoite, Swenning,* and *Cockrill* joined the *Bogue* at 1430 off Cape Henry. Task Group 22.3 was en route to Bermuda in compliance with CINCLANT 221416. Running into heavy seas, the task group entered the swept channel at Bermuda at 0929 on December 28. The carrier anchored in Port Royal Bay at 1055. Conferences were held on the island at their arrival to brief for more friendly submarine exercises to commence on January 2, 1945.[7]

The New Year's celebration of 1945 was rather mild aboard the carrier, with the entertainment of radio baritone Conrad Thubault. The crews of VC-95 were looking forward to the Allied exercises with the Italian submarine *Atropo* with the escort *PCE 846*. On January 1 at 0705, the USS *Swenning* headed out the Bermuda channel en route to New York to repair an engine problem, while the *Bogue, Willis, Janssen,* and *Wilhoite* departed to the anti-submarine exercise area. At 1500 refresher landings were begun and by 1629 some 12 Avenger refresher landings had been completed. Then later, at 2120, the escorts *Haverfield* and *Cockrill* joined the task group.

The next morning at 0833, Lieutenant (jg) L. Groninger in his FM-2 #10 on takeoff went over the side at the number two 20 mm gun sponson. The aircraft sank immediately, but thankfully the pilot was picked up by the plane guard escort *Cockrill*. The pilot received only minor injuries and mild shock. At 1055 nine Avengers and nine FM-2s conducting refresher landings had been completed. Then the anti-submarine Exercise 16 commenced. The exercise was completed with the submarine not tracked on sonobuoys and escorts received no contact.

On January 3 after a 24-hour delay caused by bad weather, one day and two night exercises were successfully completed. Since the night flights were given the same routine flights focus as day missions, the pilots began to feel that with good weather, the night exercises were no more hazardous than day flights.

The numbered exercises included all the various scenarios involved in locating and prosecuting submarines in daylight and at night. The aircraft would attempt to locate by HF/DF and/or sonobuoy pattern, as well as vectoring in the TG 22.3 escorts to have them redetect and track the contact by radar, sonobuoy, sonar, or visibility to the simulated attack position. The *Bogue* aircraft and the land-based Bermuda Group Patrol planes were also utilized. Lack of submarine locating from errors in dropping the sonobuoy patterns or other situations was encountered.

On January 5, the exercises were conducted until the *Bogue* and escorts headed back to Bermuda. The *Bogue* anchored in Port Royal Bay at 1220. At Bermuda conferences were held to cover the completed exercises and the upcoming exercises. On the 7th, the Bermuda "Lily Bowl" football game between the Navy and Army teams chosen from personnel in the area was held. The Navy won the game 32 to 6 with the outstanding skills of Lieutenant (jg) "Jack" McQuary, the carrier's LSO. If not engaged in flights for pilots and aircrewmen, classes were held in recognition, communications, ASW, the sonobuoy, and other Allied subjects. A two-hour-per-day program was conducted each day throughout the remainder of the cruise.

On the 9th, the task group headed to the exercise area for a series of three exercises. Though the weather was poor, the flying continued. That day they worked with the *Atropo* submarine. The next two days an additional submarine, the USS *R-9*, joined the exercises. On January 12, the task group was back at Port Royal Bay to review the exercises' progress at another set of conferences. The use of the expendable radio sonobuoy was a major focus. Plans were made to conduct a joint exercise with the USS *Croatan*.

On the morning of January 13, 1944, at 0931, Task Group 22.3 with *Bogue* and her escorts departed Bermuda from the anchorage at Port Royal Bay en route to the exercise area. At noon the task group joined

13. 11th Cruise

with Task Group 22.5 with the USS *Croatan* and her escorts for the joint exercise with the Italian submarine *Speri*. At 1405 a flight of four Avengers was launched. At 1533 Ensign Poland in Avenger #4 sighted the submarine bearing 210°T from the *Bogue* at the distance of 60 miles. The *Haverfield*, *Wilhoite*, and *Cockrill* of TG 22.3 were vectored to the contact. At 1656 two more Avengers were launched as B Flight to assist in the prosecution of the submarine by monitoring the sonobuoy pattern. Three escorts of TG 22.5 were also vectored to the scene. At 1818 TG 22.3, less the *Haverfield*, *Wilhoite*, and *Cockrill*, set off en route to New York in compliance with CINCLANT 091609 of January. At 1855 the USS *Snowden*, an escort from TG 22.5, gained a sonar contact on the Italian submarine. After A and B Flights were recovered at 2050, the joint exercise was completed with the *Speri*.[8]

The next day at 0200, the escorts *Haverfield*, *Wilhoite*, and *Cockrill* rejoined TG 22.3 as it continued en route to New York. The rest of the day was taken up with simulated attacks on the task group ships. At 0834 four squadron FMs were launched to act as Combat Air Patrol over the ships. Six squadron TBMs were launched as the "enemy" striking force was heading to the ships to "attack" with simulated bombs and torpedoes at 0944 while C.I.C. vectored the airborne FMs to engage the TBMs. Four additional FMs were launched at that time to support engaging the attacking TBMs. After the Combat Air Patrol problem was completed, the TBMs laid simulated sonobuoy patterns using dye markers. Beginning at 1145 all planes were recovered aboard.

On January 16 at 0608, the task group entered the swept channel at New York. By 1043 the *Bogue* was anchored in Federal Anchorage 23 on the Upper Bay, New York. The next day the carrier was moved to tie up at 1305 at the Brooklyn Navy Yard to Pier K, berth 20, New York for a four-day stay. The squadron received liberty each afternoon after the mornings were spent in ground training.

On January 20, 1945, at 1924, the *Bogue* with Task Group 22.3 departed New York en route to NAS Quonset Point, Rhode Island, in compliance with CINCLANT Speed Letter A-4–3 (0059) of January 15, 1945. At 0436 the next day, TG 22.3 detached *Willis*, *Wilhoite*, and *Janssen* to Casco Bay, Maine. At 0500 the *Bogue*, *Haverfield*, *Cockrill*, and *Swenning* entered the swept channel at Narragansett Bay. An hour and a half later, the carrier launched 11 Avengers and eight FMs en route to NAS Quonset Point, Rhode Island. At 0934 the *Bogue* anchored in Berth 54 East Passage, Narragansett Bay while the three escorts proceeded to Melville, Rhode Island. The *Bogue* left the anchorage at 1322 and steamed to moor on the starboard side to Quonset Pier, Quonset Point. Then, 26 pilots from V-F(N)52 and 16 pilots from VBF88 came aboard the carrier for qualification landings. At 2030 the *Bogue* took aboard eight F4Us and eight F6Fs.

During the next 16 days, the squadron took part in an intense training program. On the 22nd at 0831, the *Bogue* stood out of the Narragansett Bay Channel, followed at 1057 with Task Unit 28.2.2 (*Bogue, Haverfield, Swenning,* and *Cockrill*), en route to the carrier qualifications area. There, 68 F4U carrier qualification landings from 1219 to 1654 were completed.

As weather permitted, a minimum of 20 hops were flown each day involving strafing, squadron tactics, radar runs, searchlight runs, and sonobuoy work. Lectures were conducted by Air Combat Intelligence officers fresh from duty in the Pacific on recognition classes, operations, and tactics current in that area. These lectures covered accounts of various actions in the Battle of Leyte Gulf.

On January 23, TU 28.2.2 continued carrier qualification landings (from 0801 to 1354) with 23 F4U and 34 F6F landings. The next two days, no one flew due to rough weather. On the 26th, 139 carrier qual landings were completed. At 1822 VT 88 #6 returned to NAS Quonset Point for an emergency landing. On the 27th, no carrier qual flights were flown due to poor weather. At 1048 COMFAIR Quonset requested CTU 28.2.2 to investigate a ship in distress at 39° 36' N, 69° 07' W. The *Haverfield* was vectored to the location and at 1219 she reported that the S.S. *Warrior* was taking on water and the crew might have to abandon ship. The escort requested help and the *Swenning* was vectored in. At 1439 the S.S. *Warrior*, escorted by *Haverfield* and *Swenning*, were en route to New York. The *Bogue* and *Cockrill* headed back to Quonset Point.

The next morning, the *Haverfield* and *Swenning* were escorting the S.S. *Warrior* to New York when at 0115 the *Swenning* was released to proceed back to Melville. At 0323 the *Bogue* and *Cockrill* entered Narragansett Bay Channel. At 0753 the carrier launched one SB2C and three F4Us to fly to NAAS Otis Field. At 1010 the carrier was moored to the pier at Quonset Point. The *Haverfield* was released as escort to the *Warrior*. The *Willis, Janssen,* and *Wilhoite* departed from Casco Bay en route to join the *Bogue*. At 1930 *Cockrill* headed to New York to repair a main engine casualty. The end of the day at 1950, the escorts *Haverfield* and *Swenning* were en route to Casco Bay.

On the 29th, the *Bogue* departed its mooring and rendezvoused

13. 11th Cruise

with escorts *Willis*, *Janssen*, and *Wilhoite* at 0945 off Brenton Reef Lightship for more carrier qualification landings, completing 168 day landings. No night operations were conducted because of the poor weather. The next day at 0639, TU 28.2.2 commenced carrier qual landings, completing 186 landings. On January 31, 1945, TU 28.2.2 completed 47 night and 116 day landings by 1755.

On Thursday, February 1, 1945, Task Unit 28.2.2 continued its carrier qualifications in the operations area off NAS Quonset Point, Rhode Island, in company with *Willis*, *Janssen*, and *Wilhoite*. At 0759 the *Bogue* commenced flight operations for qualifications. At 0810 a fighter plane was attempting to take off when it crashed and fell into the water. As plane guard, the *Wilhoite* attempted to rescue the pilot. Spotted at 0814, the pilot was floating head below the water. There was no sign of life as the ship came alongside the body from windward with no way on. When they came close enough to attempt to rescue, the ship rolled heavily away from the body, sucking it under the bilge keel. The *Wilhoite* searched until 1300, when CTU 28.2.2. verbally ordered to abandon the search.

The *Janssen* had moved up to assume the plane guard position from the *Wilhoite* when at 1154 a fighter plane attempted a landing and fell over the starboard side of the carrier into the water. The *Janssen* maneuvered at various courses and sped to the rescue. The pilot was close aboard the port bow at 1200 when all engines were stopped. Seeing that the pilot was drowning, Lieutenant (jg) Charles O. Sloane, Jr., dived overboard into the water with a lifeline and life belt to attempt to bring the pilot aboard. With extremely adverse weather conditions, including winds at 35 knots, heavy and choppy seas, and a water temperature of 36 degrees, it was nearly impossible to hold the ship steady. After several attempts to tow the pilot to the ship, Lieutenant (jg) Sloane was hauled from the water unconscious, with the pilot in the water showing no signs of life at this time (or at any time was he able to help himself). Attempts were continued to get the pilot aboard from alongside the lee side of the starboard beam, but he drifted under the ship and soon appeared astern. Engines had already been stopped. A 186-foot Coast Guard Cutter had come in the vicinity and tried to pick up the body. After one futile attempt, the body disappeared and did not reappear. The *Willis* and the Coast Guard cutter were left in the area while the *Janssen* rejoined the *Bogue*.

The carrier quals were continued Friday, February 2, through Sunday, February 4. On early Monday, February 5, the Task Unit 28.2.2

entered the Narragansett Bay Channel when the *Bogue* detached the escorts at 0854 as they steamed independently to the fuel dock at Melville. The orders were received that the squadron was to reembark aboard the *Bogue*, with the exception of the pilots needed to fly the aircraft back to Norfolk.

On February 6, the Task Unit 28.2.2 joined up at Brenton Reef Lightship and at 0908 joined up as TG 22.3 with *Haverfield* and *Swenning* (less *Cockrill*) and headed out to sea from Narragansett Bay en route to Norfolk. On the 7th, the *Bogue* as CTG 22.3 detached Escort Division 51 escorts (less the *Cockrill*) en route to New York Navy Yard at Brooklyn, New York. The *Bogue* tied up at NOB, Norfolk when VC-95 disembarked to be quartered at NAS East Field, Norfolk. All hands were granted 10 days leave starting the 9th prior to preparation for its next cruise.[9]

On February 9, 1945, the *Bogue* got underway en route to New York to ferry 60 P-51 aircraft to the United Kingdom. The next day, the carrier moored at Staten Island, New York. The fighters were immediately loaded aboard the *Bogue*. The following day at 0702, the *Bogue* departed Staten Island and joined convoy CU-58 en route to Liverpool. The convoy consisted of 25 ships, including the USS *Card* (CVE-11), which was also ferrying aircraft. The convoy commodore was aboard the USS *General W.M. Weigel*. The convoy was escorted by Task Group 61.6.2. with nine escorts.

After an uneventful cruise, the *Bogue* was moored at 0953 on February 23 at Gladstone Dock 2, Northwest, Liverpool, England. The 60 P-51 fighter planes were unloaded. The *Bogue* remained moored as before until 1321 on March 2, 1945, when the carrier left Gladstone Dock. Later, at 1510, the *Bogue* and *Card* departed from Bar Light Ship and stood out of St. Georges Channel to anchor in the River Mersey. On March 3 at 1700, the convoy UC-58B (from Liverpool to New York) formed, with the *Bogue* initially taking position 23. The convoy consisted of 14 ships and four escorts from TG 61.6.2.

On March 12, 1945, at 0010, the *Card* and *Bogue*, escorted by the USS *Hurst*, detached from convoy UC-58B to proceed to Norfolk in compliance with CINCLANT 120309 of March. Later, at 1304, the *Bogue* entered the swept channel at Norfolk, and by 1950 she was moored to Pier 5, berth 76 at the NOB Norfolk.[10]

At 1046 on March 15, the *Bogue*, escorted by the USS *Simpson*, departed the NOB Norfolk. At 1640 the group departed en route to NAS Quonset Point, Rhode Island, in compliance with CINCLANT 131546.

13. 11th Cruise

The *Bogue* was directed to conduct carrier quals training landings. The next day, the *Bogue*, with escort *Simpson*, entered Narragansett Bay Channel at 2028.

Early the next day on March 17 at 0046, the *Bogue* and her escort anchored at 41° 21' N, 71° 24' W due to fog. Later, at 0730, the group left the anchorage and headed into Quonset Point, where the *Bogue* moored to Quonset Point Pier at 0916. The next day, the *Bogue* headed to the carrier quals area, joining with the escorts *Haverfield*, *Janssen*, and *Swenning* at 1046 off Brenton Reef Light ship to form Task Unit 28.2.2. At the end of the operational day, the *Bogue* had supported 156 day landings by 1855.

On March 19, the *Bogue* commenced carrier qual landings at 0644. At 1519 F6F #323, piloted by Ensign D.S. Parkins, crashed into the sea when his engine failed on takeoff just as he cleared the flight deck. The plane sank immediately, but thankfully Parkins was picked up uninjured by the plane guard USS *Swenning*. By 1832 the *Bogue* landed 287 day landings. Later, at 1857, the *Swenning* came alongside the *Bogue* to transfer Ensign Parkins. At 2258, 32 night landings had been completed.

The next day, 137 day landings had been completed. Night landings were commenced at 1930. The next morning, March 21, at 0201, the carrier had completed 57 night landings. The TU 28.2.2 was en route to Quonset Point in compliance with CTG 28.2 201434. The *Bogue* entered Narragansett Bay Channel and at 1045 she detached *Haverfield*, *Swenning*, and *Janssen* to proceed to Melville. At 1205 the carrier was moored to the Quonset Point Pier at Quonset Point.

The carrier remained moored the next day, but on March 23 the *Bogue* departed Quonset Point after rendezvousing with the escort USS *Broome* at 1154 at Brenton Reef Light Ship en route to Norfolk, Virginia. The carrier had received orders to break off sooner than expected from the carrier qualifications work to prepare for an operational cruise.[11]

14

The Last ASW Combat Cruise

"A bitter and truculent group of Nazis."

In the late fall of 1944, rumors and scattered intelligence indicated that the Germans were equipping U-boats with V-1 pulse jet-powered pilotless flying bombs to be launched against East Coast cities. The rumors were claimed by German spies like Oscar Mantel, who had been captured in the sinking of *U-1229* with 40 other survivors on August 20, 1944, in the Grand Banks of Newfoundland, about 300 miles southeast of Cape Race, by pilots of VC-42 from the USS *Bogue* Task Group. Mantel had been en route to be dropped off on the coast of Maine.

After a voyage from Horton, Norway, during a snowy, 20°F night of November 29/30, *U-1230* landed two German agents, Erich Gimpel and William Colepaugh, at Hancock Point near Bar Harbor, Maine. They were on a mission to transmit information on Allied ship movements to Axis handlers. In less than 40 hours after landing in Maine, they were at Grand Central Station in New York City. Colepaugh soon confessed he was a spy to a friend who turned him in to the FBI. The FBI arrested Gimpel in Times Square on New Year's Eve of 1944. The prisoners told U.S. interrogators that a group of rocket-equipped submarines were being readied for use against the East Coast.[1]

Using photographic and other intelligence, the 10th Fleet and the British Admiralty discounted the threat. But in January 1945, German Minister of Armaments and War Production Albert Speer claimed in a propaganda broadcast that V-1s and V-2s would hit New York by the beginning of February.

On January 3, 1945, the COMINCH sent an ULTRA Naval Message to the U.K. Admiralty as follows:

ACTION TO ADMIRALTY FOR OIC X FROM COMINCH X F-21 SERIAL 412 X ULTRA X THE TWO AGENTS LANDED FROM U-1230, COLEPAUGH ALIAS

14. The Last ASW Combat Cruise

CALDWELL AND GIMPEL ALIAS GREEN, HAVE BEEN CAPTURED AND INTERROGATED BY FBI X PRELIMINARY VERBAL REPORT INDICATES THEY WERE LANDED BY RUBBER BOAT PM/29 NOV AT FRENCHMAN'S BAY, MAINE X U-1230 DEPARTED KIEL 26 SEPT AND TOOK 54 DAYS IN ATLANTIC PASSAGE SUGGESTING U/BOAT HAD ARRIVED OFF COAST SEVERAL DAYS BEFORE LANDING AGENTS X LATTER WILL BE INTERROGATED BY NAVY AS SOON AS MAY BE IN VIEW OF ANY INDIRECT LIGHTING WHICH SUCH INTERROGATION MAY CAST ON 171402 NOV X[2]

Since back in the beginning of November 1944, an intensive search for enemy submarines was conducted within a radius of 400 kilometers from New York. On December 10, 1944, the mayor of New York, Fiorello La Guardia, publicly reported that Germany was considering an attack on New York. La Guardia's speech and the statements of the captured spies received considerable coverage in the media. Despite this, on December 11, 1944, the U.S. War Department and the U.S. Army reported to President Roosevelt that the probability of such an attack was so low that it did not justify diverting resources from other tasks.

This estimate provided by the Army was not supported by the Navy. On January 6, 1945, the finalized plan called *Operation Teardrop* was established and included participation in the Navy, as well as United States Army Air Forces and Army units, which were responsible for shooting down attacking aircraft and missiles.

Commander of the Atlantic Fleet (CINCLANT) Vice Admiral Jonas Ingram (succeeded Admiral Ingersoll on November 15, 1944) was at a press conference aboard a warship anchored in New York Harbor on January 8, 1945. His announcement warned the public about the threat of missile attacks and said that significant forces were gathered for the defense. The speech was reported in the *New York Times* the next day:

"Gentlemen, I have reason to assume that the Nazis are getting ready to launch a strategic attack on New York and Washington by robot bombs. I am here to tell you these attacks are not only possible, but probable as well, and that the East Coast is likely to be buzz bombed within the next 30 or 60 days. The thing to do is not to get excited about it. [They] might knock out a high building or two, might create a fire hazard, and most certainly would cause casualties. But [they] cannot seriously affect the progress of the war. It may only be 10 or 12 buzz bombs, but they may come before we can stop them."[3]

A primary element of Operation Teardrop was the establishment of two naval task forces that would operate in the mid–Atlantic as barriers against U-boats approaching the East Coast. Each of these two "barrier forces" was made up of two ASW CVEs and about 20 destroyer escorts. Each barrier force could cover only about 120 nautical miles, so the success of the operation depended heavily on intelligence and sources such as high-frequency direction finding (HF/DF) to be in the right place at the right time.

In early March 1945, decryption of German Enigma-coded radio transmissions confirmed the Germans were commencing an offensive U-boat operation against the East Coast. Beginning about March 14, a total of nine German Type IX U-boats (all equipped or retrofitted with snorkels) left their bases in German-occupied Norway en route to the East Coast of the United States and Canada. Six U-boats were designated *Gruppe Seewolf* (*U-518*, *U-546*, *U-805*, *U-858*, *U-880*, and *U-1235*) and were ordered to New York and southward, while *U-530* and *U-548* (which departed in early March) were initially ordered to operate off Canada. The ninth U-boat, *U-881*, departed later from Norway, on April 9, and was ordered to join the group.[4]

On March 24, 1945, the *Bogue*, escorted by the USS *Broome*, entered the swept channel at Norfolk. Thus began the *Bogue's* preparation work to participate in its last combat ASW cruise as part of Operation Teardrop. At 0816 the *Broome* was detached to proceed independently. The *Bogue* was moored at Pier 7, berth 76 at NOB Norfolk at 1000. The next day, the *Bogue* moved to the Norfolk Navy Yard to moor to Pier 5, berth 33 at Portsmouth. For real repair work, the *Bogue* was relocated on March 27 to Drydock 4 in the Norfolk Navy Yard. She departed the drydock at 1002 on the 31st to return to moor to Pier 4, berth 29 at the Norfolk Navy Yard.[5]

On April 5, 1945, COMINCH sent an ULTRA Naval Message to the U.K. Admiralty as follows:

> ACTION TO ADMIRALTY FOR OIC X FROM COMINCH X F-21 SERIAL 436 X ULTRA X FOR YOUR INFORMATION INTEND TO ESTABLISH CVE BARRIER PATROL AGAINST WESTBOUND U/BOATS BEGINNING 9 APRIL ON 120 MILE FRONT CENTERED AT 48–30N 30W X IT WOULD BE HELPFUL IF AZORES BASED A/C AVOIDED SWEEPS THROUGH U/BOAT AREA TO PREVENT ALERTING THEM PREMATURELY AND COMPROMISING RENDEZVOUS X[6]

The *Bogue* left the yard on a post-repair trial run on April 6 to moor to Pier 5 at NOB Norfolk. On April 9, the planes and personnel of VC-19 reported aboard the *Bogue*. On the 10th, the *Bogue* left the NOB to conduct HF/DF calibration and anchored in Lynnhaven Roads. On April 11 at sea, VC-19, commanded by Lieutenant Commander William Wood South, was embarked aboard the *Bogue* with three FM-2 Wildcats and 16 TBM-3 Avengers.

14. The Last ASW Combat Cruise

German Type IX submarine docking at Tromsø, Norway, during the latter part of World War II. Note the boat's unofficial insignia and ice floes. The U-boats composing *Gruppe Seewolf* in April 1945 were Type IXs based in occupied Norway. They were all fitted with snorkel arrays, which were retracted into a compartment under the upper-deck plates to starboard rear of the sail when not in use. (Naval History and Heritage Command Photo, Catalog #NH 41374.)

Lieutenant Commander South was born on July 14, 1918, in Atoka, Oklahoma. When he was age six, his family moved to Dunkard, Pennsylvania, where he attended grammar school. He graduated from high school in Paint Marion, Pennsylvania. In 1934 he enrolled at Washington and Jefferson College majoring in prelegal studies. South entered the U.S. Naval Academy in Annapolis in the early summer of 1936. He graduated and received a commission as an ensign on June 6, 1940. He served aboard the USS *Chicago* assigned to engineering duty. On December 16, 1942, he was detached with orders to report for flight training, which he completed in December 1943. Following operational training, he was sent to Fort Lauderdale, Florida, as an instructor. South was promoted to lieutenant commander in October 1944.[7]

Task Group 22.3 with the *Bogue* (with Captain George J. Dufek as CTG) and CORTDIV 51 (which included the *Haverfield, Janssen,*

Willis, Wilhoite, Swenning, and *Cockrill*) was en route to the Quonset Pointe NAS, Rhode Island, area for refresher ASW training with the submarine USS *Mackerel*. This movement was in compliance with CINCLANT 090646. En route, VC-19 planes did additional exercises laying sonobuoy patterns and conducting bombing and rocket firing practice on a spar towed behind the ship.[8]

The task group steamed to the exercise area bounded by latitudes 40° 10' and 40° 40' N and longitudes 69° 30' and 70° 45' W. After arrival, the ASW training exercises covered all aspects of submarine search and prosecution of enemy submarines.

On April 16 at 1016, Task Group 22.3 departed Narragansett Bay, Rhode Island, moving on a course along latitude 40 N to longitude 45 where the ships of Barrier Two would rendezvous with Task Groups 22.4 and 22.8 and Task Unit 22.7.1, all under the tactical command of CTG 22.3. The members of Barrier Two rendezvoused on April 20 as the barrier operating plans were passed to all ships and the force was preparing the sweep eastward.

The formation for Barrier Two was a north-south 120-mile patrol line of destroyer escorts separated by five-mile intervals with the two escort carriers stationed just 25 miles behind the line of DEs. The USS *Core* (CVE-13) anchored the northern end of the line, and the *Bogue* was stationed at the southern end. The VC squadrons flew searches 80 miles east and west of the barrier, overlapping in the center line. The barrier was initially set at the 45th meridian as the line swept east until they reached the 41st meridian.

The northern section of Barrier Two was Task Group 22.4 under Captain R.S. Purvis's USS *Core* (with VC-12 aboard) with her escorts *Moore, Sloat, Tomich, J. Richard Ward, Otterstetter*, and *Keith*. Additional escorts included *Pillsbury, Pope, Flaherty, Chatelain, Neunser*, and *Frederick C. Davis* organized as Task Unit 22.7.1 under Commander Frederick S. Hall.

The southern section of Barrier Two was formed around the *Bogue's* Task Group 22.3 (with VC-19 aboard) with escorts of CORTDIV 51 as well as with Task Group 22.8 escorts *Otter, Hubbard, Varian*, and *Hayter* commanded by Commander Jack F. Bowling, Jr.[9]

While the Barrier Two ships had been preparing and steaming to their assigned locations, on Barrier One the CVEs *Mission Bay* (with VC-95) and *Croatan* (with VC-55) were rendezvousing at midmorning on April 8. The following day, Barrier One was forming along 30° 00' W between 49° 30' and 47° 30' N.

14. The Last ASW Combat Cruise

Barrier One, commanded by Captain John R. Ruhsenberger, was also made up of northern and southern sections. The northern section was composed of Task Group 22.1 and TG 22.14. TG 22.1 consisted of the *Mission Bay*, also under the command of Captain Ruhsenberger, and CORTDIV 9 (under Commander Evan W. Yancey) with escorts *D.L. Howard, Farquhar, J.R.Y. Blakely, Hill, Fessenden*, and *H.C. Jones*. Also in the northern section was the all-Coast Guard unit, Task Group 22.14. It was commanded by Commander Reginald H. French as COMCORTDIV 46 with ships *Pride, Menges, Mosley*, and *Lowe*.

The southern section consisted of Task Groups 22.5 and 22.13. TG 22.5 was made up of Captain Kenneth Craig's *Croatan* with his screening escorts of Commander Gaibattista's COMCORTDIV 13 with *Frost, Huse, Inch, Snowden, Stanton*, and *Swasey*. Task Group 22.13 and dual-designated CORTDIV 79 under Commander Morgan H. Harris was the *Carter, N.A. Scott, Muir*, and *Sutton*.[10]

Barrier One destroyer escorts were set up in a 120-nautical-mile-long barrier separated by 10-mile intervals in the mid–Atlantic south of Iceland at 30 degrees west, with the two escort carriers and four escorts each operating about 40–50 nautical miles behind.

As the *Gruppe Seewolf* U-boats moved slowly across the Atlantic under Schnorchel, their progress was being monitored at 10th Fleet. In the North Atlantic, Barrier One naval forces encountered terrible weather with heavy fog and waves that looked like liquid mountains. It was so bad, over 100 sailors aboard the *Croatan* were injured when a heavy roll during a meal sent the entire mess deck flying. These sea conditions hurt carrier operations enough but there was also no decent HF/DF fixes or sightings until April 15 at 2135 when the destroyer escort *Stanton* in the *Croatan* screen detected a radar contact at 3,500 yards in heavy fog (5,000 yards off the *Croatan* bow). The *Stanton* closed to 1,000 yards with her sonar operators locked on the contact and turned on a searchlight to see the *U-1235* running on the surface because the seas were too heavy to use the Schnorchel. *U-1235* dived immediately as the *Stanton* (assisted by the *Frost*) made her first of three hedgehog attacks at 2147. At 0333 on April 16, *U-1235* was hit by the hedgehog charges, which ended in significant underwater explosions. The *U-1235*, commanded by Kapitanleutnant Franz Barsch, was sunk with all 57 hands on its first cruise in position 42° 54' N, 30° 25' W.

Just 40 minutes later that early morning of the 16th and 1.5 miles from the last location of the *U-1235*, the *Frost* saw a radar contact on their scope. They first thought the contact was the *U-1235*, but it was the

U-880. The U-boat had been heading directly at the task group as they were prosecuting the *U-1235*. She then realized her situation and turned around to escape. The *Frost* fired a star shell, but it failed to illuminate the target due to the dense fog.

At 500 yards from the *U-880*, the *Frost* used her searchlight to see the U-880 running on the surface in the fog. The seas were too heavy to change course and perhaps ram or bring the three-inch main battery guns to bear, as the *U-880* dived after a few hits from small-caliber rounds, as all sonar was lost. The *Stanton* and *Huse*, and then the *Swasey*, assisted the *Frost* in probing to regain a sonar contact. The *Frost* was able to gain a sonar contact at 0122 at a range of 300 yards and after opening the range, the *Frost* fired a volley of hedgehogs with no success.

At 0406 the *Stanton* took its turn and fired a hedgehog barrage, which resulted in a massive explosion four minutes later, knocking the sailors aboard the *Stanton* off their feet. It was even felt 15 nautical miles away on the *Croatan*. Several other escorts involved also fired their hedgehog patterns, but they were not required. The *U-880* was already dead. The U-boat was sunk in position 47° 18' N, 30° 26' W with all 49 hands lost. She was commanded by Kapitanleutnant Gerhard Schötzau.[11]

Admiral Ingram wanted to make sure to keep up with the remaining U-boats and ordered Barrier One to shift to the west-southwest. Captain Ruhsenberger directed that the rate of the retirement of the barrier to be at 100 miles per day, which he estimated was the speed of the U-boats using Schnorchel. On the 19th, Barrier One stopped at a center of 44° 30' N, 38° 00' W.

The weather was still bad, and for the pilots of VC-55 and VC-95, it was dangerous to search for U-boats. The weather problems resulted in landing crashes. The worse accident for the *Croatan* occurred on the 18th when Lieutenant Mansell in his Avenger came in for landing at night in sheets of rain, with the flight deck pitching. He had an oil leak coating the windshield as he approached. He tried to land several times but could not see the deck. Finally, he had the LSO to cut by radio on his final attempt. He had his head out of the cockpit to see the deck and LSO, but his googles blew off, which almost blinded him. The *Croatan* hit a wave that shot the deck upward. Marsell's landing gear hit the ramp just below the flight deck, which sheared off both struts as the plane bounced down the deck. When he stopped, the plane was cut in half at the turret but thankfully the crew was able to exit the plane safely.

14. The Last ASW Combat Cruise

On the night of April 18–19, a U.S. Navy PB4Y-1 (B24) Liberator from VPB-115 was flying from Terceira, Azores, and sighted *U-805* some 50 nautical miles from the *Mission Bay* on the surface using his plane's Leigh Light (a large carbon-arc searchlight). The submarine submerged before the Liberator could confirm it was an enemy sub. Unfortunately, the *U-805* did not reach Barrier One until later that afternoon. The *U-805* had been concerned by so much U.S. radio traffic and headed to the north to move around the area.

The planes from *Croatan* and her escorts were still hot after the *U-805*. On April 21, the *Mosley* gained a radar contact that evening, but it soon disappeared. A short time later the escort gained a sonar contact and attacked with depth charges. The sonobuoys picked up four explosions. The *Lowe* and *J.R.Y. Blakely* joined in with their attacks, resulting in a few more explosions heard over sonobuoys, but the *U-805* was able to escape.

Late on that same evening, the *Croatan* and her escorts were preparing to break off from Barrier One, and at 2200 in light fog illuminated by moonlight, the *Croatan* set a new course for Argentia. Fifty minutes later, the *Carter* (the flagship of Commander Harris's TG 22.13) gained a sonar contact on *U-518* in heavy sea conditions. Since she was out of position, the *Carter* radioed the escort *Neal A. Scott* that then obtained her own sonar contact and headed in the attack of hedgehog charges. Two "muted" explosions were heard, which confirmed the *U-518* was at least hurt.

The *Carter* took over, having maintained her own sonar contact, and came in at 2309 to fire a full hedgehog pattern. Sixteen seconds later, three explosions were heard. This was followed by a major underwater explosion that was so violent that the *Carter's* engineering officer ordered her auxiliary boiler, evaporator, and steam lines secured. Eleven seconds later, another massive underwater explosion occurred that was heard three miles away. *U-518* was lost with all 56 hands. It was commanded by Oberleutnant Hans-Werner Offermann northwest of the Azores in position 46° 26' N, 38° 23' W.[12]

On April 21 the *Croatan* left for Argentia, as did the *Mission Bay*. On the 23rd during landing operations, an Avenger landed hard on the *Mission Bay*. The plane missed the wires, bounded over the barriers, and crashed into another Avenger parked on the port side of the carrier flight deck. Both Avengers went over the side. The crew from the landing plane were rescued from the icy waters, but a pilot and seaman working on the parked plane were killed and a second seaman was seriously injured. This was a sad end to what was a most successful Barrier One mission.[13]

As Barrier One ships steamed to Argentia on April 21, 1945, the Barrier Two force relieved them to find and attack the *Gruppe Seewolf* U-boats. The scouting line of TG 22.3, TG 22.4, TU 22.7.1, and TG 22.8 was first sweeping along a course of 075°T at a speed 12 knots that morning. At 0600 the line changed course to 107°T, followed at 1105 by establishing the center of the Barrier Two line at 43° 00' N, 41° 00' W in compliance with CINCLANT 201937.

On April 23, Admiral Dönitz sent an order to dissolve *Gruppe Seewolf*, requiring them to proceed to the U.S. East Coast independently. He was not aware that three of his original six U-boats had already been sunk.

The *Bogue* aircraft from VC-19 planes attacked two positive and one probable contact during this period and also assisted planes from the *Core* in a fourth contact. There were also six "disappearing radar blips" that were investigated with sonobuoys but were later abandoned. Task Group 22.3 escorts attacked one probable sonar contact and were engaged in investigating various sonar, radar, and sightings, but all were eventually deemed as non-submarine. The scouting line escorts detected three contacts, but they too were evaluated as non-submarine.

On April 23, several contacts were reported by planes of Barrier Two, but none of these contacts resulted in positive prosecutions. An Avenger from the *Core* had detected possible submarine sounds on its sonobuoys and dropped a depth bomb on what was believed was a Schnorchel wake. When two escorts were vectored to the scene, they found only a dead whale.

At 1307 Avenger #7 with Lieutenant Commander William W. South, the skipper of VC-19, saw *U-546* in the process of surfacing on a bearing 042°T from the *Bogue* at a distance of 74 miles at 43° 05' N, 40° 20' W. South attacked with depth bombs immediately as the submarine dived below the water. He returned to lay a standard sonobuoy pattern and received positive contact. He expanded the pattern, and a barrier box of sonobuoys was laid with six on a side, on spacing four miles and 12 miles from the point of the attack. At 1332 two Avengers were launched to assist South. All available escorts were vectored to the scene. The sonobuoy yielded submarine contact until 1509 on the original pattern, then ceased. At 1710 the escorts arrived on scene and began to conduct sweeps throughout the night. Aircraft were monitoring the sonobuoys and making radar and visual searches until the weather forced an end to the flying at 1935.

14. The Last ASW Combat Cruise

Kapitänleutnant Paul Just of *U-546* sighted the *Core* on April 24 and began to maneuver his submarine to make a torpedo attack by moving through the escort carrier's screening escorts. At 0829 the destroyer escort USS *Frederick C. Davis* detected the *U-546* on sonar at the close range of 2,000 yards ahead. Although general quarters was not sounded, the guns and hedgehog projectors were manned and ready to be fired. Alert to the presence of the *Davis*, *U-546* began to submerge as she passed starboard next to the escort. The officer of the deck, Lieutenant (jg) John F. McWhorter, decided to order a hard right turn, which unfortunately broke contact with *U-546* with the noise of its own "Foxer" acoustic torpedo countermeasure system.

Kapitänleutnant Just immediately launched a T-5 acoustic homing torpedo using her stern tube at 650 yards. The German torpedo hit the port side of the *Davis* in the engineering spaces, exploding and killing the commanding officer (Lieutenant Commander James R. Crosby, Jr.), the OOD Lieutenant (jg) John F. McWhorter, others on the bridge, and many of the men in the forward part of the ship. In only a few seconds, the engineering spaces and the crew berthing compartments flooded. The wardroom was blown upward, which killed all the officers still having breakfast, and the steward's mates. Just one officer in the

USS *Frederick C. Davis* (DE-136) with steam up but not underway (note jack flying at the bow). Courtesy of the U.S. Naval Institute, Annapolis, Maryland. (Naval History and Heritage Command Photo, Catalog #NH 91425.)

combat information center survived the disaster. Ensign Philip K. Lundeberg, the damage control officer (DCO), was sleeping aft just over the screws of the *Frederick C. Davis* when he was jolted awake by a tremendous crashing sound. (He would later earn a PhD in history from Harvard University under Professor Samuel Eliot Morison. His thesis would be the basis for *The Atlantic Battle Won*, the 10th volume of Morison's *History of United States Naval Operations in World War II*.) The *Davis* broke in half nine minutes after it was hit by the torpedo and the bow went underwater six minutes later. Of the crew of 192, sadly 126 died. The USS *Frederick C. Davis* was the last U.S. Navy warship sunk in the Atlantic Theater in World War II.

On April 25, 1945, COMINCH sent an ULTRA Naval Message to the U.K. Admiralty as follows:

ACTION TO ADMIRALTY FOR OIC X FROM COMINCH X F-21 SERIAL 444 ULTRA X PARA ONE X MY 443 F.C.DAVIS SUNK WHILE INVESTIGATING SOUND CONTACT X AFTER CONTACT REGAINED NUMEROUS HH AND CREEPING ATTACKS MADE DURING DAY ON U/B AT 450 TO 600 FEET X 242044 LOVE DOG FORCED TO SURFACE FROM DAMAGE AND EXHAUSTION AND SUNK BY GUNFIRE OF TU 22.7.1 IN 43–54N 40–22W X 33 SURVIVORS INCLUDING C.O. PAUL JUST X PRELIMINARY INTERROGATION INDICATES SAME U/B SANK F.C.DAVIS X PARA TWO X YOUR 1645 PARA 3 AGREE U.S.S. O'TOOLE ATTACK PROBABLY ACCOUNTED FOR OBOE ITEM X TENTATIVELY CONSIDER TWO UNKNOWNS POSSIBLY OBOE JIG AND LOVE VICTOR LIQUIDATED RESPECTIVELY BY ATTACK OF 22.5 ON 16 APRIL AND OF 22.13 AT 220106 X YOUR PARA 6 QUERY 2518 SINCE 2519 MENTIONED IN CC&CS 171610 X[14]

When Commander R.F.S. Hall, the escort screen commander aboard the *Pillsbury*, spotted the explosion of the *Davis*, he ordered the escorts *Hayter* and *Neunzer* to prosecute the *U-546* while the *Flaherty* was directed to rescue survivors of the *Davis*. As the *Flaherty* moved toward the *Davis*, she detached the submarine at close range moving through the wreckage to cover their escape. The *Hayter* took over the rescue assignment and the *Flaherty* continued to move to attack the *U-546*.

The *Pillsbury* regained contact with the submarine and directed *Flaherty* to a hedgehog attack at 0951, but it missed. The *Flaherty* mistook the *U-546's* sonar decoy (a *Pillenwarfer*—a canister filled with calcium hydride, which, when mixed with seawater, created a hydrogen bubble cloud) to be a torpedo launch and alerted the *Hayter* to break off rescue efforts temporarily. At 1025 *Flaherty* conducted another unsuccessful hedgehog attack and the *U-546* escaped.

By 1156, when the *Flaherty* regained contact, there were nine

14. The Last ASW Combat Cruise

escort destroyers searching for the target submarine. The *Varian, Janssen, Hubbard, Neunzer, Chatelain,* and *Flaherty* all made multiple attacks that were likewise unsuccessful, but the constant action kept the *U-546* down and its crew tiring as the submarine's batteries were getting low. Unknown to the Barrier Two attacking escorts, the *U-546* had been damaged in an earlier attack, which required them to use the main pumps to control flooding. This blanked out the hydrophones. Finally, at 1810 a hedgehog charge from the *Flaherty* blew a 150-inch hole in the submarine's pressure hull, smashed the bridge, and ruptured the batteries, which caused chlorine gas to leak. It took one more hedgehog attack to force the *U-546* to surface at 1838 and fire a torpedo at the *Flaherty*. Thankfully it missed as the *Flaherty* responded by firing two torpedoes, which also missed. Then the *Pillsbury, Keith, Neunzer,* and *Varian* began firing aggressively at the *U-546's* conning tower. Kapitänleutnant Just called to abandon the boat as his men jumped into the frigid sea. At 1845 on April 24, 1945, after ten and a half hours of attacks, the *U-546* rolled over and sank at 43° 53' N, 40° 07' W, south-southeast of Cape Farewell, Greenland. The next day at 1600, the *Varian* came alongside the *Bogue* to receive the prisoners of war. The transfer was completed 58 minutes later when the *Varian* steamed off en route to Argentia in compliance with CINCLANT 251612. At 1530 the barrier established 60 miles south and north of the center at 42° 30" N, 43° 00' W.

Kapitänleutnant Just with 32 crewmen had survived the sinking and were rescued by the U.S. ships. Twenty-six Germans died. Professor and author Samuel Eliot Morison described the survivors as "a bitter and truculent group of Nazis, who refused to talk until after they had been landed at Argentia." While aboard Navy ships, the *U-546* survivors received considerate treatment, but when the *Varian* arrived at Argentia, Newfoundland, on April 27, Kapitänleutnant Just, the first officer, and six other crewmen who were considered to be specialists were separated and subjected to solitary confinement and continual exercises and, when totally exhausted, were beaten with rubber batons. The skipper of the *Varian*, Lieutenant Commander Leonard A. Myhre, was a witness to the beating of Kapitänleutnant Just and lodged a strong protest.

On April 28, two interrogators arrived from Washington thought to be from the joint Army-Navy interrogation center at Fort Hunt, south of Alexandria, Virginia. They reported to the 10th Fleet that the Germans would not reveal anything. The prisoners of war were taken to Fort Hunt, where they continued to be subjected to beatings. The records from Fort Hunt were burned after the war. It was eventually confirmed that no U-boats had been fitted with V1 or V2 rockets.[15]

From April 26 forward, the barrier centered at 41° 00' N, 50° 00' W was being maintained by TG 22.3, TG 22.4, TU 22.7.1, and TU 22.8, less the *Varian*, in compliance with CINCLANT 260226. The barrier was retiring at a speed of nine knots on a course of 254°T still looking for U-boats. Various contacts were discovered as the days passed, only to be later abandoned. On May 2 at 1405, Lieutenant (jg) M.B. Wheeler, Jr., in Avenger #14 reported a disappearing radar contact off 33 miles from the ship at 30° 51' N, 51° 37' W bearing 322°T. He laid a sonobuoy pattern and reported indications. He attacked the indications as six more Avengers headed to the scene. Escorts from the scouting line were also vectored to the scene. Searches continued but, as too familiar, at 2055 the search was abandoned.

The next day, the *Varian* was ordered by CINCLANT to depart Argentia and rejoin the Task Group 22.3. At 1009 Ensign M. Union in an Avenger was landing aboard the *Bogue* but went over the starboard side of the island. The *Cockrill* as plane guard rescued the pilot and crew with no injuries encountered. That same day, the *Janssen* at 1508 reported a possible periscope bearing 005°T from the ship. Five escorts were ordered to the search area, but by 1942 the search was abandoned. At 2046 CTG 22.3 was ordered by CINCLANT to operate the groups at his discretion to maintain a barrier against westbound and eastbound in areas by longitude 49° to 53° west and latitude 40° to 42° north extending to 43° north after TG 22.1 and TG 22.4 passed.

On May 4, the *Hubbard* and *Hayter* with survivors of the *Davis* detached to Argentia at 1220. They were delayed one day due to a contact from Lieutenant (jg) T.E. Jenkins at 1815 the previous day. No more positive contacts resulted in U-boat prosecutions through May 8 by TG 22.3, TG 22.4, TU 22.7.1, or TG 22.8.[16]

On May 2, Admiral Ingram split the Barrier Two force in two—one to patrol along longitude 50° and the other along longitude 50° 30' W. No submarines were found in these areas. By this time, the Barrier One Task Groups had already reached Argentia. Admiral Ingram was concerned that the two remaining *Gruppe Seewolf* U-boats were still not sunk, so he ordered the *Croatan* and *Mission Bay* with their escorts out of Argentia to form a new barrier. Back on April 8, *U-881* sailed from Norway on her first patrol as a late addition to the *Gruppe Seewolf*. Delayed by a snowstorm, on Wednesday, May 2, at 1736, the *Mission Bay* departed with Task Group 22.1 accompanied by Destroyer Escort

14. The Last ASW Combat Cruise

Division Nine from Argentia in compliance to CINCLANT 012246 en route to the assigned operating area in the vicinity of 42° 45' N, 45° 00' W. Aboard the carrier were 12 Avengers and three FM fighters from VC-95.

On the morning of May 6 at 0520, the *U-881* was lining up to attack the *Mission Bay* when the USS *Farquhar* reported a sonar contact at 1,300 yards. The first sounds were weak, but at 900 yards the echoes became strong. The *Farquhar* raced to the contact and dropped a 13-charge pattern at 0535. At 0552 the *Howard* and *Hill* were vectored to the scene, as was Ensign Cook at 0603, who laid a sonobuoy pattern. Seven explosions were heard by Ensign Cook and *Farquhar* on the purple buoy at 0610, followed five minutes later by two more explosions. Task group escorts joined in the search for any more sounds of the submarine, but there was none. It wasn't until after the war that analysis confirmed *U-881* went down with all 54 hands. The *U-881*, under the command of Kapitänleutnant der Reserve Karl-Heinz Frischke, was sunk May 6 southwest of the Grand Banks at 43° 18' N, 47° 44' W. The *U-881* was the last U-boat sunk by U.S. forces in the Battle of the Atlantic in World War II.[17]

Before the war ended in the western Atlantic, there was a short battle in sight of the New England coast. At 1740 on May 5, the *U-853* sank the collier USS *Black Point*, killing 12 men, including a naval armed guard, Boatswain's Mate Second Class Lonnie Whitson Lloyd. He would be the last U.S. sailor killed in the Battle of the Atlantic. The *Black Point* would be the last U.S. flagship lost in the Battle of the Atlantic. Thankfully, 35 men were rescued by the Yugoslavian freighter SS *Kamen*. As the freighter moved into the rescue, the *U-853* was sighted, and the position was reported by radio.

In response, the USS *Ericsson* (DD-440) was vectored to the scene with other ships from the group, *Atherton* (DE-169) and *Amick* (DE-168), and Coast Guard frigate *Moberly* (PF-63). Quickly beginning to search for the submarine, the *Atherton* gained a sonar contact off five nautical miles to the east of Block Island. The escort destroyer dropped a pattern of nine magnetic depth charges at 2028, with one exploding. She then conducted two hedgehog attacks but did not hear explosions in the shallow depths of 103 feet. The ships, which eventually totaled 11 from the U.S. Navy and Coast Guard, continued to prosecute the *U-853*. Even two blimps (*K-16* and *K-58*) from NAS Lakehurst, New Jersey, arrived to fire rockets and drop sonobuoys. Debris soon came up from the attacks and at 1230 the next morning a diver from the submarine rescue ship

Penguin (ASR-12) reported that the pressure hull and interior hull were split open, and bodies were visible. The *U-853*, under the command of Oberleutnant Helmut Frömsdorf, was sunk on May 6 with the loss of its crew of 54 at position 41° 13' N, 71° 27' W. Though many accounts even today cite the *U-853* as the last U-boat sunk in World War II, it wasn't until after the war that analysis confirmed the *U-881* actually was the last to be sunk. Naval divers had identified the remains of *U-853* and discovered the *U-881* had been sunk several hours after the *U-853*.[18]

Back on April 30, 1945, while the Soviet Red Army was moving through the rubble of Berlin, Adolf Hitler committed suicide. As specified in his last will and testament, the commander in chief of the Kriegsmarine, Admiral Karl Dönitz, was named as the German head of state, minister of war, and supreme commander of the German armed forces. On May 2, Admiral Dönitz messaged his U-boats, "In order to save hundreds of thousands of Germans from annihilation and slavery, carry on with your old rigor."[19]

In the morning of May 4, Dönitz gave orders to cancel *Regenbogen* (code name for scuttling of warships and U-boats) and sent a personal note to his submarine force:

> My U-boat men, six years of U-boat warfare lie behind us. You have fought like lions. A crushing superiority has compressed us into a very narrow area. The continuation of the struggle is impossible from the bases which remain. U-boat men, unbroken in your warlike courage, you are laying down your arms after a heroic fight which knows no equal. In reverent memory we think of our comrades who have sealed their loyalty to the Fuehrer and the Fatherland with their death. Comrades, maintain in the future your U-boat spirit with which you have fought at sea, bravely and unflinchingly, during the long years for the welfare of our Fatherland. Long live Germany.—Your Grand Admiral.[20]

On the evening of May 4, Dönitz gave orders for all German warships still at sea to cease hostilities and return home, effective 0800 on May 5. Apparently, *U-881* never received this order. On May 7 in Rheims, France, Germany surrendered unconditionally. The surrender documents included the phrase, "All forces under German control to cease active operations at 2301 Central European Time on 8 May 1945."[21]

On May 23, 1945, Grossadmiral Karl Dönitz was arrested. This ended his role as the head of the German government, known as the Flensburg Government, when it was dissolved by the Allies. He was tried at the Nuremberg Trials for major war crimes but was found not guilty of committing crimes against humanity. He was found guilty of

14. The Last ASW Combat Cruise

committing crimes against peace and crimes against the laws of war and served only 10 years in prison.[22]

On October 1, 1956, he was released from Spandau Prison and taken in a limousine to a Berlin apartment where his wife was waiting. He retired to the small village of Aumuhle in Schleswig-Holstein in northwest Germany. There, he began to write his memoir, *Zehn Jahre, Zwanzig Tage* (*Ten Years, Twenty Days*), first published in Germany in 1958 and translated into English in 1959. Karl Dönitz died of a heart attack at his home in Aumuhle on Christmas Eve, December 24, 1980. His funeral on January 6, 1981, was attended by 2,500 people, not only by many former German servicemen, including 100 holders of the Knight's Cross of the Iron Cross, but also foreign naval officers, including members of the British Royal Navy. But a representative of the German defense ministry was not in attendance. He was buried in Waldfriedhof Cemetery without military honors.[23]

On May 9, 1945, the *Bogue* Task Group 22.3 with TG 22.4, TU 22.7.1, and TG 22.8, less *Hubbard* and *Hayter*, were continuing to search for U-boats on a barrier of 60° 00' W meridian between latitudes 39° 00' and 41° 00' N. With the cessation of hostilities and in compliance with CINCLANT 092258, the three task groups in tactical command of CTG 22.3 were released. At 2215 that day, the Task Group 22.3 was en route to New York. The task group entered the swept channel at New York on May 11 at 1437 and 18 minutes later Escort Division 51 was detached. The *Bogue* was moored to Pier 88 at North River, New York City at 1844, where she would remain for the next eight days. On May 19, she moved to anchor in Graves End Bay to discharge aviation gasoline.

In compliance with CINCLANT 171419, on May 20 at 1413, the *Bogue*, escorted by *Janssen* and *Willis*, departed from Point Zebra en route to Norfolk. At 1434 the *Bogue* launched 13 Avengers and two FMs of VC-19 to NAS Norfolk. They landed at 1645. VC-19 was detached from the USS *Bogue*.

On May 21, 1945, the *Bogue* entered the swept channel at Norfolk at 0127. Detaching the *Willis* and *Janssen* at 0630, just over an hour later the *Bogue* was anchored in Hampton Roads to remove ammunition. At 1615 the carrier got underway, mooring to Pier 4, berth 30 at the Norfolk Navy Yard at Portsmouth. She remained there until May 31.

This ended the last ASW combat cruise of the USS *Bogue*.[24]

When Dönitz ordered his U-boats to surrender, there were still 49 at sea. Most of these boats surrendered. In total, 181 surrendered and 217 were destroyed by their own crews. The British Admiralty

Assessment Committee, in conjunction with the 10th Fleet, made quite accurate assessments of U-boat losses within a few units. The actual total score was 1,179 U-boats employed with 699 sunk by Allied action and 82 by marine casualty or from unknown causes.

On the afternoon of May 28, 1945, the U.S. Navy and the British Admiralty issued this joint announcement: "Effective at 2001 this date, Eastern Standard Time, (0001 May 29 Greenwich Mean Time), no further trade convoys will be sailed. Merchant ships by night will burn navigation lights at full brilliancy and need not darken ship."[25]

Year	German Submarines Sunk
1939 (4 months)	9
1940	22
1941	35
1942	85
1943	237
1944	241
1945 (4 months)	153
Totals	782

Summary Statistics of the Battle of the Atlantic from Admiral King.[26]

The cost of the Battle of the Atlantic was high on both sides. The Germans estimated that they lost 32,000 submariners in their U-boats.[27] Some 2,603 merchant ships had been sunk, totaling over 13.5 million tons, as well as 175 Allied naval vessels. The Allies lost 30,248 merchant seamen.[28] Over 700 Allied aircraft (mostly British) were lost on anti-submarine sorties. Even after the war had ended, leftover mines continued to sink ships and inflict casualties for many years.[29]

15

Transport Duty

"Operation Magic Carpet."

The *Bogue* had remained moored at the Norfolk Navy Yard at Portsmouth until June 10, 1945, when she departed on a post-repair trial run to Yorktown, Virginia, to moor to the pier at the Naval Mine Depot at 1419 to load and unload ammunition. With the ammunition loaded aboard, at 1302 the next day, she steamed to the calibration area and anchored in Chesapeake Bay at 1509.

On June 12, with calibration complete, the *Bogue* was en route to the NOB Norfolk to moor at Pier 5, berth 56 at 0745. On the 15th at noon, the carrier departed Buoy XS en route to Staten Island in compliance with COMFAIRNORFOLK 131353 of June 1945. The next day, the *Bogue* entered the swept channel at New York and moored to Pier 14 at Staten Island to start loading army planes for transport to Cristobal in the Canal Zone.

June 19 saw the *Bogue* depart from Buoy A en route to Cristobal. Arriving at Cristobal on the 24th, the *Bogue* unloaded the Army planes and reported for duty to the Commander in Chief Pacific Fleet (CINCPACFLT) and the Commander Carrier Transport Squadron Pacific (COMCARTRANSRONPAC). The carrier was designated as TU 12.9.6. The carrier departed Cristobal and transited the Panama Canal on June 27 en route to San Diego.[1]

The carrier was en route to San Diego in compliance with COMPASEAFRON Secret Dispatch 262135 of June. On July 5 at 0540, the *Bogue* entered the swept channel at San Diego and moored later at 0709 to Pier H at North Island. The next day, she received Operation Order in COMFAIRWESTCOAST Secret Dispatch 061802 of July.

On the 7th, the *Bogue* began loading 63 planes and cargo for transport to Pearl Harbor. Also, 59 officers and 237 enlisted men reported aboard for transportation. The next day the carrier departed North Island, San Diego, en route to Pearl Harbor.

USS *Bogue*

On July 14, the *Bogue* (Task Unit 19.9.19) entered the channel at Pearl Harbor and moored to Pier F-5 at Ford Island at 1730. The carrier disembarked the loaded passengers. The next day, the *Bogue* departed Ford Island en route to Guam in compliance with COMCARTRANSRONPAC Secret Dispatch 150210 of July 1945. She crossed the International Date Line at 1900 on the 18th. The carrier arrived at Guam and moored to Buoy 705, Apra Harbor at 0953 on July 25. The passengers were disembarked, and aircraft and cargo were unloaded. At 1400 the next day, the aircraft and cargo had been unloaded, and different aircraft were loaded aboard. At 1616 the carrier departed Guam en route to Pearl Harbor in compliance with COMAIRPACSUBCOMFWD Secret Dispatch 051319.[2]

At 0847 on August 4, the *Bogue* entered Pearl Harbor and moored at Pier F-13 at Ford Island. It completed unloading and loading aircraft at 1430. The next morning, at 0800, the carrier departed Ford Island en route to Alameda, California, in compliance with COMCARTRANSRONPAC Secret Dispatch 042022. The 11th saw the *Bogue* steam under the Golden Gate Bridge and moor to Pier 2 at NAS, Alameda at 0938. The carrier began unloading aircraft.

On August 15, 1945, Victory over Japan (VJ) Day was proclaimed (although the signing of the official instrument of surrender did not occur until September 2, 1945, aboard the USS *Missouri*, in Tokyo Bay). The USS *Bogue* was moored at Naval Air Station Alameda, California.

On August 18 at 1703, the loading of aircraft, cargo, and a CASU unit was completed, and the *Bogue* departed NAS Alameda en route to Adak, Alaska, in compliance with COMWESTSEAFRON Dispatch 132330.

The carrier arrived at Adak and moored to Pier 3 at 1107 on the 25th. The aircraft were unloaded by 1600 and the *Bogue* moved to the anchorage and moored to Pier Buoy 3, Kulak Bay, Adak. On the 29th, the carrier loaded aircraft and about 500 passengers for the purpose of demobilization and reassignment. The carrier departed en route to Seattle, Washington, at 1105 in compliance with COMA1SEAFRON Secret Dispatch 290232.[3]

On September 3 at 1543, the *Bogue* arrived at Seattle and moored to Pier 91 to disembark passengers. The next day, the carrier left Seattle en route to Alameda in compliance with COMA1SEAFRON Secret Dispatch 290242. It arrived at NAS Alameda on the 6th and moored to Pier 2 at 1240 to begin unloading aircraft.

On September 7, 1945, Captain Jesse S. McClure relieved Captain G.J. Dufer as the commanding officer of the USS *Bogue*.

15. Transport Duty

Passengers were embarked on the 10th by 1432 as the *Bogue* departed en route to Pearl Harbor in compliance with COMWESTSEAFRON Order A4–3.NG 4 (WSF-11-IN) of September 9. The purpose was to transport passengers for duty outside the Continental United States. The carrier arrived at Ford Island, Pearl Harbor, on September 16 and at 1130 she was moored to Pier F10 at Ford Island. The passengers were disembarked.

The 200 officers and 500 men returning to the United States as passengers either for demobilization or reassignment were embarked. At 0710 the *Bogue* departed Pearl Harbor en route to Alameda in compliance with COMCARTRANSRONPAC Dispatch 180202. She arrived at 1239 on the 23rd to moor at Pier 2, NAS Alameda, and disembarked passengers.

The *Bogue* steamed underway on September 27 to drydock YDF 71, Drydock #2 at the United Engineering Company, Alameda.[4] The carrier left the drydock on October 4, 1945, to moor at Pier 5 United Engineering Company at Alameda at 1156. The *Bogue* departed Pier 5 and moved to NAS Alameda and moored to Pier 2 at 0735 on October 9.

On October 11, the *Bogue* loaded aircraft and embarked passengers and steamed en route to Pearl Harbor in compliance with COMWESTSEAFRON Movement Order #847. They arrived at Ford Island on October 17 to moor at Pier F12 at 1201 to unload the aircraft and disembarked the passengers. On October 18, 1945, the *Bogue* embarked the passengers and loaded mail.[5]

The *Bogue* then joined what was known as the Operation Magic Carpet fleet returning servicemen from the Pacific areas. On February 15, 1946, Commander Paul Clayton Griggs relieved Captain McClure as the captain of the USS *Bogue*. After that service in Operation Magic Carpet, on November 30, 1946, the carrier was placed out of commission in reserve at Tacoma, Washington. On June 12, 1955, the carrier was redesignated as CVHE-9 and was "stricken" from the Navy List (fulfills an important function in international law in that warships are required by article 29 of the United Nations Convention on the Law of the Sea) on March 1, 1959. In 1960, she was sold to the Hyman-Michaels Company of Chicago, Illinois, and towed from Bremerton to Everett, Washington, for scrapping.[6]

16

USS *Bogue* Legacy

"For extraordinary heroism in action against enemy submarines in the Atlantic Area in 1943 and 1944."

As renowned World War II naval author Samuel Eliot Morison wrote in the preface to his volume X *The Atlantic Battle Won, May 1943–May 1945*, "Antisubmarine warfare in the Atlantic is perhaps the most absorbing and interesting aspect of naval warfare in World War II. It was unremitting, subject to constant ups and downs, and fought on three levels—on the surface of the ocean, under the sea, and in the air; a war fought by scientists, inventors, naval construction, and ordnance experts, as well as by sailors and aviators."[1] When the Atlantic Battle against the U-boat began for the British, it was primarily focused on the defensive aspects of protecting convoy merchant vessels with naval escort ships. On both sides of the Atlantic, a limited number of mostly land-based aircraft patrolled over the convoys as best they could. As the battle progressed, the emergence of the ASW escort carrier, with its destroyer escorts organized as task groups, shifted the major focus to offensive operations designed to search and attack U-boats during the day or night.

Some of the key developments in operational tactics and technologies that underpinned this Allied ASW operational shift from defense to offense were as follows:

- Centralization of Atlantic convoy management and control.
- The U.S. Navy establishment of the centralized ASW organization for the Atlantic with the new 10th Fleet tasked to coordinate communication of Ultra and HF/DF and other intelligence information on U-boats among the U.K., Canadian, and U.S. forces.
- The rapid employment of available merchant ship hulls to speed the building of the initial escort carriers for ASW missions.

16. USS Bogue *Legacy*

- The U.S. Navy development of the concept of a "composite squadron" aboard an escort carrier made up of pilots and ground crews trained to fly and maintain one or the other of two different type aircraft.
- Continual optimization of the number of torpedo bomber versus fighter aircraft complements deployed aboard ASW escort carriers.
- Establishment of hunter-killer groups defined around an escort carrier with destroyer escorts as the primary ASW force defending convoys and engaging in aggressive offensive warfare against U-boats.
- Deployment of the first American ASW acoustic homing torpedo (MK-24 *Fido*).
- Deployment of the Allied Foxer noise-making decoy to defeat U-boat homing torpedoes.
- Use of sonobuoys (underwater microphones that pick up underwater sounds and transmit them to the aircraft) to detect and locate U-boats.
- Allied ASW aircraft use of flares and eventually mounted searchlights to illuminate surfaced U-boats at night.
- Deployment of advanced (microwave) airborne air-to-surface vessel (ASV) radar to locate surfaced U-boats.

While the Allied ASW forces continually moved ahead to eliminate the U-boat threat in the Battle of the Atlantic, the Germans used all available tactics and technologies to counter the Allied moves, including the deployment of the passive electric acoustic homing torpedoes aboard U-boats (GNAT) and the Schnorchel (a pipe system that enabled a periscoping submarine to operate its diesel engines) on U-boats, thus providing almost unlimited underwater range. These changes were useful but could not overcome the combined advantages held by the Allied ASW forces. The ever-increasing number of U.S., Canadian, and U.K. ASW ships and aircraft, as well as the additional skills and experiences gained by the naval personnel fighting U-boats, meant there was no magic German advancement that could overcome their plunge toward defeat.

Certainly, in the struggle to successfully accomplish the goal of defeating the German U-boat threat in the Atlantic, the USS *Bogue* and her escorts, as well as the other hunter-killer escort carrier groups, were among the major ASW contributors to that effort. In the Battle of the

Atlantic, U.S. escort carriers sank a total of 55 U-boats (1942–1, 1943–27, 1944–22, 1945–5). The *Bogue* and her escorts conducted more than 25 attacks on enemy submarines, sinking 11 German and two Japanese submarines, making her the most successful anti-submarine carrier in World War II.[2]

In support of these ASW operations, the USS *Bogue* steamed over 200,000 miles and made more than 7,000 landings on her flight deck. During these operations, 163 officers and 3,295 men served aboard the carrier. Nothing sums up the contribution to ASW efforts more than the words from the Presidential Unit Citation:

> For extraordinary heroism in action against enemy submarines in the Atlantic Area in 1943 and 1944. Carrying out powerful and sustained offensive action during a period of heavy German undersea concentrations threatening our uninterrupted flow of supplies to the European theater operations, these six Anti-Submarine Task Groups tracked the enemy wolf packs relentlessly and, by unwavering vigilance and persistent aggressiveness of all units involved sank a notable number of hostile U-boats. The gallantry and superb teamwork of the officers and men who fought the embarked planes and who manned the BOGUE and her escort vessels were largely instrumental in forcing the complete withdrawal of enemy submarines from supply routes essential to the maintenance of our established military supremacy.[3]

Appendix A

USS *Bogue*
Commanding Officers

Captain Giles Elza Short	USNA 1919	26 Sept. 1942–9 July 1943
Captain Joseph Brantley Dunn	USNA 1922	9 July 1943–23 April 1944
Captain Aurelius Bartlett Vosseller	USNA 1924	23 April 1944–5 Oct. 1944
Captain George John Dufek	USNA 1925	5 Oct. 1944–7 Sept. 1945
Captain Jesse Samuel McClure	USNA 1926	7 Sept. 1945–15 Feb. 1946
Commander Paul Clayton Griggs	NAVCAD 1936	15 Feb. 1946–30 Nov. 1946

Ref: *Ron Reeves & Wolfgang Hechler; USS* Bogue *Reunion Group; Jeffrey S. Griggs; Skip Duett.*

Appendix B

USS *Bogue*
Executive Officers and Department Heads

Executive Officers *Commander Dunn*   *Commander Quinn*   *Commander Smith*   *Commander Griggs*

Air

CDR Monroe	CDR Mathews	LCDR Moore
LCDR Carroll	LCDR Quinn	LCDR Laster

Navigation	*Gunnery*	*Engineering*	*Communications*
LCDR Angrick	LCDR Hoyt	CDR Wolfenberg	LCDR Greene
CDR Phillips	LT Everall	LT White	LCDR Phillips
LT Everall	LT Roberts	LT Williamson	LT Munns
CDR Clifford	LCDR Caley		LT (jg) Owens
LT Lawrence	LT Ross		

Supply	*C and R*	*Medical*	*Chaplains*
LT Grassino	LCDR Goodhue	LCDR Mote	LT Hewitt
LT Blackwell	LCDR Holzapfel	CDR Austin	LT Trussell
LT Beverett	LT Yattergren	LCDR Pennington	
		LT (jg) Westfall (Temporary)	
		LCDR Eisberg	
		CDR Stewart	

Ref: *USS Bogue CV-9 Cruise Book 1942–1945, p 49.*

Appendix C

USS *Bogue*
Composite Squadrons (VC) Aboard

Squadron	Commanding Officer	Dates
VC-9	Lieutenant Commander William McClure Drane	Nov. 22, 1942–Aug. 23, 1943
VC-19	Lieutenant Commander Claude Weaver Stewart	Sept. 3, 1943–Dec. 29, 1943
VC-95	Lieutenant Commander John F. Adams	Feb. 24, 1944–April 20, 1944
VC-69	Lieutenant Commander Jesse Dean Taylor	May 2, 1944–July 3, 1944
VC-42	Lieutenant Commander Joseph Thomas Yavorsky	July 23, 1944–Sept. 24, 1944
VC-95	Lieutenant Commander John F. Adams	Oct. 18, 1944–Feb. 9, 1945
VC-19	Lieutenant Commander William W. South	April 9, 1945–May 20, 1945

Appendix D

USS *Bogue*
Presidential Unit Citation

The Secretary of the Navy
Washington

The President of the United States takes pleasure in presenting the PRESIDENTIAL UNIT CITATION to the following Six Anti-Submarine Task Groups which operated with the U.S.S. *Bogue* as Flagship:

Task Group 21.2, USS *Bogue, Lea, Greene, Belknap, Osmond Ingram, George E. Badger*, and VC-9.	20 Apr–20 June 1943, Atlantic Area.
Task Group 21.13. USS *Bogue, Osmond Ingram, George E Badger, Clemson*, and VC-9.	12 July–23 Aug. 1943, Atlantic Area.
Task Group 21.13. USS *Bogue, Osmond Ingram, George E Badger, Clemson, Du Pont*, and VC-19.	14 Nov.–29 Dec. 1943, Atlantic Area.
Task Group 22.2. USS *Bogue, Haverfield, Swenning, Willis, Janssen, P.N. Robinson*, and VC-69.	4 May–3 July 1944, Atlantic Area.
Task Group 22.3. USS *Bogue, Haverfield, Swenning, Willis, Janssen, Wilhoite*, and VC-42.	1 Aug.–24 Aug. 1944, Atlantic Area.
Task Group 22.11, USS *Bogue, Haverfield, Swenning, Willis, Hobson* (until 25 March), *Janssen* (until 7 Apr.), and VC-95.	26 Feb.–19 Apr. 1944, Atlantic Area.

for service as set forth in the following

CITATION:

"For extraordinary heroism in action against enemy submarines in the Atlantic Area from April 20, 1943, to August 24, 1944,

Appendix D. USS **Bogue**

carrying powerful and sustained offensive action during a period of heavy German undersea concentrations threatening our uninterrupted flow of supplies to the European theater of operations, these Six Anti-Submarine Task Groups tracked the enemy packs relentlessly and, by the unwavering vigilance and persistent aggressiveness of all units involved, sank a notable number of hostile U-boats. The gallantry and superb teamwork of the officers and men who fought the embarked planes and who manned the BOGUE and her escort vessels were largely instrumental in forcing the complete withdrawal of enemy submarines from supply routes essential to the maintenance of our established military supremacy."

For the President,
James Forrestal
Secretary of the Navy

Appendix E

USS *Bogue*
Task Organization in the Atlantic 1943–45

(Dates in parentheses indicate new ship or air squadron, or new commanding officer, joined. Missions with no important events are omitted.)

BOGUE, Captain Giles E. Short
(I) 5 Mar.–18 June 1943: 5 missions
VC-9: 12 F4F-4 (Wildcat); 8 (12 after 23 Apr.) TBF-1 (Avenger),
Lt. Cdr. William McClure Drane
Screen Commander, Lt. Cdr. Doyle M. Coffee (CORTDIV 1)
Destroyers
Belknap, Lt. Cdr. Coffee; *George E. Badger*,* Cdr. W.H. Johnsen; (15 May)
Lt. T.H. Byrd; (23 Apr.) *Greene*, Lt. Cdr. L.J. Beilis; (13 May) Lt. Cdr. J. S. Lewis; *Osmond Ingram*, Lt. Cdr. N.J. Sampson; (23 Apr.–2 May) *Lea*, Lt. Cdr. D.I. Thomas; (30 May) *Clemson*, Lt. Cdr. E.W. Yancey.

BOGUE, Captain Joseph B. Dunn
(II) 12 July–25 Dec. 1943: 6 missions
VC-9: Same types of planes, **Lt. Cdr. Drane**
(5 Sept.) VC-19: 9 FM-1 (Wildcat), 13 TBF-1C, **Lt. Cdr. C.W. Stewart**
Screen Commander, Lt. Cdr. E.W. Yancey (CORTDIV 1)
Destroyers
George E. Badger, Lt. Byrd; *Clemson*,** Lt. W.F. Moran; *Osmond Ingram*, Lt. Cdr. N.J. Sampson; (14 Nov.) Lt. Cdr. R.F. Miller; (29 Sept.) *Du Pont*, Cdr. J.G. Marshall; (14 Nov.) Lt. E.M. Higgins.

---

* Not in 23 April–2 May crossing.
** Detached 30 Sept., back 15 Nov.

Appendix E. USS Bogue

(III) 26 Feb.–12 Apr. 1944: 2 missions
VC-19; Same types of planes, **Lt. Cdr. J.F. Adams**
Screen Commander, Cdr. T.S. Lank (CORTDIV 51)
Destroyer Escorts
Haverfield, Lt. Cdr. J.A. Mathews; *Janssen*, Lt. Cdr. E. Cross,
Willis, Lt. Cdr. G.R. Atterbury; *Swenning*, Lt. R.E. Peek; *Hobson*,
Lt. Cdr. Kenneth Loveland.

BOGUE, Captain Aurelius B. Vosseller
(IV) 5 May–24 Sept. 1944: 4 missions
VC-69: 9 FM-2, 12 TBM-1C (Avenger), **Lt. Cdr. Jesse D. Taylor USNR**
(1 Aug.) VC-42: 9 FM-2, 14 TBM-1C, **Lt. Cdr. J.T. Yavorsky**
Screen Commander, Cdr. Lank
Destroyer Escorts
Haverfield, *Janssen*, *Willis*, as above; (to 30 June) *Francis M. Robinson*,
Lt. J. E. Johansen; (1 Aug.) *Wilhoite*, Lt. Cdr. E.B. Roth.

BOGUE, Captain George J. Dufek
(V) 15 Apr.–11 May 1945: Barrier Force Mission
VC-19: 3 FM-2, 16 TBM-3, **Lt. Cdr. W.W. South**
Screen Commander, Cdr. Lank
Destroyer Escorts
Haverfield, Lt. Cdr. R.W. Dudley; *Janssen*, Lt. Cdr. S.G. Rubinow;
Willis, Lt. Cdr. J.M. Gunn; *Wilhoite*, Lt. R.C. Moore; *Swenning*,
Lt. Cdr. R.E. Peek; *Cockrill*, Lt. Cdr. J.H. Castle; *Otter*, Lt. Cdr.
J. M. Irvine with Cdr. J.F. Bowling (CORTDIV 62) embarked; *Hubbard*,
Cdr. L.C. Mabley; *Varian*, Lt. Cdr. L.A. Myhre; *Hayter*, Lt. Cdr.
Frederick Huey.

REF: Morison, Samuel Eliot, *History of United State Naval Operations in World War II, Vol. X, The Battle of the Atlantic Won, May 45–May 45*, Oxford University Press: London, 1956, 430–431.

Appendix F

USS *Bogue*

Submarines Sunk or Contacted by Bogue *Task Groups*

Submarine losses credited to USS *Bogue* (CVE-9), her embarked aircraft squadrons, DD & DE escorts assigned

	Submarine	*Date(s)*	*Location*	*Brief details*
1	**U-569**	22-May-43	S of Cape Farewell	VC-9: Sub scuttled by crew. 25 survivors, 21 men lost.
2	**U-217**	5-Jun-43	WSW of Azores	VC-9: no survivors (50 lost).
3	**U-118**	12-Jun-43	SSW of Azores	VC-9: 15 survivors, 43 men lost. Had received 11 injured crewmembers from *U-758*.
4	**U-613**	23-Jul-43	S of Azores	USS *George E. Badger* (AVD-3): Surface depth charge attack. No survivors (48 lost).
5	**U-527**	23-Jul-43	S of Azores	VC-9: 13 survivors (40 lost). Caught *U-648* & *U-527* on surface to refuel. *U-648* dove & escaped air attack. *U-527* stayed to fight and was sunk.
6	**U-86**	29-Nov-43	E of Azores	VC-19: no survivors (50 lost).
7	**U-172**	13-Dec-43	NNW of Cape Verde Islands	VC-19, USS *George E. Badger* (DD-196), USS *Osmond Ingram* (DD-255), USS *Clemson* (DD-186): 46 survivors (14 lost). Caught *U-219* & *U-172* refueling. *U-219* dived & escaped. *U-172* sunk.
8	**U-850**	20-Dec-43	SW of Azores	VC-19: No survivors (66 lost).

Appendix F. USS Bogue

	Submarine	Date(s)	Location	Brief details
9	**U-575**	13-Mar-44	N of Azores	VC-95, USS *Haverfield* (DE-393), USS *Hobson* (DD-464), HMCS *Prince Rupert*: There were survivors.
10	**RO-501**	13-May-44	NW Cape Verde Is.	Japanese, ex-German *U-1224*. USS *Francis M. Robinson* (DE-220).
11	**I-52**	24-Jun-44	W of Cape Verde Is.	Japanese. VC-69: No survivors. Mixed Japanese crew & German techs. *U-530* in support of *I-52* was in area but escaped search.
12	**U-1229**	20-Aug-44	SSE Cape Race	VC-42: 41 survivors, include spy Mantel (18 lost).
13	**U-546**	24-Apr-45	SSE Cape Farwell	VC-19, USS *Bogue* (CVE-9), USS *Core* (CVE-13), DE escorts: sub sank USS *Frederick C. Davis* (DE-136). There were survivors.

Submarines known to be contacted by aircraft, DD and DE escorts of USS *Bogue* (CVE-9) Task Groups, but not destroyed

	Submarine	Date(s)	Location	Brief details
1	**U-336**	7-Mar-43	West of Ireland	VC-9: First sighting & attack by *Bogue* group. Depth bombs failed release. "No Joy."
2	**U-468**	21-Apr-43	S Cape Farewell	VC-9: Heavy flak drove a/c off. Lost contact.
3	**U-231**	21-May-43	SE Cape Farewell	VC-9: Attack damaged conning tower. Sub returned to Brest.
4	**U-305**	22-May-43	S Cape Farewell	VC-9: Sub spotted 3 times. Severely damaged, managed temporary repair & escape.
5	**U-641**	22-May-43	SW Azores	VC-9: Flak damaged a/c in aerial attack. Escaped contact.
6	**U-603**	4-Jun-43	SW Azores	VC-9: Contact escorting convoy to Africa. Depth bombs failed to damage.
7	**U-758**	8-Jun-43	W of Azores	VC-9: Attacked and damaged U-758 which escaped and transferred 11 injured to U-118 (sunk Jun 12, 1943).

Appendix F. USS *Bogue*

	Submarine	Date(s)	Location	Brief details
8	*U-648*	23-Jul-43	W Azores	VC-9: Caught *U-648* & *U-527* on surface to refuel. *U-648* dived & escaped air attack. *U-527* stayed to fight and was sunk.
9	*U-764*	29-Nov-43	W of Cape Finisterre	VC-19: Attacked but escaped to Brest for repairs.
10	*U-238*	30-Nov-43	W of Spain	VC-19: A/c attack caused sub recall to Brest. 2 crew killed, 5 wounded.
11	*U-219*	12-Dec-43	NNW Cape Verde Is.	VC-19: Caught *U-219* & *U-172* refueling. *U-219* dived & escaped. *U-172* sunk by Bogue DDs.
12	*U-530*	23–24 Jun 1944	W Cape Verde Islands	VC-69: *U-530* in support of Japanese *I-52* was in area but escaped search.
13	*U-802*	15 Aug– 2 Sep 1944	Grand Bank	VC-42: Spotted twice. Subsequently attacked. Escaped undamaged.
14	*U-881*	23-Apr-45	En route to U.S. East Coast	Probably the U-boat sighted by an Avenger of VC-19: Dived & escaped. Did not heed surrender: sunk by USS *Farquhar* (DE-139) on May 6, 1945.

References:

TDCS Ralph Hiestand, USN (Ret), USS Bogue Association Co-historian.
U–Boat Operations of the Second World War, vols. 1 and 2, by Kenneth Wynn (Naval Institute Press).
U–Boats Destroyed—German Submarine Losses in the World Wars, by Paul Kemp (Naval Institute Press).
Hunter-Killer, by William T. Y'Blood (Naval Institute Press).
The USS Bogue *Hunter-Killer Groups*, by Forest Garner (August 1997).
USS Bogue *(CVE-9) Reunion Assoc.*, "Bogue's Rogues" Newsletter, "Historically Speaking," by ex-crewmen Ralph Hiestand & Bill Glenzer.

Appendix G

Chart of U-boat Losses 1939–1945

	Jan	Feb	Mar	Apr	May	Jun	Jul	Aug	Sep	Oct	Nov	Dec	Total
1939									2	5	1	1	**9**
1940	2	5	3	4	1	1	2	2	1	1	2		**24**
1941			5	2	1	4		4	2	2	5	10	**35**
1942	3	2	7	2	4	3	12	9	10	16	13	5	**86**
1943	7	18	15	17	42	16	38	25	10	26	19	8	**241**
1944	14	22	24	21	23	24	23	32	20	9	7	15	**234**
1945	14	21	29	48	24								**136**
Total U-boats lost													**765**

Ref: *Chart of U-boat losses 1939–1945, Uboat.net.*

Chapter Notes

Introduction

1. *SS Athenia: Wartime Spirit*, published Oct. 5, 2017, 7:23 p.m. by *The Maritime Executive*, Carroll, Francis M., "The Sinking of USS *Athenia*," *Legion Magazine*, August 30, 2019.
2. Y'Blood, William T., *Hunter-Killer: U.S. Escort Carriers in the Battle of the Atlantic*, Naval Institute Press, 1.
3. *Allied Merchant Ship Losses 1939 to 1943*, Office of War Information, OWI 3789, Washington, November 28, 1944.
4. Winston S. Churchill, *The Second World War* (London: Cassell, 1948–1953), vol. V, 6.
5. *Royal Canadian Navy Convoy Escorts: Sept–Dec 1940*, Loyal Edmonton Regiment Military Museum, lermuseum.org/second-world-war-1939–45/1940/royal-canadian-navy-convoy-escorts-sept-dec-1940.
6. *Lend-Lease and Military Aid to the Allies in the Early Years of World War II*, Office of the Historian, Foreign Service Institute, U.S. Department of State, history.state.gov/milestones/1937–1945/lend-lease, Seidl, Mark, *The Lend-Lease Program*, 1941–1945, fdrlibrary.org/lend-lease.
7. Goette, Richard, "Britain and the Delay in Closing the Mid-Atlantic 'War Gap' During the Battle of the Atlantic," *The Northern Mariner/Le marin du nord*, XV No 4 (October 2005), 19–20.

Chapter 1

1. Morison, Samuel Eliot, *The Atlantic Battle Won, May 1943–May 1945, History of U.S. Naval Operations in WWII, Volume X*, Oxford University Press, 1956, 37–38.
2. Morison, Samuel Eliot, *The Atlantic Battle Won, May 1943–May 1945, History of U.S. Naval Operations in WWII, Volume X*, Oxford University Press, 1956, 38.
3. Lane, Frederic C., *Ships for Victory: A History of Shipbuilding under the U.S. Maritime Commission in World War II*, Johns Hopkins University Press, 1950.
4. Petrescu, Relly; Petrescu, Florian (February 2013), *The Aviation History Norderstedt*: Books on Demand GmbH., 196.
5. Chesneau, Roger (1998), *Aircraft Carriers of the World: 1914 to the Present*, London, England: Brockhampton Press, 216.
6. Jane, Frederick Thomas; Prendergast, Maurice; Parkes, Oscar (1961), *Jane's Fighting Ships*, Santa Barbara, California: Jane's Publishing Company Limited, 320.
7. Konstam, Angus (2019), *British Escort Carriers 1941–1945*, Oxford, United Kingdom: Osprey Publishing Ltd., 23.
8. *Ibid.*, 29–30.
9. *Dictionary of American Naval Fighting Ships*, Bogue, NHHC, www.history.navy.mil/research/histories/ship-histories/danfs/b/bogue-i.html, *Bogue-Class Escort Carrier*, Wikipedia, 1–3.
10. Morison, Samuel Eliot, *The Atlantic Battle Won, May 1943–May 1945, History of U.S. Naval Operations in WWII, Volume X*, Oxford University Press, 1956, 38–40.
11. *Dictionary of American Naval Fighting Ships*, Bogue, NHHC, www.

Notes—Chapters 2 and 3

history.navy.mil/research/histories/ship-histories/danfs/b/bogue-i.html, Bogue-*Class Escort Carrier*, Wikipedia, 1–3, *USS* Bogue *War Diary 9/26/42–10/31/42*, Commanding Officer USS *Bogue*, 9 July 1945, Serial 083.

12. *USS Intrepid History 1943 to 1963, Twenty Intrepid Years Cruise Book*, Intrepid Museum, 79.

13. USS Bogue War Diary 9/26/42–10/31/42, Commanding Officer USS *Bogue*, 9 July 1945, Serial 083.

14. *USS* Bogue *War Diary 11/1–30/42*, Commanding Officer USS *Bogue*, National Archives Identifier: 134052117, 1–19.

15. *Extract from Interview of Commander Jack Monroe, USN, Air Officer, USS* Bogue *in the Bureau of Aeronautics*, April 6, 1943, 1.

16. *USS* Bogue *War Diary 11/1–30/42*, Commanding Officer USS *Bogue*, National Archives Identifier: 134052117, 20–24.

17. *Escort Scouting Squadron Nine (VGS-9) / Composite Squadron Nine (VC-9)*, www.asisbiz.com/usn/VC-9-and-VGS-9.html, Menary, Robert F., and Spear, Moncrieff J., *VC-9: First in the Battle of the Atlantic*, Nook Ebook, 8–9.

18. Menary, Robert F., and Spear, Moncrieff J., *VC-9: First in the Battle of the Atlantic*, Nook Ebook, 8–9.

19. *Ibid.*

20. Menary, Robert F., and Spear, Moncrieff J., *VC-9: First in the Battle of the Atlantic*, Nook Ebook, 84–85.

21. *USS* Bogue *War Diary 11/1–30/42*, Commanding Officer USS *Bogue*, National Archives Identifier: 134052117, 24–30.

22. *USS* Bogue *War Diary 12/1–31/42*, Commanding Officer USS *Bogue*, National Archives Identifier: 134043340, 1–9.

23. Menary, Robert F., and Spear, Moncrieff J., *VC-9: First in the Battle of the Atlantic*, Nook Ebook, 8.

24. *Ibid.*

25. *USS* Bogue *War Diary 12/1–31/42*, Commanding Officer USS *Bogue*, National Archives Identifier: 134043340, 10–26.

26. *Ibid.*, 27–31.

Chapter 2

1. Garner, Forest and Hiestand, Ralph, *The USS* Bogue *Hunter-Killer Groups*, u-boat.net, *Extract from Interview of Commander Jack Monroe, USN, Air Officer, USS* Bogue *in the Bureau of Aeronautics*, April 6, 1943, 1.

2. *USS* Bogue *War Diary 1/1–31/43*, Commanding Officer USS *Bogue*, National Archives Identifier: 134061170, 1–31.

3. Richards, Denis, and St. G. Saunders, Hilary, *Royal Air Force 1939–1945 II (1954)*.

4. Morison, Samuel Eliot, *The Atlantic Battle Won: May 1943–May 1945, Vol. X*, Oxford University Press, London, 1956, 12–13.

5. *CCS papers, 155/1, Conduct of the War in 1943*, Casablanca Conference, Vol. 1, 16.

6. Churchill, *The Second World War IV*, 913–914.

7. Morison, Samuel Eliot, *The Atlantic Battle Won: May 1943–May 1945, Vol. X*, Oxford University Press, London, 1956, 19–23.

8. *Ibid.*, 23–24.

9. *Ibid.*, 26–29.

10. *USS* Bogue *War Diary 2/1–28/43*, Commanding Officer USS *Bogue*, National Archives Identifier: 134107407, 1–7.

11. *Ibid.*, 7–28.

Chapter 3

1. uboat.net/allies/warships/ship/4231.html, *USS* Bogue *War Diary 3/1–31/43*, Commanding Officer USS Bogue, National Archives Identifier: 134129103, 1–4, *Convoy HX-228*, Wikipedia, en.wikipedia.org/w/index.php?title=Convoy_HX_228&oldid=1040933358.

2. *Extract from Interview of Commander Jack Monroe, USN, Air Officer, USS* Bogue *in the Bureau of Aeronautics*, April 6, 1943, 1.

3. *USS* Bogue *War Diary 3/1–31/43*, Commanding Officer USS *Bogue*, National Archives Identifier: 134129103, 5–10.

4. Y'Blood, William T., *Hunter-Killer:*

U.S. Escort Carriers in the Battle of the Atlantic, Naval Institute Press, 35–36, Menary, Robert F., and Spear, Moncrieff J., *VC-9:First in the Battle of the Atlantic*, Nook Ebook, 11.

5. USS Bogue *War Diary 3/1–31/43*, Commanding Officer USS *Bogue*, National Archives Identifier: 134129103, 11–12.

6. *Convoy HX-228*, Wikipedia, *en.wikipedia.org/w/index.php?title=Convoy_HX_228&oldid=1040933358*.

7. *SS Jonathan Sturges*, navylog.navymemorial.org/jonathan-sturges, USS Bogue *War Diary 3/1–31/43*, Commanding Officer USS *Bogue*, National Archives Identifier: 134129103, 13–14., *Madeloma*, uboat.net/allies/merchants/ships/2696.html, *SS Jonathan Sturges*, uboat.net/allies/merchants/ships/2695.html, Menary, Robert F., and Spear, Moncrieff J., *VC-9:First in the Battle of the Atlantic*, Nook Ebook, 11.

8. USS Bogue *War Diary 3/1–31/43*, Commanding Officer USS *Bogue*, National Archives Identifier: 134129103, 12–25, Menary, Robert F., and Spear, Moncrieff J., *VC-9:First in the Battle of the Atlantic*, Nook Ebook, 11.

Chapter 4

1. USS Bogue *War Diary 3/1–31/43*, Commanding Officer USS *Bogue*, National Archives Identifier: 134129103, 25–41.

2. Menary, Robert F., and Spear, Moncrieff J., *VC-9:First in the Battle of the Atlantic*, Nook Ebook, 11.

3. *Ibid.*

4. *Ibid.*

5. *Ibid.*, 11–12.

6. USS Bogue *War Diary 3/1–31/43*, Commanding Officer USS *Bogue*, National Archives Identifier: 134129103, 25–41, Menary, Robert F. and Spear, Moncrieff J., *VC-9:First in the Battle of the Atlantic*, Nook Ebook, 11.

Chapter 5

1. *Extracts from Interview of Commander Jack Monroe, USN, Air Officer,* USS Bogue *in the Bureau of Aeronautics, April 6, 1943*, 2–3.

2. *History of the USS* Bogue *(CVE9), Chronology of the USS Bogue, Enclosure B*, Commanding Officer, USS *Bogue*, December 25, 1944, 4–5, USS Bogue *War Diary 4/1–30/43*, Commanding Officer USS *Bogue*, National Archives Identifier: 134186123, 11–28.

3. Menary, Robert F., and Spear, Moncrieff J., *VC-9:First in the Battle of the Atlantic*, Nook Ebook, 12.

4. USS Bogue *War Diary 4/1–30/43*, Commanding Officer USS *Bogue*, National Archives Identifier: 134186123, 24–28.

5. Menary, Robert F., and Spear, Moncrieff J., *VC-9:First in the Battle of the Atlantic*, Nook Ebook, 12–13.

6. USS Bogue *War Diary 4/1–30/43*, Commanding Officer USS *Bogue*, National Archives Identifier: 134186123, 31–33.

7. Y'Blood, William T., *Hunter-Killer: U.S. Escort Carriers in the Battle of the Atlantic*, Naval Institute Press, 39.

8. *Ibid.*, 39–40, Morison, Samuel Eliot, *The Atlantic Battle Won: May 1943–May 1945, Vol. X*, London: Oxford University Press, 1956, 80.

9. *Interview of Captain Short, USN, C.O. USS* Bogue, *LT. Commander Drane, Air Group Commander*, USS *Bogue*, NAVAIR June 22, 1943, 4.

10. USS Bogue *War Diary 5/1–31/43*, Commanding Officer USS *Bogue*, National Archives Identifier: 134237156, 14–25.

11. USS Bogue *War Diary 5/1–31/43*, Commanding Officer USS *Bogue*, National Archives Identifier: 134237156, 25, Y'Blood, William T., *Hunter-Killer: U.S. Escort Carriers in the Battle of the Atlantic*, Naval Institute Press, 40, Menary, Robert F., and Spear, Moncrieff J., *VC-9: First in the Battle of the Atlantic*, Nook Ebook, 15, Morison, Samuel Eliot, *The Atlantic Battle Won: May 1943–May 1945, Vol. X*, London: Oxford University Press, 1956, 80.

12. Bishop, John, "The U-boat Meets Its Master," *Saturday Evening Post*, 18 September 1943, 80.

13. USS Bogue *War Diary 5/1–31/43*,

Notes—Chapter 6

Commanding Officer USS *Bogue*, National Archives Identifier: 134237156, 26, Menary, Robert F., and Spear, Moncrieff J., *VC-9: First in the Battle of the Atlantic*, Nook Ebook, 15–16, Morison, Samuel Eliot, *The Atlantic Battle Won: May 1943– May 1945, Vol. X*, London: Oxford University Press,1956, 80.

14. Menary, Robert F., and Spear, Moncrieff J., *VC-9: First in the Battle of the Atlantic*, Nook Ebook, 16–17, Morison, Samuel Eliot, *The Atlantic Battle Won: May 1943–May 1945, Vol. X*, London: Oxford University Press, 1956, 80–81.

15. USS Bogue *War Diary 5/1–31/43*, Commanding Officer USS *Bogue*, National Archives Identifier: 134237156, 26–27, Y'Blood, William T., *Hunter-Killer: U.S. Escort Carriers in the Battle of the Atlantic*, Naval Institute Press, 40–45, *U-569*, uboat.net/boats/u569.htm, Menary, Robert F., and Spear, Moncrieff J., *VC-9: First in the Battle of the Atlantic*, Nook Ebook, 18.

16. Menary, Robert F., and Spear, Moncrieff J., *VC-9: First in the Battle of the Atlantic*, Nook Ebook, 18–19.

17. USS Bogue *War Diary 5/1–31/43*, Commanding Officer USS *Bogue*, National Archives Identifier: 134237156, 28–35.

18. Menary, Robert F., and Spear, Moncrieff J., *VC-9: First in the Battle of the Atlantic*, Nook Ebook, 20.

19. USS Bogue *War Diary 5/1–31/43*, Commanding Officer USS *Bogue*, National Archives Identifier: 134237156, 28–35, Menary, Robert F., and Spear, Moncrieff J., *VC-9: First in the Battle of the Atlantic*, Nook Ebook, 12.

Chapter 6

1. USS Bogue *War Diary 5/1–31/43*, Commanding Officer USS *Bogue*, National Archives Identifier: 134237156, 36.

2. Y'Blood, William T., *Hunter-Killer: U.S. Escort Carriers in the Battle of the Atlantic*, Naval Institute Press, 33.

3. Morison, Samuel Eliot, *The Atlantic Battle Won: May 1943–May 1945, Vol. X*, London: Oxford University Press, 1956, 108.

4. *Ibid.*, 83–84.

5. *Ibid.*, 108.

6. Short-Lived Halt in Atlantic U-Boat War, *Daily Chronicles of World War II*, Berlin, Germany, May 24, 1943, *U-954*, https://www.uboat.net/boats/u954.htm.

7. Y'Blood, William T., *Hunter-Killer: U.S. Escort Carriers in the Battle of the Atlantic*, Naval Institute Press, 33, 45.

8. Bogue *Action Report, Serial 002*, 2, *Communications Intelligence*, Vol. II, 105.

9. Y'Blood, William T., *Hunter-Killer: U.S. Escort Carriers in the Battle of the Atlantic*, Naval Institute Press, 49–50, Russell, Commander Jerry C., USN, *Ultra and The Campaign Against The U-Boats in World War II, Studies in Cryptology*, NSA, Document SRH-142, Record Group 457, Records of the National Security Agency, 16.

10. Y'Blood, William T., *Hunter-Killer: U.S. Escort Carriers in the Battle of the Atlantic*, Naval Institute Press, 50–53, *U-217*, uboat.net/boats/u217.htm.

11. Menary, Robert F., and Spear, Moncrieff J., *VC-9: First in the Battle of the Atlantic*, Nook Ebook, 24.

12. Y'Blood, William T., *Hunter-Killer: U.S. Escort Carriers in the Battle of the Atlantic*, Naval Institute Press, 52–54, USS Bogue *War Diary 6/1/43 to 7/31/43*, Commanding Officer USS *Bogue*, National Archives Identifier: 135908518, 12–13, U-488, uboat.net/boats/u488.htm, Menary, Robert F. and Spear, Moncrieff J., *VC-9: First in the Battle of the Atlantic*, Nook Ebook, 23–24.

13. Menary, Robert F., and Spear, Moncrieff J., *VC-9: First in the Battle of the Atlantic*, Nook Ebook, 23–24.

14. *Ibid.*, 24–26.

15. Y'Blood, William T., *Hunter-Killer: U.S. Escort Carriers in the Battle of the Atlantic*, Naval Institute Press, 55–60.

16. Menary, Robert F., and Spear, Moncrieff J., *VC-9: First in the Battle of the Atlantic*, Nook Ebook, 27.

17. Menary, Robert F., and Spear, Moncrieff J., *VC-9: First in the Battle of the Atlantic*, Nook Ebook, 27–29, *Report*

Notes—Chapters 7, 8 and 9

on the Interrogation of Survivors from U-118 Sunk on 12 June 1943, ONI 250 Series-G/Serial 15, Navy Department, Office of the Chief of Naval Operations, August 23, 1943, 1.

18. Menary, Robert F., and Spear, Moncrieff J., *VC-9: First in the Battle of the Atlantic*, Nook Ebook, 29.

19. Menary, Robert F., and Spear, Moncrieff J., *VC-9: First in the Battle of the Atlantic*, Nook Ebook, 29, *USS* Bogue *War Diary 6/1/43 to 7/31/43*, Commanding Officer USS *Bogue*, National Archives Identifier: 135908518, 18–28.

Chapter 7

1. *USS* Bogue *War Diary 6/1/43 to 7/31/43*, Commanding Officer USS *Bogue*, National Archives Identifier: 135908518, 29–47.
2. *Joseph Brantley Dunn, USN*, uboat.net/allies/commanders/3763.html.
3. *USS* Bogue *War Diary 6/1/43 to 7/31/43*, Commanding Officer USS *Bogue*, National Archives Identifier: 135908518, 49–71.
4. Menary, Robert F., and Spear, Moncrieff J., *VC-9: First in the Battle of the Atlantic*, Nook Ebook, 31.
5. Y'Blood, William T., *Hunter-Killer: U.S. Escort Carriers in the Battle of the Atlantic*, Naval Institute Press, 79.
6. *U-613*, www.uboat.net/boats/u613.htm, Y'Blood, William T., *Hunter-Killer: U.S. Escort Carriers in the Battle of the Atlantic*, Naval Institute Press, 78–79.
7. Y'Blood, William T., *Hunter-Killer: U.S. Escort Carriers in the Battle of the Atlantic*, Naval Institute Press, 78–80, Menary, Robert F., and Spear, Moncrieff J., *VC-9: First in the Battle of the Atlantic*, Nook Ebook, p 31, *USS* Bogue *War Diary 6/1/43 to 7/31/43*, Commanding Officer USS *Bogue*, National Archives Identifier: 135908518, 71, *U-527*, www.uboat.net/boats/u527.htm.
8. *USS* Bogue *War Diary 6/1/43 to 7/31/43*, Commanding Officer USS *Bogue*, National Archives Identifier: 135908518, 73.
9. *USS* Bogue *War Diary 6/1/43 to 7/31/43*, Commanding Officer USS *Bogue*, National Archives Identifier: 135908518, 73–85, Y'Blood, William T., *Hunter-Killer: U.S. Escort Carriers in the Battle of the Atlantic*, Naval Institute Press, 81.
10. *USS* Bogue *War Diary 8/1–31/43*, Commanding Officer USS *Bogue*, National Archives Identifier: 135927307, 1–12.
11. Y'Blood, William T., *Hunter-Killer: U.S. Escort Carriers in the Battle of the Atlantic*, Naval Institute Press, 81–82.
12. *USS* Bogue *War Diary 8/1–31/43*, Commanding Officer USS *Bogue*, National Archives Identifier: 135927307, 11–38.

Chapter 8

1. *USS* Bogue *War Diary 8/1–31/43*, Commanding Officer USS *Bogue*, National Archives Identifier: 135927307, 37–38.
2. *The Technologies*, uboat.net/technical/torpedoes.htm, *History of the USS* Bogue, CO USS *Bogue*, December 25, 1944, Y'Blood, William T., *Hunter-Killer: U.S. Escort Carriers in the Battle of the Atlantic*, Naval Institute Press, 100–101.
3. Y'Blood, William T., *Hunter-Killer: U.S. Escort Carriers in the Battle of the Atlantic*, Naval Institute Press, 100–101, *USS* Bogue *War Diary 10/1–31/43*, Commanding Officer USS *Bogue*, National Archives Identifier: 135967545, 1–24, *Enclosure B, Chronology of the USS* Bogue, *History of the USS* Bogue, CO USS *Bogue*, December 25, 1944, 8–9, *History of Composite Squadron Nineteen*, Commanding Officer VC-19, January 6, 1945, National Archives Identifier: 77650539, 1–2.

Chapter 9

1. *USS* Bogue *War Diary 10/1–31/43*, Commanding Officer USS *Bogue*, National Archives Identifier: 135967545, 1–24, *Enclosure B, Chronology of the USS* Bogue, *History of the USS* Bogue, CO USS *Bogue*, December 25, 1944, 8–9.
2. *Grumman F4F Wildcat (Aviation*

Notes—Chapter 10

History History), www.aviation-history.com/grumman/f4f.html.

3. Y'Blood, William T., *Hunter-Killer: U.S. Escort Carriers in the Battle of the Atlantic*, Naval Institute Press, 119.

4. Y'Blood, William T., *Hunter-Killer: U.S. Escort Carriers in the Battle of the Atlantic*, Naval Institute Press, 119–120, *Enclosure B, Chronology of the USS* Bogue, *History of the USS* Bogue, CO USS *Bogue*, December 25, 1944, 9.

5. *USS* Bogue *War Diary 12/1–31/43*, Commanding Officer USS *Bogue*, National Archives Identifier: 78234710, 1–5.

6. Y'Blood, William T., *Hunter-Killer: U.S. Escort Carriers in the Battle of the Atlantic*, Naval Institute Press, 120.

7. Lundeberg, Dr. Philip K., *American Anti-submarine Operations in the Atlantic, May 1943–May 1945*, Harvard University, ProQuest Dissertations Publishing, 1954, 581.

8. *USS* Bogue *War Diary 12/1–31/43*, Commanding Officer USS *Bogue*, National Archives Identifier: 78234710, 6.

9. *Arnold Hague Convoy Database*, convoyweb.org.uk/gus/index.html?gus.php?convoy=16!~gusmain, *USS* Bogue *War Diary 12/1–31/43*, Commanding Officer USS *Bogue*, National Archives Identifier: 78234710, 6.

10. *USS* Bogue *War Diary 12/1–31/43*, Commanding Officer USS *Bogue*, National Archives Identifier: 78234710, 7.

11. *Report of Sinking of Enemy Submarine*, CO USS *George E. Badger* (DD-96), Serial 005–43, December 17, 1943, 1–2, *USS* Bogue *War Diary 12/1–31/43*, Commanding Officer USS *Bogue*, National Archives Identifier: 78234710, 8, Y'Blood, William T., *Hunter-Killer: U.S. Escort Carriers in the Battle of the Atlantic*, Naval Institute Press, 120–121.

12. *Report of Sinking of Enemy Submarine*, CO USS *George E. Badger* (DD-96), Serial 005–43, December 17, 1943, 2.

13. *Report of Sinking of Enemy Submarine*, CO USS *George E. Badger* (DD-96), Serial 005–43, December 17, 1943, 2–3, *USS* Bogue *War Diary 12/1–31/43*, Commanding Officer USS *Bogue*, National Archives Identifier: 78234710, 8–9,

Y'Blood, William T., *Hunter-Killer: U.S. Escort Carriers in the Battle of the Atlantic*, Naval Institute Press, 121–123.

14. Lundeberg, Dr. Philip K., *American Anti-submarine Operations in the Atlantic, May 1943–May 1945*, Harvard University, ProQuest Dissertations Publishing, 1954, 585.

15. Bradshaw, Harold G., LTJG, *Oral Histories of Sinking of U-172*, *Oral History-Battle of the Atlantic, 1941–1945*, NHHC.

16. Bradshaw, Harold G., LTJG, *Oral Histories of Sinking of U-172*, *Oral History-Battle of the Atlantic, 1941–1945*, NHHC, *Appendix D, History of the USS* Bogue *(CVE9)*, CO USS *Bogue*, December 25, 1944, f, g, h, i, j, Y'Blood, William T., *Hunter-Killer: U.S. Escort Carriers in the Battle of the Atlantic*, Naval Institute Press, 124, *USS* Bogue *War Diary 12/1–31/43*, Commanding Officer USS *Bogue*, National Archives Identifier: 78234710, 11.

17. *USS* Bogue *War Diary 12/1–31/43*, Commanding Officer USS *Bogue*, National Archives Identifier: 78234710, 11.

18. Ibid., 12–16.

Chapter 10

1. *USS* Bogue *War Diary 1/1–31/44*, Commanding Officer USS *Bogue*, National Archives Identifier: 78289709, 1–10.

2. *Ralph Hiestand Correspondence*, *USS* Bogue *War Diary 2/1–29/44*, Commanding Officer USS *Bogue*, National Archives Identifier: 778439453, 1–10.

3. *USS* Bogue *War Diary 2/1–29/44*, Commanding Officer USS *Bogue*, National Archives Identifier: 778439453, 4–10.

4. *Composite Squadron Ninety Five History*, CO. VC-95, January 1, 1945, *Enclosure A (2): Squadron History, Narrative*, 1–2.

5. *Appendix A: Lt. Cmdr. John Adams, USNR-Commanding Officer, Composite Squadron Ninety Five History*, CO. VC-95, January 1, 1945, *John F. "Jack" Adams*, sunjournal.com, June 4, 2010.

Notes—Chapter 11

6. USS Bogue *War Diary 3/1–31/44*, Commanding Officer USS *Bogue*, National Archives Identifier: 7855644, 1–7.

7. USS Bogue *War Diary 3/1–31/44*, Commanding Officer USS *Bogue*, National Archives Identifier: 7855644, 8, Y'Blood, William T., *Hunter-Killer: U.S. Escort Carriers in the Battle of the Atlantic*, Naval Institute Press, 151–152, *Appendix E, History of the USS* Bogue *(CVE9)*, CO USS *Bogue*, December 25, 1944, (J) (K) (L).

8. *Report on the Survivors from U-575 Sunk 13 March 1944*, Final Report-G/Serial 32, Op-16-Z, Navy Department, Office of Naval Operations, Washington, 92–93.

9. USS Bogue *War Diary 3/1–31/44*, Commanding Officer USS *Bogue*, National Archives Identifier: 7855644, 9–17, *Composite Squadron Ninety Five History*, Commanding Officer VC-95, January 1, 1945, 3.

10. USS Bogue *War Diary 3/1–31/44*, Commanding Officer USS *Bogue*, National Archives Identifier: 7855644, 3–8.

11. *Composite Squadron Ninety Five History, Narrative*, Commanding Officer VC-95, January 1, 1945, 3–5.

12. USS Bogue *War Diary 4/1–22/44*, Commanding Officer USS *Bogue*, National Archives Identifier: 78597691, 1–15, USS Bogue *War Diary 4/23–30/44*, Commanding Officer USS *Bogue*, National Archives Identifier: 78393838, 1.

Chapter 11

1. Vice Admiral Aurelius B. Vosseller, U.S. Navy, Retired, 24 September 1956 in Biographies, 20th century collection, Navy Department Library. NHHC.

2. USS Bogue *War Diary 5/1 to 6/30/44*, Commanding Officer USS *Bogue*, National Archives Identifier: 78480260, 1–6, Y'Blood, William T., *Hunter-Killer: U.S. Escort Carriers in the Battle of the Atlantic*, Naval Institute Press, 215–216.

3. German submarine U-1224, militaryhistory.fandom.com/wiki/German_submarine_U-1224, *Sensuikan! IJN Submarine RO-501* (ex-U-1224), www.combinedfleet.com/RO-501.htm.

4. USS Bogue *War Diary 5/1 to 6/30/44*, Commanding Officer USS *Bogue*, National Archives Identifier: 78480260, 6–7.

5. *History of the USS* Bogue *(CVE9)*, CO USS *Bogue*, December 25, 1944, 10–11, Y'Blood, William T., *Hunter-Killer: U.S. Escort Carriers in the Battle of the Atlantic*, Naval Institute Press, 217.

6. USS Bogue *War Diary 5/1 to 6/30/44*, Commanding Officer USS *Bogue*, National Archives Identifier: 78480260, 8–18.

7. *Action Report on the Operations Concerning the Loss by Enemy Action of the U.S.S. Block Island on 29 May 1944*, Commander Task Group 21.11 (CO USS *Block Island*), 29 June 1944, USS *Block Island* (CVE 21), uboat.net/allies/merchants/ship/3255.html, Y'Blood, William T., *Hunter-Killer: U.S. Escort Carriers in the Battle of the Atlantic*, Naval Institute Press, 178–180, 217, *U-549*, Uboat.net.

8. USS Bogue *War Diary 5/1 to 6/30/44*, Commanding Officer USS *Bogue*, National Archives Identifier: 78480260, 20–30.

9. Hackett, Bob, Kingsepp, Sander, *IJN Submarine I-52: Tabular Record of Movement*, www.combinedfleet.com/I-52.htm, Edwards, Paul M., *Between the Line of World War II: Twenty-One Remarkable People and Events*, McFarland, 2010, 48–52.

10. USS Bogue *War Diary 5/1 to 6/30/44*, Commanding Officer USS *Bogue*, National Archives Identifier: 78480260, 30–35.

11. Hackett, Bob, Kingsepp, Sander, *IJN Submarine I-52: Tabular Record of Movement*, www.combinedfleet.com/I-52.htm.

12. *Appendix F, History of the USS* Bogue, CO USS *Bogue*, December 25, 1944, (L) (M) and (N).

13. Y'Blood, William T., *Hunter-Killer: U.S. Escort Carriers in the Battle of the Atlantic*, Naval Institute Press, 217–219, USS Bogue *War Diary 5/1 to*

Notes—Chapters 12 and 13

6/30/44, Commanding Officer USS *Bogue*, National Archives Identifier: 78480260, 36–37.

14. USS Bogue *War Diary 5/1 to 6/30/44*, Commanding Officer USS *Bogue*, National Archives Identifier: 78480260, 37–42.

15. *CTG 22.2 Action Report*, serial 0022, 7.

16. Ibid., 7–8.

17. *Narrative, History of the USS* Bogue, CO USS *Bogue*, December 25, 1944, 11.

18. *Enclosure (B), COMCORTDIV 51 Conf. ltr, CED51/A12–1(4), Serial 101*, dated 30 June 1944, CTG 22.2, 051, June 3, 1944, 19.

Chapter 12

1. USS Bogue *War Diary 7/1–31/44*, Commanding Officer USS *Bogue*, National Archives Identifier: 78588379, 1–7.

2. *History of Composite Squadron Forty-Two from 15 April 1943 to 24 September 1944*, CO VC-42, 28 December 1944, NAID 77651225, 1–10.

3. *Chapter Seven, History of Composite Squadron Forty-Two from 15 April 1943 to 24 September 1944*, CO VC-42, 28 December 1944, NAID 77651225, 1-4.

4. Y'Blood, William T., *Hunter-Killer: U.S. Escort Carriers in the Battle of the Atlantic*, Naval Institute Press, 239.

5. *Chapter Seven, History of Composite Squadron Forty-Two from 15 April 1943 to 24 September 1944*, CO VC-42, 28 December 1944, NAID 77651225, 1–7.

6. *Chapter Seven, History of Composite Squadron Forty-Two from 15 April 1943 to 24 September 1944*, CO VC-42, 28 December 1944, NAID 77651225, 7, USS Bogue *War Diary 7/1- 31/44*, Commanding Officer USS *Bogue*, National Archives Identifier: 78588379, 8–11.

7. *Chapter Seven, History of Composite Squadron Forty-Two from 15 April 1943 to 24 September 1944*, CO VC-42, 28 December 1944, NAID 77651225, 8–11, Y'Blood, William T., *Hunter-Killer: U.S. Escort Carriers in the Battle of the Atlantic*, Naval Institute Press, 240–241.

8. *Chapter Seven, History of Composite Squadron Forty-Two from 15 April 1943 to 24 September 1944*, CO VC-42, 28 December 1944, NAID 77651225, 8–15.

9. *Rescue Operations and Preliminary Report of Prisoners*, CO USS *Janssen* (DE 396), File No. DE396/AI6–3, August 21, 1944, 2.

10. *Final Report-G/Serial 46, Report on the Interrogation of Survivors from U-1229 Sunk 20 August 1944*, Navy Office of the CNO, 27 September 1944, 2–8.

11. Ibid., 13–15.

12. Ibid., 9–10.

13. *Chapter Seven, History of Composite Squadron Forty-Two from 15 April 1943 to 24 September 1944*, CO VC-42, 28 December 1944, NAID 77651225, 18.

14. USS Bogue *War Diary 8/1–31/44*, Commanding Officer USS *Bogue*, National Archives Identifier: 139733677, 14–16.

15. *Chapter Seven, History of Composite Squadron Forty-Two from 15 April 1943 to 24 September 1944*, CO VC-42, 28 December 1944, NAID 77651225, 18–20.

16. Ibid.

17. USS Bogue *War Diary 8/1–31/44*, Commanding Officer USS *Bogue*, National Archives Identifier: 139733677, 18–19, USS Bogue *War Diary 9/1–30/44*, Commanding Officer USS *Bogue*, National Archives Identifier: 1344362199, 1–24, *Chapter Seven, History of Composite Squadron Forty-Two from 15 April 1943 to 24 September 1944*, CO VC-42, 28 December 1944, NAID 77651225, 20–26.

18. *U.S. Fleet Anti-Submarine Bulletin of September 1944*, 12.

19. *Chapter Seven, History of Composite Squadron Forty-Two from 15 April 1943 to 24 September 1944*, CO VC-42, 28 December 1944, NAID 77651225, 27–28.

Chapter 13

1. *Chapter 7, Seventh Period Schnorchel U-Boats Operate in British Home Waters*,

Notes—Chapter 14

June 1944–End of War, Antisubmarine Warfare in World War II, Operations Evaluation Group Report No. 51, Officer of CNO, Wash., 1946, 63–79.
  2. ComInch message, Serial 003093, 23 October 1944 (in CVE Antisubmarine Operations).
  3. *George J. Dufek Biography*, howold.co/person/george-j-dufek/biography.
  4. *Composite Squadron Ninety Five History*, CO VC-95, Serial VC95/A12, January 1, 1945, 1–16, NAID 77659033, *USS Bogue War Diary 10/1/1944 to 11/4/1944*, Commanding Officer USS *Bogue*, National Archives Identifier: 78644260, 1–12.
  5. *Composite Squadron Ninety Five History*, CO VC-95, Serial VC95/A12, January 1, 1945, National Archives Identifier: 77659033, 15–16, *USS* Bogue *War Diary 11/5–30/44*, Commanding Officer USS *Bogue*, National Archives Identifier: 78687318, 1–12.
  6. *USS* Bogue *War Diary 12/1–31/44*, Commanding Officer USS *Bogue*, National Archives Identifier: 139796797, 1–13.
  7. *Composite Squadron Ninety Five History*, CO VC-95, Serial VC95/A12, January 1, 1945, National Archives Identifier: 77659033, 17–18, *USS* Bogue *War Diary 12/1–31/44*, Commanding Officer USS *Bogue*, National Archives Identifier: 139796797, 13–16.
  8. *Composite Squadron Ninety Five History-Period 1 January 1, 1945 to March 31 1945*, CO VC-95, Serial VC95/A12(61), April 1, 1945, National Archives Identifier: 77659033, 1–3, *USS* Bogue *War Diary 1/1–31/45*, Commanding Officer USS *Bogue*, National Archives Identifier: 139839480, 1–8.
  9. *Composite Squadron Ninety Five History-Period 1 January 1, 1945 to March 31 1945*, CO VC-95, Serial VC95/A12(61), April 1, 1945, National Archives Identifier: 77659033, 1–3, *USS* Bogue *War Diary 1/1–31/45*, Commanding Officer USS *Bogue*, National Archives Identifier: 139839480, 1–17.
  10. *USS* Bogue *War Diary 3/1–31/45*, Commanding Officer USS *Bogue*, National Archives Identifier: 139949661, 1–5, Convoy CU.58, CU/TCU Convoy Series, Arnold Hague Convoy Database, convoyweb.org.uk, Convoy UC.58B, UC Convoy Series, Arnold Hague Convoy Database, convoyweb.org.uk, *USS* Bogue, *Unit History for December 1944, January, February 1945*, CO USS *Bogue*, Serial CVE9, National Archives Identifier: 77688216, 1–2.
  11. *USS* Bogue *War Diary 3/1–31/45*, Commanding Officer USS *Bogue*, National Archives Identifier: 139949661, 6–10, *Unit History for March, April, May, June, July and August 1945*, CO USS *Bogue*, Serial CVE9/A12–1, September 6, 1945, National Archives Identifier: 77688216, 1–3.

Chapter 14

  1. Sassaman, Richard, *Nazi Spies Come Ashore, America in WWII, October 1, 2005*, thefreelibrary.com/Nazi+spies+come+ashore.-a0401096032.
  2. *COMINCH—Admiralty Operational Intelligence Center Serial Messages January 3, 1945*, Uboatarchive.net.
  3. *Operation Teardrop*, GlobalSecurity.org.
  4. Hinsley, F.H.; Ransom, C.F.G.; Knight, R.C. (1988), *British Intelligence in the Second World War: Its Influence on Strategy and Operations. Volume Three, Part II*, London: Her Majesty's Stationery Office, 625–626, Blair, Clay (1998), *Hitler's U-Boat War, The Hunted, 1942–1945* (Modern Library ed.), New York: Random House, 686–687.
  5. *USS* Bogue *War Diary 3/1–31/45*, Commanding Officer USS *Bogue*, National Archives Identifier: 139949661, 10–11.
  6. *COMINCH—Admiralty Operational Intelligence Center Serial Messages April 5, 1945*, Uboatarchive.net.
  7. *History of Composite Squadron Nineteen, 1 January 1945 to 31 March 1945*, Commander VC-19, 13 April 1945, National Archives Identifier: 77650539, 4.
  8. *USS* Bogue *War Diary 4/1–30/45*, Commanding Officer USS *Bogue*, National Archives Identifier: 139997162, 1–3, *History of Composite Squadron*

Notes—Chapter 14

Nineteen, 1 April 1945–14 June 1945, CO VC-19, National Archives Identifier: 77650539, 1–2.

9. *Unit History for March, April, May, June, July and August 1945*, CO USS *Bogue*, Serial CVE9/A12–1, September 6, 1945, National Archives Identifier: 77688216, 1–3, Y'Blood, William T., *Hunter-Killer: U.S. Escort Carriers in the Battle of the Atlantic*, Naval Institute Press, 263, 267.

10. Y'Blood, William T., *Hunter-Killer: U.S. Escort Carriers in the Battle of the Atlantic*, Naval Institute Press, 260, 261.

11. Y'Blood, William T., *Hunter-Killer: U.S. Escort Carriers in the Battle of the Atlantic*, Naval Institute Press, 263--265, Cox, Samuel J., *H-047–1: The Last Battle of the Atlantic-Operation Teardrop*, Naval History and Heritage Command, May 2020, *U-1235*, Uboat.net, *U-880*, Uboat.net.

12. Y'Blood, William T., *Hunter-Killer: U.S. Escort Carriers in the Battle of the Atlantic*, Naval Institute Press, 265–267, Cox, Samuel J., *H-047–1: The Last Battle of the Atlantic-Operation Teardrop*, Naval History and Heritage Command, May 2020, *U-518*, Uboat.net.

13. *CTG 22.1 Action Report*, Serial 0044, 4, *Enclosure A*, 48, *VC-95 History*, Serial 089, 28 June 1945, *Narrative*, 2–3.

14. *COMINCH—Admiralty Operational Intelligence Center Serial Messages April 25, 1945*, Uboatarchive.net.

15. Cox, Samuel J., *H-047–1: The Last Battle of the Atlantic-Operation Teardrop*, Naval History and Heritage Command, May 2020, *USS* Bogue *War Diary 4/1–30/45*, Commanding Officer USS *Bogue*, National Archives Identifier: 139997162, 10–14, *Unit History for March, April, May, June, July and August 1945*, CO USS *Bogue*, Serial CVE9/A12–1, September 6, 1945, National Archives Identifier: 77688216, 3–4, Y'Blood, William T., *Hunter-Killer: U.S. Escort Carriers in the Battle of the Atlantic*, Naval Institute Press, 268–271, *U-546*, Uboat.net.

16. *USS* Bogue *War Diary 4/1–30/45*, Commanding Officer USS *Bogue*, National Archives Identifier: 139997162, 15–18, *USS* Bogue *War Diary 5/1–31/1945*, Commanding Officer USS *Bogue*, National Archives Identifier: 140006798, 1–8.

17. Cox, Samuel J., *H-047–1: The Last Battle of the Atlantic-Operation Teardrop*, Naval History and Heritage Command, May 2020, *U-881*, uboat.net, Y'Blood, William T., *Hunter-Killer: U.S. Escort Carriers in the Battle of the Atlantic*, Naval Institute Press, 271, *USS Mission Bay War Diary 5/1–31/1945*, *Enclosure A*, Commanding Officer USS *Mission Bay*, National Archives Identifier: 101719743, 1, 7–8.

18. Cox, Samuel J., *H-047–1: The Last Battle of the Atlantic-Operation Teardrop*, Naval History and Heritage Command, May 2020, *U-853*, uboat.net, King, Admiral Ernest J., *U.S. Navy at War 1941–1945, Third Report*, December 3, 1945, 205 note 12.

19. Communications Intelligence, Vol II, 235.

20. Turner, Barry, *Karl Dönitz and the Last Days of the Third Reich*, Icon Books Ltd: London, 2015.

21. Cox, Samuel J., *H-047–1: The Last Battle of the Atlantic—Operation Teardrop*, H-Gram 047, Naval History and Heritage Command, May 2020.

22. Cox, Samuel J., *H-047–1: The Last Battle of the Atlantic—Operation Teardrop*, H-Gram 047, Naval History and Heritage Command, May 2020.

23. Sheldon, Natasha, *The Last Führer: 9 Facts about Karl Dönitz, Hitler's Successor*, historycollection,com, June 26, 2017.

24. *Unit History for March, April, May, June, July and August 1945*, CO USS *Bogue*, Serial CVE9/A12–1, September 6, 1945, National Archives Identifier: 77688216, 4–5, *USS* Bogue *War Diary 5/1–31/1945*, Commanding Officer USS *Bogue*, National Archives Identifier: 140006798, 9–12, *History of Composite Squadron Nineteen, 1 April 1945–14 June 1945*, CO VC-19, National Archives Identifier: 77650539, 1–2.

25. Morison, Samuel Eliot, *History of United State Naval Operations in World War II, Vol. X, The Battle of the Atlantic*

Won, May 43–May 45, London: Oxford University Press, 1956, 359–361.

26. King, Admiral Ernest J., *U.S. Navy at War 1941–1945, Third Report*, December 3, 1945, 206.

27. *Konteradmiral Godt speech at Hamburg War Memorial on May 16, 1954* (translated by Commander H.T. Hardenburg, USNR).

28. Hughes, Terry, and Costello, John, *The Battle of the Atlantic*, New York: Dial Press, 1977.

29. Cox, Samuel J., *H-047–1: The Last Battle of the Atlantic—Operation Teardrop, H-Gram 047, Naval History and Heritage Command, May 2020*.

Chapter 15

1. *USS* Bogue *War Diary 6/1–30/45*, Commanding Officer USS *Bogue*, National Archives Identifier: 101718124, 1–6.

2. *USS* Bogue *War Diary 7/1–31/45*, Commanding Officer USS *Bogue*, National Archives Identifier: 101776772, 1–10, *Unit History for March, April, May, June, July and August 1945*, CO USS *Bogue*, Serial CVE9/A12–1, September 6, 1945, National Archives Identifier: 77688216, 2.

3. *USS* Bogue *War Diary 8/1–31/45*, Commanding Officer USS *Bogue*, National Archives Identifier: 83556436, 1–9.

4. *USS* Bogue *War Diary 9/1–30/45*, Commanding Officer USS *Bogue*, National Archives Identifier: 83573340, 1–7.

5. *USS* Bogue *War Diary 10/1–18/45*, Commanding Officer USS *Bogue*, National Archives Identifier: 77557294, 1–4.

6. *Bogue*, DANFS. Navy Department, Naval History and Heritage Command, 30 January 2006, Yarnall, Paul (20 September 2019*), USS BOGUE* (ACV-9), www.navsource.org.

Chapter 16

1. Morison, Samuel Eliot, *History of United State Naval Operations in World War II, Vol. X, The Battle of the Atlantic Won, May 43–May 45*, London: Oxford University Press,1956, 359–361.

2. Y'Blood, William T., *Hunter-Killer: U.S. Escort Carriers in the Battle of the Atlantic*, Naval Institute Press, 282–283.

3. *USS* Bogue *CV-9 Cruise Book 1942–1945*, ix.

Bibliography

Action Report on the Operations Concerning the Loss by Enemy Action of the U.S.S. Block Island on 29 May 1944, Commander Task Group 21.11 (CO USS *Block Island*), June 29, 1944.
Allied Merchant Ship Losses 1939 to 1943, Office of War Information, OWI 3789, Washington, November 28, 1944.
Appendix A: Lt. Cmdr. John Adams, USNR-Commanding Officer, Composite Squadron Ninety Five History, CO. VC-95, January 1, 1945.
Appendix D, History of the USS Bogue *(CVE9)*, CO USS *Bogue*, December 25, 1944, f, g, h, i, j.
Appendix E, History of the USS Bogue *(CVE9)*, CO USS *Bogue*, December 25, 1944 (J) (K) (L).
Appendix F, History of the USS Bogue, CO USS *Bogue*, December 25, 1944 (L) (M) and (N).
Arnold Hague Convoy Database, convoyweb.org.uk/gus/index.html?gus.php?convoy=16! ~gusmain.
Bishop, John, "The U-boat Meets Its Master," *Saturday Evening Post,* September 18 and 25, 1943.
Blair, Clay (1998), *Hitler's U-Boat War, The Hunted, 1942–1945*, New York: Random House.
Bogue *Action Report, Serial 002.*
Bogue, DANFS. Navy Department, Naval History and Heritage Command, January 30, 2006.
Bogue-*Class Escort Carrier*, Wikipedia.
Bradshaw, Harold G., LTJG, *Oral Histories of Sinking of U-172, Oral History-Battle of the Atlantic, 1941–1945*, NHHC.
Carroll, Francis M., "The Sinking of SS *Athenia*," *Legion Magazine*, August 30, 2019.
CCS papers, 155/1, Conduct of the War in 1943, Casablanca Conference, Vol. 1.
Chapter 7, Seventh Period Schnorchel U-Boats Operate in British Home Waters, June 1944–End of War, Antisubmarine Warfare in World War II, Operations Evaluation Group Report No. 51, Officer of CNO, Wash., 1946.
Chapter Seven, History of Composite Squadron Forty-Two from 15 April 1943 to 24 September 1944, CO VC-42, December 28, 1944, NAID 77651225.
Chesneau, Roger (1998), *Aircraft Carriers of the World: 1914 to the Present*, London, England: Brockhampton Press.
Churchill, Winston S. *The Second World War.* London: Cassell, 1948–1953..
COMINCH—Admiralty Operational Intelligence Center Serial Messages January 3, 1945, Uboatarchive.net.
COMINCH—Admiralty Operational Intelligence Center Serial Messages April 5, 1945, Uboatarchive.net.
COMINCH—Admiralty Operational Intelligence Center Serial Messages April 25, 1945, Uboatarchive.net.

Bibliography

COMINCH message, Serial 003093, 23 October 1944 (in CVE Antisubmarine Operations).
Communications Intelligence, Vol. II.
Composite Squadron Ninety Five History, CO. VC-95, January 1, 1945, Enclosure A (2): Squadron History, Narrative.
Composite Squadron Ninety Five History, Narrative, Commanding Officer VC-95, January 1, 1945.
Composite Squadron Ninety Five History-Period 1 January 1, 1945, to March 31 1945, CO VC-95, Serial VC95/A12(61), April 1, 1945, National Archives Identifier: 77659033.
Convoy CU.58, CU/TCU Convoy Series, Arnold Hague Convoy Database, convoyweb.org.uk, Convoy HX-228, Wikipedia, en.wikipedia.org/w/index.php?title=Convoy_HX_228&oldid=1040933358.
Convoy UC.58B, UC Convoy Series, Arnold Hague Convoy Database, convoyweb.org.uk.
Cox, Samuel J., H-047–1: The Last Battle of the Atlantic—Operation Teardrop, H-Gram 047, NHHC, May 2020.
CTG 22.1 Action Report, Serial 0044, Enclosure A, VC-95 History, Serial 089, June 28, 1945, Narrative.
CTG 22.2 Action Report, serial 0022.
Dictionary of American Naval Fighting Ships, Bogue, NHHC, www.history.navy.mil/research/histories/ship-histories/danfs/b/bogue-i.html.
Dufek, George J., Biography, howold.co/person/george-j-dufek/biography.
Edwards, Paul M., Between the Line of World War II: Twenty-One Remarkable People and Events, McFarland, 2010.
Enclosure (B), COMCORTDIV 51 Conf. ltr, CED51/A12–1(4), Serial 101, dated 30 June 1944, CTG 22.2, 051, June 3, 1944.
Enclosure B, Chronology of the USS Bogue, History of the USS Bogue, CO USS Bogue, December 25, 1944.
Escort Scouting Squadron Nine (VGS-9) / Composite Squadron Nine (VC-9), www.asisbiz.com/usn/VC-9-and-VGS-9.html.
Extract from Interview of Commander Jack Monroe, USN, Air Officer, USS Bogue in the Bureau of Aeronautics, April 6, 1943.
Final Report-G/Serial 46, Report on the Interrogation of Survivors from U-1229 Sunk 20 August 1944, Navy Office of the CNO, 27 September 1944.
Garner, Forest, and Hiestand, Ralph, The USS Bogue Hunter-Killer Groups, u-boat.net.
German submarine U-1224, militaryhistory.fandom.com/wiki/German_submarine_U-1224.
Goette, Richard, "Britain and the Delay in Closing the Mid-Atlantic 'Air Gap' During the Battle of the Atlantic," The Northern Mariner/Le marin du nord, XV No 4 (October 2005), 19–41.
Grumman F4F Wildcat (Aviation History History), www.aviation-history.com/grumman/f4f.html.
Hackett, Bob, and Sander Kingsepp, IJN Submarine I-52: Tabular Record of Movement, www.combinedfleet.com/I-52.htm.
Hinsley, F.H., C.F.G. Ransom, and R.C. Knight, (1988), British Intelligence in the Second World War: Its Influence on Strategy and Operations. Volume Three, Part II, London: Her Majesty's Stationery Office.
History of Composite Squadron Forty-Two from 15 April 1943 to 24 September 1944, CO VC-42, 28 December 1944, NAID 77651225.
History of Composite Squadron Nineteen, 1 April 1945–14 June 1945, CO VC-19, National Archives Identifier: 77650539.
History of Composite Squadron Nineteen, 1 January 1945 to 31 March 1945, Commander VC-19, 13 April 1945, National Archives Identifier: 77650539.
History of the USS Bogue (CVE9), Chronology of the USS Bogue, Enclosure B, Commanding Officer, USS Bogue, December 25, 1944.

Bibliography

History of the USS Bogue *(CVE9)*, CO USS *Bogue*, December 25, 1944.
History of the USS Bogue, CO USS *Bogue*, December 25, 1944.
Hughes, Terry, and John Costello, *The Battle of the Atlantic*, New York: Dial Press, 1977.
Interview of Captain Short, USN, C.O. USS *Bogue, LT. Commander Drane, Air Group Commander*, USS *Bogue*, NAVAIR June 22, 1943.
Jane, Frederick Thomas, Maurice Prendergast, Oscar Parkes (1961), *Jane's Fighting Ships*, Santa Barbara, California: Jane's Publishing Company Limited.
John F. "Jack" Adams, sunjournal.com, June 4, 2010.
Joseph Brantley Dunn, USN, uboat.net/allies/commanders/3763.html.
King, Admiral Ernest J., *US Navy at War 1941–1945, Third Report*, December 3, 1945.
Konstam, Angus (2019), *British Escort Carriers 1941–1945*, Oxford, United Kingdom: Osprey Publishing Ltd.
Konteradmiral Godt speech at Hamburg War Memorial on May 16, 1954 (translated by Commander H.T. Hardenburg, USNR).
Lane, Frederic C., *Ships for Victory: A History of Shipbuilding under the U.S. Maritime Commission in World War II*, Johns Hopkins University Press, 1950.
Lend-Lease and Military Aid to the Allies in the Early Years of World War II, Office of the Historian, Foreign Service Institute, US Department of State, history.state.gov/milestones/1937–1945/lend-lease.
Lundeberg, Dr. Philip K., *American Anti-submarine Operations in the Atlantic, May 1943–May 1945*, Harvard University, ProQuest Dissertations Publishing, 1954.
Madeora, uboat.net/allies/merchants/ships/2696.html.
Menary, Robert F., and Moncrieff J. Spear, *VC-9: First in the Battle of the Atlantic*, Nook Ebook.
Morison, Samuel Eliot, *The Atlantic Battle Won, May 1943–May 1945, History of US Naval Operations in WWII, Volume X*, Oxford University Press, 1956.
Narrative, History of the USS Bogue, CO USS *Bogue*, December 25, 1944.
Operation Teardrop, GlobalSecurity.org.
Petrescu, Relly, and Florian Petrescu (February 2013), *The Aviation History Norderstedt*: Books on Demand GmbH.
Ralph Hiestand Correspondence.
Report of Sinking of Enemy Submarine, CO USS *George E. Badger* (DD-96), Serial 005–43, December 17, 1943.
Report on the Interrogation of Survivors from U-118 Sunk on 12 June 1943, ONI 250 Series-G/Serial 15, Navy Department, Office of the Chief of Naval Operations, Aug 23, 1943.
Report on the Survivors from U-575 Sunk 13 March 1944, Final Report-G/Serial 32, Op-16-Z, Navy Department, Office of Naval Operations, Washington.
Rescue Operations and Preliminary Report of Prisoners, CO USS *Janssen* (DE 396), File No. DE396/AI6-3, August 21, 1944.
Richards, Denis, and Hilary St. G. Saunders, *Royal Air Force 1939–1945 II (1954)*.
Royal Canadian Navy Convoy Escorts: Sept–Dec 1940, Loyal Edmonton Regiment Military Museum, lermuseum.org/second-world-war-1939–45/1940/royal-canadian-navy-convoy-escorts-sept-dec-1940.
Russell, Commander Jerry C., USN, *Ultra and The Campaign Against The U-Boats in World War II, Studies in Cryptology*, NSA, Document SRH-142, Record Group 457, Records of the National Security Agency.
Sassaman, Richard, *Nazi Spies Come Ashore, America in WWII, October 1, 2005*, thefreelibrary.com/Nazi+spies+come+ashore.-a0401096032.
Seidl, Mark, *The Lend-Lease Program*, 1941–1945, fdrlibrary.org/lend-lease.
Sensuikan! IJN Submarine RO-501 (ex-U-1224), www.combinedfleet.com/RO-501.htm.
Sheldon, Natasha, *The Last Führer: 9 Facts about Karl Dönitz, Hitler's Successor*, historycollection.com, June 26, 2017.

Bibliography

Short-Lived Halt in Atlantic U-Boat War, Daily Chronicles of World War II, Berlin, Germany, May 24, 1943.
SS Athenia: Wartime Spirit, published Oct. 5, 2017, 7:23 p.m. by *The Maritime Executive*.
SS Jonathan Sturges, navylog.navymemorial.org/jonathan-sturges.
SS Jonathan Sturges, uboat.net/allies/merchants/ships/2695.html.
The Technologies, uboat.net/technical/torpedoes.htm.
Turner, Barry, *Karl Dönitz and the Last Days of the Third Reich*, Icon Books Ltd: London, 2015.
U.S. Fleet Anti-Submarine Bulletin of September 1944.
U-1235, Uboat.net.
U-217, Uboat.net
U-488, Uboat.net
U-518, Uboat.net.
U-527, Uboat.net
U-546, Uboat.net.
U-549, Uboat.net.
U-569, Uboat.net
U-613, Uboat.net
U-853, Uboat.net.
U-880, Uboat.net.
U-881, Uboat.net.
U-954, Uboat.net
Unit History for March, April, May, June, July and August 1945, CO USS *Bogue*, Serial CVE9/A12–1, September 6, 1945, National Archives Identifier: 77688216.
USS Block Island (CVE 21), uboat.net/allies/merchants/ship/3255.html.
USS Bogue *CV-9 Cruise Book 1942–1945*, ix.
USS Bogue, *Unit History for December 1944, January, February 1945*, CO USS *Bogue*, Serial CVE9, National Archives Identifier: 77688216.
USS Bogue *War Diary 1/1–31/42*, Commanding Officer USS *Bogue*, National Archives Identifier: 134061170.
USS Bogue *War Diary 1/1–31/44*, Commanding Officer USS *Bogue*, National Archives Identifier: 78289709.
USS Bogue *War Diary 1/1–31/45*, Commanding Officer USS *Bogue*, National Archives Identifier: 139839480.
USS Bogue *War Diary 10/1/1944 to 11/4/1944*, Commanding Officer USS *Bogue*, National Archives Identifier: 78644260.
USS Bogue *War Diary 10/1–18/45*, Commanding Officer USS *Bogue*, National Archives Identifier: 77557294.
USS Bogue *War Diary 10/1–31/43*, Commanding Officer USS *Bogue*, National Archives Identifier: 135967545.
USS Bogue *War Diary 11/1–30/42*, Commanding Officer USS *Bogue*, National Archives Identifier: 134052117.
USS Bogue *War Diary 11/5–30/44*, Commanding Officer USS *Bogue*, National Archives Identifier: 78687318.
USS Bogue *War Diary 12/1–31/42*, Commanding Officer USS *Bogue*, National Archives Identifier: 134043340.
USS Bogue *War Diary 12/1–31/43*, Commanding Officer USS *Bogue*, National Archives Identifier: 78234710.
USS Bogue *War Diary 12/1–31/44*, Commanding Officer USS *Bogue*, National Archives Identifier: 139796797.
USS Bogue *War Diary 2/1–28/43*, Commanding Officer USS *Bogue*, National Archives Identifier: 134107407.
USS Bogue *War Diary 2/1–29/44*, Commanding Officer USS *Bogue*, National Archives Identifier: 778439453.

Bibliography

USS Bogue *War Diary 3/1–31/43*, Commanding Officer USS Bogue, National Archives Identifier: 134129103.
USS Bogue *War Diary 3/1–31/44*, Commanding Officer USS *Bogue*, National Archives Identifier: 7855644.
USS Bogue *War Diary 3/1–31/45*, Commanding Officer USS *Bogue*, National Archives Identifier: 139949661.
USS Bogue *War Diary 4/1–22/44*, Commanding Officer USS *Bogue*, National Archives Identifier: 78597691.
USS Bogue *War Diary 4/1–30/43*, Commanding Officer USS *Bogue*, National Archives Identifier: 134186123.
USS Bogue *War Diary 4/1–30/45*, Commanding Officer USS *Bogue*, National Archives Identifier: 139997162.
USS Bogue *War Diary 4/23–30/44*, Commanding Officer USS *Bogue*, National Archives Identifier: 78393838.
USS Bogue *War Diary 5/1–6/30/44*, Commanding Officer USS *Bogue*, National Archives Identifier: 78480260.
USS Bogue *War Diary 5/1–31/1945*, Commanding Officer USS *Bogue*, National Archives Identifier: 140006798.
USS Bogue *War Diary 5/1–31/43*, Commanding Officer USS *Bogue*, National Archives Identifier: 134237156.
USS Bogue *War Diary 6/1/43–7/31/43*, Commanding Officer USS *Bogue*, National Archives Identifier: 135908518.
USS Bogue *War Diary 6/1–30/45*, Commanding Officer USS *Bogue*, National Archives Identifier: 101718124.
USS Bogue *War Diary 7/1- 31/44*, Commanding Officer USS *Bogue*, National Archives Identifier: 78588379.
USS Bogue *War Diary 7/1–31/45*, Commanding Officer USS *Bogue*, National Archives Identifier: 101776772.
USS Bogue *War Diary 8/1–31/43*, Commanding Officer USS *Bogue*, National Archives Identifier: 135927307.
USS Bogue *War Diary 8/1–31/44*, Commanding Officer USS *Bogue*, National Archives Identifier: 139733677.
USS Bogue *War Diary 8/1–31/45*, Commanding Officer USS *Bogue*, National Archives Identifier: 83556436.
USS Bogue *War Diary 9/1–30/44*, Commanding Officer USS *Bogue*, National Archives Identifier: 1344362199.
USS Bogue *War Diary 9/1–30/45*, Commanding Officer USS *Bogue*, National Archives Identifier: 83573340.
USS Bogue *War Diary 9/26/42–10/31/42*, Commanding Officer USS *Bogue*, 9 July 1945, Serial 083.
USS Intrepid History 1943 to 1963, Twenty Intrepid Years Cruise Book, Intrepid Museum.
USS Mission Bay War Diary 5/1–31/1945, *Enclosure A*, Commanding Officer USS *Mission Bay*, National Archives Identifier: 101719743.
Vice Admiral Aurelius B. Vosseller, U.S. Navy, Retired, 24 September 1956 in Biographies, 20th-century collection, Navy Department Library. NHHC.
Y'Blood, William T., *Hunter-Killer: US Escort Carriers in the Battle of the Atlantic*, Naval Institute Press.
Yarnall, Paul (20 September 2019*), USS BOGUE* (ACV-9), www.navsource.org.

Index

Abwehr agent 111
FNFL *Aconit* (corvette) 26
ACV-9 (auxiliary aircraft carrier) 6
Adak 150
Adams, Lieutenant Commander John F. "Jack" 81, 84
Admiralty 20, 46, 86
USS *Ahrens* (DE- 575) 93, 95
Air Anti-Submarine Development Unit Atlantic Fleet (AIRASDEVLANT) 22
Air Combat Intelligence 128
Air Group 29 81
Air Group Four 13
Air Medal 91, 115
Aircraft Submarine Warfare Development Detachment, Quonset Point, Rhode Island 92
Alameda 150, 151
Alameda, California 150
Alameda Naval Air Squadron 102
Alexandria 61, 64
Alexandria, Virginia 143
Algeria 122
Allied ASW aircraft 153
Allis-Chambers steam turbine engine 4
Ambrose channel 78
American Anti-submarine Operations in the Atlantic, May 1943–May 1945 73
American ASW acoustic homing torpedo 70
USS *Amick* (DE-168) 145
Annapolis 11
anti-submarine Exercise 16 126
Anti-Submarine Measures Division 22
anti-submarine patrol aircraft 27
anti-submarine warfare (ASW) 2, 3, 19, 20
Anti-Submarine Warfare Unit, Atlantic Fleet 92
Apra Harbor 150
HMS *Archer* 4
Argentia 28, 29, 32, 36, 45, 55, 139, 140, 143, 144, 145
Argentia, Newfoundland 24, 30, 35, 114
Argentia Bay 45

Argentia Field, Newfoundland 45
HMS *Argus* (British) 3
USS *Arizona* 91
USS *Arkansas* 78, 79
Arlington, Massachusetts 81
Army Air Base 17
Army Antisubmarine Air Command 22
Army B-17 15
Army bomber number 123450 10
Army Chemical Warfare Service 103
Army planes 149
Arnold, General Hap 22, 23
"arsenal of democracy" 2
ASD (APS-3) airborne radar 118
ASD microwave radar 104
ASD Radar 123
ASDEVLANT, Quonset Point, Rhode Island 81, 100, 118, 121, 122
USS *Asheville* 89
Assistant Chief of Staff for ASW 21
ASW Development Unit Atlantic 90
ASW escort carrier 152, 153
ASW Operational Research Group (ASWORG) 22
SS *Athenia* 1
USS *Atherton* (DE-169) 145
Atlantic 1, 21, 63, 96, 98, 103, 119, 121, 125, 137
The Atlantic Battle Won, May 1943–May 1945 142, 152
Atlantic Campaign 81
Atlantic Convoy Conference in Washington 20
Atlantic Fleet 21, 46, 102
Atlantic Sea Frontiers 21
Atoka, Oklahoma 135
Atropo, Italian submarine 125, 126
Royal Navy tug *Audacious* 40
HMS *Audacity* 4
Augusta, Georgia 121
Aumuhle in Schleswig-Holstein 147
Auxiliary Vessels Board of the Navy 5
Avenger TBF-1 torpedo bomber 13, 14
AVG-9 (auxiliary aircraft ferry-escort carrier) 6

185

Index

Avonmouth 25
Azores 2, 58, 61, 64, 65, 67, 74, 94, 139

B-24 Liberator bomber 22, 23, 37
HMCS *Baddeck* 37
USS *Badger* 27, 28, 29, 31, 32, 33, 34, 40, 57, 58, 59, 61, 63, 65, 67, 68, 69, 70, 71, 72, 73, 74, 76, 77
Bahr, Kapitanlieutenant Rudolf 43
Balboa, Canal Zone 15, 16, 17
Balliett, Lieutenant (jg) Letson S. 50
Baltz, Oberleutnant Rudolf 48
Bangor, Maine 124
Bangor Bay, Belfast, Northern Ireland 39, 40
Bank of America, San Diego 10
Bank of Japan 97
Bar Harbor, Maine 132
Bar Light Ship 130
Bardon, ARM2c D.A. 107
USS *Barr* 93, 95, 96
"barrier forces" 133
Barrier One 136, 137, 138, 140
Barrier Two 136, 140, 143, 144
Barsch, Kapitanleutnant Franz 137
Bartels 113
Battle of the Atlantic 1, 47, 55, 145, 148, 153
Battleship Division 4, Battle Fleet 90
Bay of Biscay 119
Beauregard, Ensign H.B., USNR 39
Beer, Stabs Ober Steuermann Fritz 111
Behrendt, Petty Officer Rolf 98
Belfast, Northern Ireland 38, 39, 40
Belfast Harbor 39
USS *Belknap* (DD-251) 18, 23, 24, 26, 27, 28, 29, 31, 32, 34, 35, 36, 37, 38, 40, 46, 56
Bellinger, Vice Admiral P.N.L. (Commander Air Force, Atlantic Fleet) 118
Benoit, Lieutenant (jg) G.C. 124
Berlin 146, 147
Bermuda 47, 48, 67, 76, 100, 105, 106, 122, 125
Bermuda Group Patrol planes 126
Bermuda "Lily Bowl" football game 126
Bernhard, Rear Admiral A.D. 18
Bethlehem Steel Company's Shipbuilding Division 92
Bevan, Rear Admiral R.H.L. 39
Biros, Lieutenant E.W. 48
Biscay-Channel 119
"Black Friday" 47
Black Head Light 40
"Black Pit" 2
USS *Black Point* 145
Blackman, Lieutenant J.L. (air combat intelligence officer) 117, 118
Block Island 95, 96, 145
USS *Block Island* (CVE-21) 16

Boehmer, Oberleutnant Wolfgang 83, 85
Bogue class 4
Bogue Sound, North Carolina 5
Bohlen, Ensign A.D. 94
Bombing Squadron Five 6
Bombing Squadron Seven 7
Bombing Squadron Six 81
Bordeaux, France 55
Boston 20, 35, 78, 80
Boston Harbor 35
Boston Navy Yard 87
Bowling, Commander Jack F., Jr. 136
Boyd, AOM2c Rex 45
Bradshaw, Lieutenant (jg) Harold G. 73, 74, 75, 76
HMCS *Brandon* 37
Bremerton 151
Brenton Reef Light ship 129, 130, 131
Brest, France 43, 67
Brillhart, ARM3c W.S. 103
Britain 1, 2, 3, 19, 73, 152
British Admiralty 4, 132, 148
British Admiralty Assessment Committee 147
British Anti-submarine School at Bally Kelly in Northern Ireland 39
British B-17 84
British Isles 47
British LCI[L] landing craft 48
British navy 1
British Operational Intelligence Center 47
British Royal Navy 147
Brittany 97
Brodeur, Victor, Rear Admiral of the Royal Canadian Navy 20
Brokas, Lieutenant (jg) A.X. 109, 110, 115, 117, 118
Bronze Star Medal with Combat "V" 91
Brooklyn, New York 83
USS *Broome* 131, 134
Broome, Commander J.E., DSC of the Royal Navy 27, 30, 39
Brubaker, Ensign R.C. 87
Brubaker, Lieutenant (jg) 124
Bucholtz, AMM3c Harold Eugene 14, 24, 50, 51
USS *Bunker Hill* 92
Bureau of Aeronautics, Navy Department, Washington, D.C. 91
ORP *Burza* 26
Bush, Dr. Vannevar 21
Büttner, Oberleutnant (Ing.) Willy 111, 113
Byrd, Lieutenant Thomas H. 58, 59

C3 hull 4
C3-S-A1 keel design 5
C3-S-A2 keel design 5
Canada 1, 19, 134

186

Index

Canadian frigates (EG-16) 108
Canal Zone 15, 16, 149
Canary Islands 95, 96
Cape Farewell (the southern tip of Greenland) 41, 143
Cape Henry 80, 105, 125
Cape of Good Hope 98
Cape Race 111, 132
Cape St. Mary 115
Cape Saint Mary's Lighthouse 45
Cape Verde Islands 87, 92, 93, 98
Carby, Ensign H.C. 13
USS *Card* (CVE-11) 108, 130
Caribbean 2
Carrier Division 2, U.S. Fleet (USS *Saratoga*) 91
USS *Carter* 137, 139
Casablanca, French Morocco, in North Africa 60, 61, 64, 69, 85, 86, 87, 93, 95, 96
Casablanca Conference of the Combined Chiefs of Staff with Roosevelt and Churchill 20
Casco Bay 124, 128
Castillo-Bellver (freighter) 60
CASU 118, 150
CASU-21 103
Catalina plane 124
CESF 124
CFG 21.11 88
CFG 21.12 47
C.H. Wilson of the A.C.G. 106
Chamberlain, Lieutenant (jg) William F. 44, 45, 53
Chance Field 16
Chaney, Lieutenant (jg) A.H. 125
USS *Charger* 81, 122
Charleston, South Carolina 79
USS *Chatelain* 136, 143
HMS *Chelsea* 31
USS *Chepachet* (oiler) 82
Cherbourg Peninsula 120
Cherry Point Lighthouse 23
Chesapeake Bay 23, 56, 66, 78, 80, 92, 104, 149
USS *Chicago* 135
China 100
Christophersen, Oberleutnant Edwin 48
HMS *Churchill* 7
Churchill, British Prime Minister Winston 1, 20
CIC 71
CINCAIRLANT 100
CINCLANT 17, 23, 46, 47, 55, 56, 57, 61, 63, 65, 66, 68, 77, 78, 82, 87, 88, 89, 92, 95, 96, 98, 100, 103, 105, 107, 114, 115, 117, 118, 123, 124, 125, 127, 130, 136, 140, 143, 144, 145, 147
CINCLANT AD COMD 122

CINCPAC 14, 15
CINCPACFLT 6
CINCWA 41, 86
Civil Service 115
Clark, AMM3c D.L. 13
HMS *Clematis* 31
USS *Clemson* 46, 52, 55, 56, 57, 59, 60, 61, 63, 64, 65, 67, 68, 69, 72, 73, 74, 77
Clyde 78
Coast Guard (US) 145
Coast Guard Cutter 24, 129
Coastal Command (a branch of the Royal Air Force) 20
USS *Cockrill* (DE 398) 122, 124, 125, 126, 127, 128, 130, 144
Cockroft, Lieutenant (jg) T.C. 75
Colepaugh, William (German agent) 132
HMCS *Collingwood* 37
Collins, Captain 104
Colmore, Lieutenant R.L. (Air Combat Intelligence Officer) 121
Colon, Panama 17
COMA1SEAFRON 150
COMAIRLANT 18, 24, 104
COMAIRPACSUBCOMFWD 150
Combat Air Patrol (CAP) 35, 127
Combat Intelligence Division (CID) 21
Combined Chiefs of Staff 20, 21
COMCARTRANSRONPAC 150, 151
COMCORTDIV 51, 80, 122
COMCORTDIV 13 137
COMCORTDIV 46 137
COMCORTDIVONE 72
COMDESRON 15 123
COMEASTSEAFRON 77
COMFAIR Norfolk 118
COMFAIR Quonset 128
COMFAIRNORFOLK 149
COMFAIRWC 102
COMFAIRWESTCOAST 13, 15, 149
COMINCH 47, 65, 69, 132, 134, 142
Commander Air Force, U.S. Atlantic Fleet 18
Commander Air Forces, Pacific Fleet 6
Commander AIRLANT 118
Commander Carrier Division One (COMCARDIVONE) 18
Commander Carrier Transport Squadron Pacific (COMCARTRANSRONPAC) 149
Commander Destroyers, Battle Force (USS *Omaha*) 90
Commander Fleet Air Alameda 15
Commander Fleet Air West Coast (COMFAIRWESTCOAST) 10
Commander in Chief Pacific Fleet (CINCPACFLT) 149

187

Index

Commander-in-Chief, U.S. Atlantic Fleet 46
Commander-in-Chief, Western Approaches (CINCWA) 20, 38, 41
Commander Morrocan Sea Frontier (COMMORSEAFRON) 68
Commander of CORTDIV 51 101
Commander of Escort Division One (COMCORTDIVONE) 71
Commander of the 5th Naval District 77
Commander Task Group 21.11 80
Commander Tenth Fleet 21, 118
Commander Western Sea Frontier 16
Commendation Ribbon 124
COMMORSEAFRON 68, 96
COMPACSEAFRON 149
Composite Squadron Nine (VC-9) 1, 26
Composite Squadron 19 (VC-19) 63
Composite Squadron 95 Narrative 88
COMTASKFORCE 24, 26, 28
COMTASKUNIT 24.4.1 of the Mid–Ocean Carrier Escort Group 26
COMWESTSEAFRON 150, 151
Coney Island 80
Congress (US) 2
Connearney, Lieutenant (jg) J.A. 82, 87
Continental United States 151
USS *Conyngham* (DD-58) 6
convoy CU-58 130
convoy Flight 10 48
convoy GCS-7A 48
convoy GUS-7A 48, 50
convoy GUS-11 61
convoy GUS-16 64, 65
convoy GUS-23 69
convoy HX-228 26, 27, 28
convoy HX-229 64
convoy HX-235 36, 37
convoy ON-166 28, 29
convoy ON-168 27
convoy ON-184 41, 45
convoy SC-12 31, 32
convoy SC-122 64
convoy SC-130 47
convoy TU-7 80
convoy UC-58B 130
convoy UGS-9 48, 50
convoy UGS-12 56, 57, 58, 60
convoy UGS-13 61
convoy UGS-17 63
convoy UGS-24 66
convoy UGS-34 80, 82
convoy UGS-36 87
convoy UGS-49 105, 106
convoy UT-7 78, 80
Cook, Ensign 145
USS *Core* (CVE-13) 59, 75, 136, 140, 141
USS *Corry* (DD-463) 16, 17

CORTDIV 1 46
CORTDIV 9 137
CORTDIV 51 92, 135, 136
CORTDIV 79 137
Counihan, Lieutenant Commander 74
Cousins, ARM3c R.H. 94
USS *Cowie* 80
Craig, Captain Kenneth 137
Cristobal 149
USS *Croatan* 100, 103, 120, 126, 137, 138, 139, 144,
Crosby, Lieutenant Commander James R., Jr. 141
CTG 21.12 46, 48, 55, 63
CTG 21.13 57, 58, 60, 61, 62, 70
CTG 22.2 92
CTG 22.3 123, 144
CTG 22.6 107
CTF 24 31, 35, 36
CTF 69 78
CTG 92.3 41, 45
CTU 27.6.6 89
CVE-9 6, 58
CVHE-9 151
Czygan, Korvettenkapitan (Commander) Werner 54, 55

Daimler Benz 97
damage control officer (DCO) 142
USS *Davis* 144
Degaussing Barge 24
DESRON 15 123
Destroyer Escort Division Nine 145
"Destroyers for Bases" Agreement 2
Deutsche Werft 111
DeWeber, AM3c A.C. 103
Distinguished Flying Cross 115
Distinguished Service Cross 45
Distinguished Service Medal 45
Dittmer, Frank (gunner) 59
Dixfield, Maine 81
Dixon, Lieutenant (jg) Wayne A. 107, 108
USS *D.L. Howard* 137
Donahoe, Lieutenant (jg) O.J. 43, 58
Donau-Mosel 41
Dönitz, Admiral Karl 32, 41, 46, 47, 50, 61, 63, 68, 140, 146, 147
Dönitz, Peter 47
Donnelly, ART3c R.B. 106
USS *Doran* 78
Doty, Ensign Stewart E. 16, 43, 54, 58
Dow Field at Bangor 124
Drane, Lieutenant Commander William McClure 11, 14, 31, 41, 45, 49
Dufek, Captain George John J. 121, 135, 150
Dunkard, Pennsylvania 135
Dunn, Captain Joseph Brantley 56, 60, 90

188

Index

USS *Du Pont* (DD-152) 64, 65, 67, 68, 69, 70, 71, 72, 73, 74, 76

Eager, Lieutenant (jg) E.E. 39
USS *Eagle* 78
Earhart, Amelia 11
USS *Earl* 80
East Field, NAS Norfolk 103, 104, 124, 125
Eastern Aircraft Division of General Motors 66
electric acoustic homing torpedo 64
USS *Elizabeth C. Stanton* 79
Elizabeth River Channel 63
Ellingsworth, ARM3c F.E. 13
Royal Navy tug *Empire Cherub* 40
Royal Navy tug *Empire Medal* 40
USS *Endicott* 78
England 1, 147
English Channel 119
Enigma coding machine 41, 98, 134
USS *Enterprise* 7
USS *Ericsson* (DD-440) 145
Ermer, ARM2c H.A. 109, 115
HMS *Escapade* 26
escort carrier 3
Escort Division 51 130, 147
Escort Scouting Squadron Nine (VC-9) 11
Escort Scouting Squadron Nine (VGS-9) 11
USS *Essex* (CV-9) 13
USS *Eugene E. Elmore* (DE 686) 95, 96
Europe 2, 119
Europe, Mississippi 56
Everett, Washington 151
Ewerth, Kapitanleutnant Klaus 74

F4F-4 Grumman Wildcat fighter 11, 16, 24, 66
F4U carrier qualification landings 128
F6F Hellcat 66
Falke T4 torpedo 64
Fanad Head Lighthouse 38
USS *Farquhar* 137, 145
Fayal Island, Portugal 74
FBI 132
Federal Anchorage 127
USS *Fessenden* 137
Fetsch, Lieutenant (jg) Carter E. 67
Fido, MK-24 acoustic homing torpedo 70, 76, 99, 153
Fighting Squadron 2 91
Final Report on the Interrogation of Survivors from U-1229 111
Finch, ARM1c James H. 50
Fireside Chat (Roosevelt) 2
Firth of Clyde, Scotland 40, 78, 79
Fish, Price 99
Flag Officer Commanding Iceland 41

USS *Flaherty* 136, 142, 143
Fleet Air Detachment in Observation Squadron 2 91
Flemish Cap 114
Flensburg Government 146
Fleur, Lieutenant (jg) Wallace A. 74
Flinn, AOM3c J. 103
Flores 65
FM-1 66
FM-2 66, 90
FOC Gibraltar 60
Fogde, Lieutenant (jg) Frank D. 45, 51
FOGMA 86
Ford Island, Pearl Harbor 150, 151
Fort Cobbe Inland waters of the Canal Zone 16
Fort Hunt 143, 144
Fort Lauderdale, Florida 135
Fort Wool 24
Foster-Wheeler boiler 4
Fowler, Lieutenant (jg) Wilma S. 49, 50, 53
Fowler, Ensign W.S. 24
"Foxer" acoustic torpedo countermeasure system 64, 93, 95, 141, 153
France 111, 122
USS *Frances M. Robinson* (DE-220) 92, 93
USS *Frederick C. Davis* 136, 141, 142
French, Commander Reginald H. 137
French North Africa 12
Friend, Lieutenant George S., landing signal officer (LSO) 23
Frischke, Kapitänleutnant der Reserve Karl-Heinz 145
USS *Friske* (DE-143) 107
Frömsdorf, Oberleutnant Helmut 146
USS *Frost* 137, 138
Fryatt, Ensign Harry 32
Fryatt, Lieutenant (jg) H.E. 48, 53, 55, 57
Fuel Oil Dock at Manchester, Washington 8

Gaibattista, Commander 137
Gallagher, Lieutenant (jg) W.J. 67, 74
Galley, Captain 118
Gander Airport 22
Gardner, Captain M.B. 22
ORP *Garland* 26
Gaylord, Lieutenant (jg) E.C 69, 70
General Board of the Navy 4
USS *General W.M. Weigel* 130
HMS *Gentian* 31
USS *George E. Badger* 19, 23, 24, 26, 46, 56
Georges Bank 123, 124
German 1, 2, 4, 19, 47, 50, 52, 59, 60, 64, 72, 74, 85, 95, 97, 98, 110, 111, 146
German fleet 55
German Focke-Wolf 200 aircraft 60
German navy 64

189

Index

German submarine radio message 47
German Type IX U-boats 134
Germany 1, 2, 6, 119, 133, 147
Gibraltar 47, 48, 57
Gilder, S1c A.D., Jr. 103
USS *Gillespie* (DD-609) 9, 12, 13, 14
Gimpel, Erich (German agent) 132
Gladstone Dock 130
Glasgow, Scotland 78
GNAT (passive German Naval Acoustic Homing Torpedo) 64, 95, 153
Royal Navy tug *Golden Emblem* 41
Golden Gate Bridge 150
Goldman, Lieutenant Aaron 80
Goletti, Lieutenant V.J. 125
Goodwin, Ensign G. 75
Gordon, Ensign W.D. 95
Gordon, Lieutenant (jg) William "Flash" 99
SS *Graf Waldersee* (ex-German ship) 6
Grand Bank 41
Grand Banks 145
Grand Banks of Newfoundland 111, 132
Grand Central Station in New York City 132
Graves (crewman) 115
Graves End Bay 147
Graves Lighthouse 35
USS *Greene* (DD-266) 36, 38, 39, 40, 46, 56
Greenland 2, 41
Greenock 78
Griggs, Commander Paul Clayton 151
Grille (Adolf Hitler's yacht) 113
Groninger, Lieutenant (jg) L. 125
Grotta Light, Iceland 41
Group "Trutz" 47
Grumman F4F-4 "Wildcat" 12
Grumman plant 66
Gruppe Seewolf 134, 137, 140, 144
USS *Guadalcanal* 103, 118
Guam 150
Gulf of Maine 123, 124
Gulf of Mexico 59
Gulf of Paris, Trinidad, British West Indies 89
Gulf of St. Lawrence 108

Halifax 1, 20, 25
Halifax four-engine heavy bomber 96
Hall, Commander Frederick S. 136
Hall, Commander R.F.S. 142
Halsey, Rear Admiral William F. 3
Hamburg 113
Hamilton, Bermuda 107
Hampton Roads 17, 18, 24, 55, 56, 57, 61, 62, 63, 64, 66, 69, 80, 87, 100, 125, 147
Hance, Lieutenant (jg) K.P. 75
Hancock Point 132

Harbor Pilot Johnson 10
Harris, Commander Morgan H. 137, 139
Harvard University 142
HMS *Harvester* 26, 28
Hatteras 89
USS *Haverfield* (DE-393) 80, 81, 82, 83, 84, 85, 87, 89, 92, 94, 95, 96, 98, 99, 100, 105, 106, 115, 117, 122, 123, 124, 125, 127, 128, 130, 131, 135, 158, 161
USS *Hayter* 136, 142, 144, 147
USS *H.C. Jones* 137
Head, Ensign 103
HMS *Heather* 31
Hepp, Oberleutnant Horst 67
HF/DF (high-frequency direction finder network) 20, 39, 40, 41, 44, 45, 46, 48, 50, 52, 54, 56, 57, 58, 60, 64, 78, 80, 84, 92, 104, 125, 126, 134, 137, 152
Hiestand, Ralph (aviation machinist) 79
USS *Hill* 137, 145
Hirsbrunner, Lieutenant (jg) A.L. 96
Hirsch, Lieutenant (jg) W.C. 96
History of United States Naval Operations in World War II 142
Hitler, Adolf 146
USS *Hobson* 78, 79, 80, 82, 83, 84, 85, 86, 87
Hodgson, Lieutenant (jg) Edward R. 48, 60
Hoffman, LT (jg) A.J., USNR 39
Hoffman, Oberleutnant Herman 69, 70
Hoines, Ensign A.H. 82
Horta, Portugal, in the Azores 87
Horton, Norway 132
House of Commons 20
USS *Howard* 145
USS *Hubbard* 136, 143, 144, 147
Hughes, Lieutenant (jg) W.P. 124
USS *Hurst* 130
USS *Huse* (DD-145) 69, 137, 138
Hvalfjordur, Iceland 41
Hyman-Michaels Company of Chicago, Illinois 151

I-52 (Japanese) 97, 98
Iceland 40
IFF (Identification, friend or foe) 16
Illinois College 90
USS *Inch* 137
Indian Ocean 69, 98
Ingersoll, Admiral Royal J. 46, 55, 69, 101, 114, 120
USS *Ingram* 38, 40, 42, 43, 57, 60, 61, 63, 65, 67, 69, 72, 74, 77
Ingram, Vice Admiral Jonas (Commander of the Atlantic Fleet [CINCLANT]) 133, 138, 144
Ireland 1
Iron Cross 1st class 113

Index

Isle of Aran Light 38
Isthmain Steamship Company 5
Italy 3
HMCS *Itchen* 41
Iwanicki, ARM3c H.W. 108, 115

USS *J. Richard Ward* 136
Jacksonville 59
Jacksonville, Illinois 90
Jansen, Lieutenant (jg) 86
USS *Janssen* (DE-396) 80, 82, 83, 86, 87, 88, 89, 92, 96, 100, 108, 111, 115, 117, 122, 123, 124, 125, 129, 135, 143, 144, 147
Japanese 3, 100
Japanese Naval Attaché in Berlin 98
HMS *Jed* 47
Jenkins, Lieutenant (jg) T.E. 144
Jettee Delure 86, 95
Johannsen, Oberleutnant zur See der Reserve Hans 44
Johansen, Lieutenant Commander 93
Johnson, Lieutenant (jg) Robert J. 53, 54
joint Army-Navy interrogation center at Fort Hunt 143
Joint Munitions Assignment Board 6
SS *Jonathan Sturges* (Liberty cargo ship) 28
Joubert, Air Chief Marshal Sir Philip, R.A.F. Coastal Command 19
USS *J.R.Y. Blakely* 137, 139
Jupiter (collier) 3
Just, Kapitänleutnant Paul 141, 143

K-16 (blimp) 145
K-58 (blimp) 145
SS *Kamen* (Yugoslavian freighter) 145
Keane, Commander T.J. USNR 39
Keinholz, Lieutenant Q.O. 107
USS *Keith* 115, 136, 143
USS *Kendrick* (DD-612) 14, 15
Kennemund, Metrosengefreiters 60
Kiel, Germany 93
King, Admiral Ernest, Commander in Chief, United States Fleet (COM-INCH) 20, 21, 23, 29, 55, 120, 122
King George V Dock at Glasgow, Scotland 79
Kirkpatrick, Miss D. 39
USS *Knight* 80
Knight's Cross of the Iron Cross 147
knuckle 73
Koos, Lieutenant (jg) E.M. 86
Krankenhagen, Kapitänleutnant Detlev 96
Kriegsmarin 146
Kuhn, Lieutenant (jg) Roger C. 42, 43
Kulak Bay, Adak 150

L-8H searchlight 104, 118

LaFleur, Lieutenant (jg) Wallace A. 75, 76
La Guardia, Fiorello (Mayor of New York) 133
Lair, Lieutenant Carl E. 108, 115, 117, 118
Lake Washington 11
Lane, Lieutenant W.Z. 121
Lange, Kapitanleutnant Kurt 98
USS *Langley* 3, 6
Lank, Commander Theodore S. 92
La Pallice, France 42
Lapham, Ensign R.D.,USNR 10
Lark, Commander Theodore S. 101
Las Palmas 96
Laughlin, S1c Gerald 14
Law, Lieutenant (jg) R.B. 109, 116
USS *Lea* (DD-118) 35, 36, 37, 38, 39, 40, 41
Legion of Merit 92
Leigh Light (large carbon arc searchlight) 139
Lend-Lease Act 2, 4, 5
Letters of Commendation 115, 124
USS *Lexington* 3, 91
Liberty ships 4
Lidey, Ensign R.H., USNR 39
Little Placentia Harbor, Argentia, Newfoundland 25, 26, 33, 34, 45, 46
Liverpool, England 26, 28, 31, 130
Lloyd, Boatswain's Mate Second Class Lonnie Whitson 145
Locke, AMM3c D.E. 94
The Log 90
Lohman, Lieutenant (jg) R.K. 96
Lohrville, Iowa 6
Londonderry 20, 39
USS *Long Island* 4
Lorient 98
Los Coronados Island 10
Low, Rear Admiral Francis S. 20
Low Room Point 35, 36
USS *Lowe* 137, 139
Lower New York Bay 83
LSO (landing signal officer) 116
Lundeberg, Dr. Philip K. 73, 142
Lynch, AEM2c G.K. 106
Lynnhaven Roads 134

Mabry, Lieutenant (jg) 107, 109
USS *Mackerel* 136
MAD (magnetic anomaly detector) 123, 124
Madeira, Portugal 69, 96
SS *Madoera* (Dutch) 29
Maine 111, 132
Malaysia 94
M.A.N. Diesel 111
Manchester, Washington 9
Manseck, Kapitanleutnant Helmut 50, 51, 52, 55

191

Index

Mansell, Lieutenant 138
Mantel, Lieutenant Oskar (Propagandamann) 111, 132
Manteo, North Carolina 103
Mare Island Navy Yard, California 10, 15
Marineschule at Flensburg 113
Maritime Commission 5
Maritime Commission Act (MARCOM) 4
Mark VI instantaneous flare 99
Marlette, ARM3c Clarence Manly 14
Marshall, General George C. 23
USS *Maryland* 121
McAuslan, Alexander C. 27, 28, 49
McCain, Rear Admiral John S. 22
McClure, Captain Jesse S. 150, 151
McCormick, Sen. Joseph Medill 90
McCreath, Lieutenant Fowler (VC-9 Squadron Intelligence Officer) 51, 55
McGinnis, ARM3c J.J. 82
McGusty, Lieutenant (jg) 115, 116
McNarney, Lieutenant Gen. Joseph T. 22
McQuary, Lieutenant (jg) "Jack" 126
McWhorter, Lieutenant (jg) John F. 141
Medical Officer 111
Mediterranean 106
Melton, ARM3c C.G. 108
Melville, Rhode Island 127, 128, 130
USS *Menges* 137
Merchant Ship Anchorage in the Firth of Clyde, Scotland 79
Messerschmitt Me-163 "Komet" rocket fighter airplane 94
USS *Method* (AM 264) 123
Mew Island 40
Mexican border 44
Meyers, (radioman) 59
Miami, Florida 64
Mid–Ocean Carrier Escort Group 31
Mid–Ocean Escort Force Group B3 26
milchkuh or milchcow (supply and replenishment submarine tanker) 50
Miller, Lieutenant Commander Roger F. 72
Miller, Lieutenant Commander W., Jr. 5
Miller, Mrs. W., Jr. 5
USS *Mission Bay* 136, 137, 139, 145
USS *Mississippi* 90
USS *Missouri* 150
Mitsubishi Corporation 97
Mitsubishi Electric and Instrument Company 97
Mk 2 markers 108
Mk 5 (3.5-inch forward-firing aircraft rocket) 109
Mk VI depth charge 70
Mk 8 magnetic influence depth charge 93
Mk 10 Hedgehog 93
Mk XI depth bomb 108

Mk 17 depth charge 27, 29, 49
Mk 17–2 flat-nosed TNT depth charge 44
Mk 44 flat-nosed bomb 42, 44
Mk 47 depth charge 59, 75
Mk 54 torpex-filled depth bomb 109
Coast Guard frigate *Moberly* (PF-63) 145
molybdenum 98
Monogram Field 104
Monroe, Commander Jack Pendleton (USS *Bogue* air officer) 8, 10, 18, 26, 34
Monterey Bay 103
USS *Moore* 136
Moore, British Vice-Admiral Henry 20
Moore, Lieutenant W. O. 9
Morison, Professor Samuel Eliot 142, 152
SS *Mormacland* 4
SS *Mormacmail* 4
Morocco 52
Morrison, Lieutenant (jg) H. 69
Morrison, Lieutenant R.D. 98
Morrison, Third Officer S., W.R.E.N. 39
USS *Mosley* 137, 139
Mount Desert Rock 123
USS *Muir* 137
Myhre, Lieutenant Commander Leonard A. 143

N&PBL Railway Pier 63
NAAS Manteo, North Carolina 121
NAAS Otis Field 128
Nantucket Shoals 124
HMS *Narcissus* 26
Narragansett Area 82
Narragansett Bay Channel 128, 130, 131
Narragansett Bay, Rhode Island 127, 136
NAS Anacostia 6
NAS Bermuda in Port Royal Bay, South Bermuda 107
NAS Coco Solo 6
NAS East Field, Norfolk 130
NAS Kindley Field, Bermuda 123
NAS Lakehurst, New Jersey 145
National Socialist 113
Naval Air Station Alameda, California 150, 151
Naval Air Station Argentia 36, 115
Naval Air Station Dock 10, 12
Naval Air Station Norfolk, Virginia 6, 55, 65, 77, 80, 89, 117, 120, 121, 122, 147
Naval Air Station Pensacola, Florida 6, 11, 91, 122
Naval Air Station Quonset Point, Rhode Island 35, 81, 90, 127, 128, 130, 136
Naval Air Station San Diego, California 14, 91
Naval Ammunition Depot at Saint Juliens Creek in Portsmouth 24

Index

Naval Ammunition Depot at Yorktown, Virginia 83
Naval Auxiliary Air Station (NAAS) Creeds, Virginia 89, 103
Naval Auxiliary Air Station (NAAS) Pungo, Virginia 65, 121
Naval Control Services Officer at Clyde 79
Naval Intelligence 60, 113
Naval Mine Depot 149
Naval Operating Base (NOB) Argentia. 25, 114, 115
Naval Operating Base (NOB) at Norfolk 18, 19, 23, 24, 55, 56, 62, 63, 65, 66, 77, 78, 80, 89, 92, 100, 102, 103, 104, 117, 120, 122, 125, 130, 130, 134, 149
Naval Operating Base, Casablanca 60
Naval Reserve 81
Naval War College 7
Navy Department 21
Navy Department Building in Washington, D.C. 21
Navy List 151
Navy Secret Report on the Interrogation of Survivors from U-575 Sunk 13 March 1944 85
Navy Tug YT199 10
Navy Yard at Bremerton 8
Navy Yard at Philadelphia 35
Navy Yard Drydock at Portsmouth 18
Navy Yard, South Boston Annex 35
Naxof FuMB7 radar 98
Nazis 2, 133, 143
USS *Neal A. Scott* 137, 139
Nelson, Lieutenant (jg) 124
Nelson, Lieutenant G.L. 95, 98, 116
USS *Neunser* 136, 142, 143
New England 145
New York (city) 20, 26, 28, 31, 48, 78, 79, 89, 111, 123, 127, 130, 132, 133, 134, 147, 149
New York Harbor 133
New York Navy Yard 81, 83, 130
New York Times 133
Newfoundland 2, 22, 44
Newport, Arkansas 102
Nichols, Lieutenant (jg) D. 84, 86
Nihon Kogaku KK 97
1930 Naval Term 113
Noble, British Admiral Percy 20
Norfolk 48, 63, 64, 66, 77, 89, 90, 97, 100, 104, 117, 124, 130, 134, 147
Norfolk NAS Administration Building 118
Norfolk Navy Yard at Portsmouth 18, 56, 63, 66, 77, 78, 80, 89, 102, 117, 120, 122, 124, 134, 147, 149
Normandy 119
North Africa 56, 122
North African convoys 46

North America 2
North Atlantic 24, 46, 47, 64, 68, 119, 137
North Island Naval Air Station, San Diego 12
North River, New York City 123, 147
Northern Transit Area 119
Norton, Lieutenant (jg) 9
Norway 119, 120, 134
Norwegian merchant vessel 25
Nova Scotia 1, 123
NRAB, Squantum, Massachusetts 82
Nuremberg Trials 146

Oahu, Hawaii 105
Ocean View 104
Oderwerke, Stettin, Germany 113
Offermann, Oberleutnant Hans-Werner 139
Ogle, Lieutenant (jg) James E., III 67
Onice (Italian submarine) 123
Operation Magic Carpet 151
Operation Teardrop 133, 134
Operation "Torch" 12
opium 98
Orchard Bay at Illahee, Washington 8
Osaka 97
USS *Osmond Ingram* 36, 46, 55, 56
USS *Otter* 136
USS *Ottersetter* 115, 136

P-47 unloading 79
P-51 fighter planes 130
Pacific 56, 102
Pacific Air Group 125
Paint Marion, Pennsylvania 135
Panama Canal 17, 149
Panama Canal Zone 6
Papago Park, Arizona (POW camp) 44
Paris 115
Paris, AMM2c C.E. 108
Parkins, Ensign D.S. 131
USS *Patoka* 7
Patrol Squadron Six (VP-6) at Pearl Harbor 11
Patrol Squadron 55 91
Patrol Squadron 74 91
Patrol Wing Five 91
Pattie, Lieutenant Donald A. 83, 84
PBM patrol plane 61
USS *PC 1184* 89
USS *PCE 846* 123, 125
USS *PCE 847* 123
Pearl Harbor 149, 150, 151
Penang, Malaysia 93
USS *Penguin* (ASR-12) 146
Perabo 52
Perabo, Ensign P. 14
Perabo, Lieutenant (jg) Phil 51

193

Index

Pfeffer, Ensign James Oren 14
Phelps Bank 123
Philippine mahogany 100
Pierce, Lieutenant 103
Pillenwarfer (sonar decoy) 142
USS *Pillsbury* 136, 142, 143
Placentia Bay 25, 29, 36
POBRY 99
Point Comfort 24
Point Loma 13, 15
Point Loma Lighthouse 10
Point X-Ray 35
Point Z 35
Point Zebra 147
Poland, Ensign 127
Polish 1
USS *Pope* 136
Pope, Lieutenant S.W. 120, 121, 123
Port Angeles 9
Port Royal Bay, South, Bermuda 77, 100, 122, 125, 126
Port Said, Egypt 48, 61, 63, 69, 80, 87
Porter, Lieutenant (jg) W.S. 109, 110, 115, 116
Portsmouth 56, 134
Poske 113
Pratt and Whitney R-1830 engine 11
Presidential Unit Citation 114, 124, 154
USS *Pride* 137
HMCS *Prince Rupert* 84, 85
USS *Prince William* (CVE-31) 104
Puget Sound Navy Yard, Bremerton, Washington 6, 7, 8, 26
Pungo Beach 104
Purvis, Captain R.S. 136

Queenstown, Ireland 6
Quertin, Leutnant zur See 113
Quincy, Massachusetts 92
quinine 98
Quonset Point 121, 122, 128, 131

USS *R-1* 123
USS *R6* 06, 56, 106, 107, 123
USS *R-9* 126
Racon (YJ) 110
RAF Coastal Command 119
RAF Squadron 517 96
RAF Sunderland Flying Boat 38
USS *Ranger* 12, 36, 91
Rappahannock Spit in the Bay 23, 24
RDF 116
Read, Rear Admiral A.C. (Commander Fleet Air, Norfolk) 118
Readiness Condition Two 25
Reeves, Commander-in-Chief of the U.S. Fleet, Admiral J.M. 3, 6
Regenbogen (code name for scuttling of warships and U-boats) 146

Rendtel, Kapitanleutnant Horst 49
USS *Reno* 90
FNFL *Renoncule* 26
Reserve Officer Training Corps (ROTC) 121
HMCS *Restigouche* 37
Revenaugh, Lieutenant (jg) R.L. 73, 107, 108, 115
Rheims, France 146
USS *Rhind* 80
Richmond, Lieutenant (jg) R.F. 87
River Mersey 130
RO-501 93, 94
USS *Robert I. Paine* (DE-578) 95
Roberts, Lieutenant H.S. (XO) 29, 44, 45
USS *Robinson* 93, 94, 97, 98, 100
rocket-equipped submarines 132
Rockford, Illinois 121
USS *Roe* (DD-418) 69
Rogers, Lieutenant Richard S. 49
Roosevelt, President Franklin D. 1, 4, 20, 133
FNFL *Roselys* 26
Royal Air Force 20, 96
Royal Canadian Air Force 86
Royal Canadian Navy 1
Royal Navy 1, 3, 4, 5, 39, 45, 47, 55
Ruhsenberger, Captain John R. 137, 138

USS *S-39* 121
SS *Sague* 15
Saigon 13
St. Georges Channel 130
Saint John's, Newfoundland 26, 29, 115
HMCS *Saint Laurent* 42, 44
Salerno 122
HMS *Salisbury* 31
San Diego, California 9, 13, 149
San Diego Harbor 13, 14, 15, 36
San Joaquin River 103
Sands Point Naval Air Station at Seattle, Washington 11
USS *Santee* (CVE-29) 81
Santee, Lieutenant 37
USS *Saratoga* 3, 122
Savelli, Seaman 2c Armand 65
SBNO AZORES 83, 86
Schafer, Commander Alfred 98
Schlanker, Lieutenant (jg) W.H. 124
Schmaltz, ARM3c Sylvester Peter 14
Schnorchel 110, 113, 114, 116, 117, 118, 120, 123, 137, 138, 140, 153
Schotzau, Kapitanleutnant Gerhard 138
Schroeder, Ensign 116, 117
Schug, Kapitanleutnant Walter 67
Schulze, Petty Officer Kurt 98
Scinio, AOM3c D.J. 108
Scotland 78, 80
Scouting Squadron One 6

194

Index

Scouting Squadron 33 82
Scouting Squadron 101 82
Sea Devil (German wolfpack) 32
Seattle, Washington 150
Seattle-Tacoma Shipbuilding Corporation of Tacoma, Washington 5
Seitz, Commander (chief of staff of CINCAIRLANT) 118
HMS *Sennen* (sloop) 47
SF-1 radar 71
Shawmut Dairy 35
Sherbring, Lieutenant (jg) M.J. 109, 110, 115
Short, Captain Giles Elza 6, 28, 29, 39, 40, 41, 46, 47, 48, 49, 52, 56
Sicily 122
USS *Simpson* 131
Singapore 97, 98
Sissler, Lieutenant (jg) B.C. 109, 110, 112
Sixth Escort Group 41, 46
SK radar 116
Skelmore Bank Bell Buoy 40
Sloane, Lieutenant (jg) Charles O., Jr. 129
USS *Sloat* 136, 115
Smoke Bomb Experimental Project 103
USS *Snowden* 127, 137
Snyder, AMM2C Bud 45
SOC1 12
SOC-3A 8
South, Lieutenant Commander William Wood 134, 135, 140
Soviet Red Army 146
Spain 111
Spandau Prison 147
Speer, Albert (German Minister of Armaments and War Production) 132
Speri (Italian submarine) 123, 127
Sprague, Lieutenant (jg) D.G. 94, 97
Squadron VC-19 77
Squadron VC-95 80
USS *Stanton* 137, 138
Stark, Chief of Naval Operations (CNO), Admiral 3
Staten Island 78, 130, 149
Stearns, Lieutenant (jg) Robert 52, 54, 59, 60
Steel Advocate 5
Steinmetz 60
Stephens, Lieutenant Commander Stuart 102
Steward, Lieutenant (jg) Robert Lamar 23
Stewart, Lieutenant Commander Claude Weaver, USN 63
Stine, ARM1c James O. 45
stirrup-and-trough method 27
Stout, Ensign L.L. 103
Straits of Gibraltar 55
submarine rescue ship 145

Submarine Tracking Room 47
Summary Statistics of the Battle of the Atlantic from Admiral King 148
"Survival of the Blippiest" award 117
USS *Sutton* 137
Sutton, Lieutenant (jg) Johnny, Jr. 105, 106
USS *Swasey* 137, 138
HMS *Sweetbriar* 31
USS *Swenning* (DE-394) 80, 82, 83, 86, 87, 89, 92, 94, 96, 97, 98, 100, 105, 108, 115, 117, 122, 123, 124, 125, 127, 128, 130, 131, 136, 158, 161
Sydenham Aerodrome Jetty, Belfast 39, 40
Sydney 1

T2 tanker 4
T-5 acoustic homing torpedo 141
T5 *Zaunköning* version 64
Tacoma, Washington 151
Taffinder, Rear Admiral S.A. 6
Tait, Royal Navy Commander Arthur Andre 26
Task Group 21.11 82, 84, 86, 96
Task Group 21.12 87
Task Group 21.13 56, 67, 69, 73, 76, 77
Task Group 21.15 74
Task Group 22.1 137
Task Group 22.2 92, 94, 96, 97, 98
Task Group 22.3 104, 107, 115, 117, 122, 123, 124, 135, 136, 140, 147
Task Group 22.4 115, 136
Task Group 22.5 127, 137
Task Group 22.6 100
Task Group 22.8 136
Task Group 22.13 137
Task Group 22.14 137
Task Group 38.3 13
Task Group 63 61
Task Group 64 61
Task Group 92.3 36, 38
Task Unit 19.9.19 150
Task Unit 22.3.1 117
Task Unit 22.3.2 117
Task Unit 22.7.1 136
Task Unit 24.1.14 36
Task Unit 24.4.1 31
Task Unit 28.2.2 128, 130
Tate, Dr. John T. 22
Taylor, Lieutenant Commander Jesse Dean 90, 94, 97, 98, 99
TBF Grumman Avenger torpedo bomber 11
TBF-1 Avengers 24
TBM (TBF version by General Motors Corp., Eastern Aircraft Div., Linden, New Jersey) 90
TBM-1C 104
TBM-1D Avenger 104

195

Index

TBS 72
10cm radar detector 119
Tennant, Lieutenant (jg) Raymond J. 53
Tenth Fleet 21, 41, 47, 52, 58, 68, 98, 107, 115, 132, 137, 143, 148
Tenth Fleet Anti-Submarine Measures Division 22
Tenth Fleet Civilian Scientific Council 22
Tenth Fleet Convoy and Routing Division 22
Tenth Fleet Operational Division 21
Terceira, Azores 67, 139
TG 21.11 87, 89, 93
TG 21.13 72
TG 22.1 144
TG 22.3 106, 108, 115, 126, 127, 140, 144
TG 22.4 140, 144, 147
TG 22.8 140
TG 22.14 137
TG 27.8 74
TG 61.6.2. 130
Thalia Acres 104
Thebaud, U.S. Navy Captain L.H. 20
USS *Thornton* 6
Thubault, Conrad (radio baritone) 125
Times Square 132
Tokyo Bay 150
SS *Toltec* 41
USS *Tomich* 136
Torpedo Squadron 51 82
HMS *Trent* 37
TRIDENT Conference 22
Trinidad 88, 98
Triton key network 47
Tromsø, Norway 135
Trondheim 111
Trutz 48, 49, 50
TU-7 79
TU 12.9.6. 149
TU 22.7.1 140, 144, 147
TU 22.8 144
TU 24.1.16 31
TU 24.12.1 31
TU 27.1.3 123
TU 28.2.2 128, 129
tug Y.S.D. 23 (*Mary Ann*) 35
tungsten 97, 98
USS *Tuscaloosa* 35
Type C1 4
Type C2 4
Type C3 4
Type C4 4
Type IX-C submarine 111

U-30 1
U-67 59
U-86 28
U-118 51, 52, 53, 54, 55
U-172 54, 69, 70, 73
U-217 49
U-219 69
U-221 28, 64
U-228 48
U-231 41, 42
U-238 67
U-305 43
U-406 28
U-432 28
U-444 28
U-460 51, 52
U-468 42
U-488 50
U-504 113
U-518 134, 139
U-527 59
U-530 98, 134
U-546 134, 140, 141, 142, 143
U-548 134
U-549 95
U-561 113
U-569 44, 45
U-575 84, 85
U-603 48, 64
U-613 58, 59
U-641 49
U-648 59
U-653 29
U-663 32
U-707 28
U-757 28
U-758 50, 51, 52, 55, 64
U-802 107, 108
U-805 134, 139
U-850 74, 75, 76
U-853 145, 146
U-858 134
U-880 134, 138
U-881 134, 145, 146
U-954 47
U-1224 93
U-1229 110, 111, 112, 113, 114, 115, 117, 118, 132
U-1235 134, 137, 138
U-boat 1, 2, 4, 11, 19, 20, 21, 26, 32, 37, 40, 41, 42, 43, 44, 46, 47, 48, 49, 50, 51, 52, 54, 57, 58, 59, 61, 63, 64, 65, 67, 68, 69, 70, 71, 72, 75, 81, 83, 84, 85, 86, 87, 93, 94, 95, 96, 98, 99, 107, 108, 109, 110, 111, 112, 113, 114, 115, 117, 118, 119, 120, 132, 133, 137, 138, 140, 144, 145, 146, 147, 148, 152, 153, 154, 159, 164, 165, 169, 179
Uhlenbrück 113
Uhlig, Kapitanleutnant (Lieutenant Commander) Herbert 59, 60
U.K. Admiralty 132, 142
SS *Ulua* 16

Index

ULTRA 47, 54, 98, 152
ULTRA Naval Message 132, 134, 142
Underman, Lieutenant F.B. 108, 117
Union, Ensign M. 144
United Engineering Company, Alameda 151
United Kingdom 130
United Nations 20
United Nations Convention on the Law of the Sea 151
United States 1, 2, 3, 5, 19, 47, 90, 134, 151
United States Army Air Forces Anti-Submarine Command 20
United States Army Air Forces 133
United States Atlantic Fleet 45, 73
United States Congress 4
United States Shipping Board (USSB) 4
U.S. Army 133
U.S. Fleet Anti-Submarine Bulletin of September 1944 117
U.S. Joint Chiefs of Staff 21
U.S. Naval Academy in Annapolis, Maryland 6, 56, 90, 121, 135
U.S. Naval Headquarters at Brest, France 6
U.S. Navy 3, 4, 5, 29, 66, 88, 145, 148, 153
U.S. Navy PB4Y-1 (B24) Liberator 139
U.S. War Department 133
University of North Carolina at Chapel Hill 81
Uno, Japanese Commander Kanmeo 97, 98

V-1 pulse jet-powered pilotless flying bomb 132, 144
V2 rocket 132, 144
Valeich, Ensign E.L. 124
Valentine, Ensign William, Jr. 14
HMS *Vanessa* 31
USS *Varian* 136, 143, 144
VBF88 128
VC-1 67
VC-9 36, 40, 45, 54, 55, 63
VC-12 136
VC-13 104
VC-19 67, 74, 104, 134, 136, 140, 147
VC-42 102, 103, 104, 106, 110, 112, 114, 116, 117, 118, 132
VC-55 96, 136, 138
VC-69 90, 94, 98, 100, 102
VC-95 80, 81, 82, 88, 89, 121, 122, 124, 125, 130, 136, 138, 145
Vernalles 103
Vero Beach 103
Vettee Transversale 60
VF-42 108
V-F(N)52 128
VGS-9 16
VHF 42, 116
Victory Over Japan (VJ) Day 150

Virginia Beach 104
Volm, Lieutenant (jg) Bernard H. 67
Vosseller, Captain Aurelius Bartlett 90, 92, 99, 100, 101, 104, 105, 108, 114, 115, 121
VTB aircraft 101
VPB-115 139

USS *Wake Forest* 100
USS *Wake Island* 90, 107
Waldfriedhof Cemetery 147
War Department 22
S.S. *Warrior* 128
Washington and Jefferson College 135
Washington, D.C. 47, 133, 143
Watson, Lieutenant 106, 110
Wheeler, Lieutenant (jg) M.B., Jr. 108, 116, 117, 144
HMS *Whimbrel* 31
Whipple Academy 90
White, Lieutenant 60
HMS *Whitehall* 31
Whitlock, ART1c Edward A. 98
USS *Wilhoite* (DER-397) 105, 115, 116, 117, 122, 124, 125, 127, 129, 136
Wilkinson, Aerologist I.I. USN 115
William C. Gorgas 28
Williams, AMM3c H.S. 82
USS *Willis* (DE-395) 80, 82, 86, 87, 88, 89, 92, 94, 96, 97, 100, 105, 115, 117, 122, 123, 124, 125, 127, 128, 129, 135, 147, 158, 161
Willow Grove, Pennsylvania 121
Wilson, C.H. (A.C.G.) 106
Windmill Point 23
Wojcik, AEM3c C.J. 24, 48, 50, 51,
Wolf Trap 56
Wolf Trap Lighthouse 23, 24
HMS *Woodstock* 45
World War I 4, 6
World War II 1, 2, 3, 96, 111, 122, 135, 145, 146, 152
USS *Wright* (AZ-1) 6, 91
Wright Cyclone engine 11

Yancey, Commander Evan W. 137
Yard number 9, Way number 1 5
Yavorsky, Lieutenant Commander Jesse T. 103, 115, 118
York Spit channel 125
USS *Yorktown* 7, 81
Yorktown, Virginia 149
Y.S.D. 23 (Mary Ann) 45

Zaunkönig (Wren) 64
Zehn-Jahre, Zwanzig Tage (*Ten Years, Twenty Days*) 147
Zinke, Korvettenkapitän Armin 111, 112, 113

www.ingramcontent.com/pod-product-compliance
Ingram Content Group UK Ltd.
Pitfield, Milton Keynes, MK11 3LW, UK
UKHW042008140426
5217IPUK00015B/1054